An Ordinary Relationship

AN ORDINARY RELATIONSHIP

American Opposition to Republican Revolution in China

Daniel M. Crane
and
Thomas A. Breslin

UNIVERSITY PRESSES OF FLORIDA
Florida International University Press / Miami

UNIVERSITY PRESSES OF FLORIDA is the central agency for scholarly publishing of the State of Florida's university system, producing books selected for publication by the faculty editorial committees of Florida's nine public universities: Florida A&M University (Tallahassee), Florida Atlantic University (Boca Raton), Florida International University (Miami), Florida State University (Tallahassee), University of Central Florida (Orlando), University of Florida (Gainesville), University of North Florida (Jacksonville), University of South Florida (Tampa), University of West Florida (Pensacola).

ORDERS for books published by all member presses of University Presses of Florida should be addressed to University Presses of Florida, 15 NW 15th Street, Gainesville, FL 32603

Library of Congress Cataloging-in-Publication Data

Crane, Daniel M.
    An ordinary relationship.

    Bibliography, p.
    Includes index.
    1. United States—Foreign relations—China.   2. China
—Foreign relations—United States.   3. United States—
Foreign relations—1909–1913.   4. United States—
Foreign relations—1913–1921.   5. China—History—
Revolution, 1911–1912.   6. China—History—Revolution,
1913.   I. Breslin, Thomas A.   II. Title.
E183.8.C5C78   1986   327.73051   85–26452
ISBN 0–8130–0800–X

Contents

Acknowledgments

Numerous individuals and institutions have been very helpful to us as we pursued research into the activities of the governmental, business, and religious leaders involved with setting American policy toward China during this period. We are most grateful to Professors John Israel and Norman Graebner of the University of Virginia, who provided us with the grounding in Chinese and American diplomatic history needed to carry out this study and who offered invaluable guidance and criticism to us over the years as we prepared this work. A grant from the Liberty Fund and the Institute for Humane Studies made possible research into the Hornbeck Papers. Tobin N. Harvey, Patricia Hager, Sandra Mannis, Sandra Bergeson, and Barbara Lann enhanced the manuscript by their thoughtful scrutiny and sustained efforts and we remain indebted to them for their assistance. John Stack guided the manuscript through a long process of review and revision. Finally, this study could not have been completed without the encouragement, guidance, and patience of our wives, Bunty Crane and Maida Watson, and the forbearance of our children, Elizabeth, Nora, Emily, Matthew, and Brian Crane, and Moira and Brian Breslin.

Preface

DIPLOMATIC history is one of the most conservative branches of historiography, slow to absorb new information and techniques, slower still to cast off misconceptions. The history of Sino-American relations fully reflects these traits, with pernicious results for the conduct of American relations with China. Despite valiant efforts by a tiny group of historians to show that there was nothing special about America's dealings with China, the majority of their colleagues have merely amplified an old, confusing fiction that the United States and China enjoyed a "special relationship" quite different from that with other nations. This fiction destabilized Sino-American relations, embittered still further the witch-hunting of the McCarthy era, and created a climate that encouraged U.S. involvement in Vietnam.

The development of the myth of a special relationship can be traced to the earliest days of Sino-American relations, when the United States, out of weakness, seized upon the idea of cultivating China's goodwill to advance American commercial interests and to gain an edge over European competitors. John Adams noted as early as 1785, "much will depend upon the behavior of our own people who may go into those countries [of East Asia]. If they endeavor by an irreproachable integrity, humanity, and civility to conciliate the esteem of the natives, they may easily become the most favored nation; for the conduct of European nations in general . . . has given us great advantage." Hard-pressed in the early nineteenth century by powers such as Great Britain, China reciprocated American efforts to set itself apart from the Europeans as part of a divide-and-conquer strategy to resist foreign encroachment. As one Chinese official wrote in 1843, "If we treat the American barbarians courteously . . . and also take the trade of the English barbarians and give it to the American barbarians, then the American barbarians are sure to be grateful for this Heavenly Favor and will energetically oppose the English barbarians."[1] Thus, the illusion evolved that a spirit of benevolence and philanthropy characterized U.S.–China policy, along with the belief that such policies had earned China's gratitude and friendship.

On the U.S. side, the fiction that a spirit of benevolence and philanthropy characterized America's China policy and earned China's gratitude and friendship has been, in the words of Michael Hunt, "a staple of both popular and official rhetoric." Distinguished popular experts on China, such as Pearl S. Buck, S. Wells Williams, and Arthur Smith, heralded the myth and high school textbooks typically summed it up with a statement to the effect that "few nations have interested us for so long or touched our sympathies so deeply, but our interest has been primarily sentimental and humanitarian rather than political or historical." Where textbooks left off, recent secretaries of state have picked up the line: Dean Acheson ("our historic policy of friendship for China"), John Foster Dulles ("long history of cooperative friendship"), Dean Rusk ("the historic ties of friendship"). As Warren Cohen observed, this rhetoric fed the belief that "the role of the United States was different from that of the other imperialists—that the United States was the 'champion' of China's independence, seeking to protect that hapless country against European and Japanese imperialists."[2]

Doubters whose skeptical instincts are aroused by this effusive rhetoric cannot take much comfort from the work of American sinologists and diplomatic historians. The most significant American book written about China, John King Fairbank's *The United States and China*, stresses the "traditional friendship" between the United States and China and describes the U.S. actions toward China as "benevolent, seeking to give as well as get." Dorothy Borg, who as much as any historian of Sino-American relations has demonstrated the gap between American rhetoric and action in China, argues that pro-Chinese sentiment was a basic factor in America's East Asian policy between the world wars. Finally, even Paul Varg's *Making of a Myth: The United States and China 1897–1912*, which persuasively demonstrates that on the official, governmental level the "special relationship" was nothing more than a carefully crafted illusion, concludes that on the unofficial level American attitudes toward China were truly benevolent and friendly.[3]

The myth of the special relationship has gained currency in large part from diplomatic historians' neglect and misinterpretation of the 1911 Revolution, which overthrew a centuries old monarchy in favor of a republic in the world's most populous nation. These historians often assume the existence of a special relationship. The well-respected and highly influential Akira Iriye, for example, has noted that "a notion of Sino-American friendship as a distinct phenomenon dates from the republican revolution of 1912." Similarly, Benson Grayson has observed that "the warm spot in most American hearts for the Chinese Republic dating back to the Revolution of 1911–12 lasted until the establishment of the Communist regime in Peking almost fifty years later." Or, as Foster Rhea Dulles concluded, the Chinese Revolution "drew tighter our bonds with the Chinese people."[4]

A search through the historical literature for the substance of the special relationship is inevitably fruitless but hardly surprising since Charles Neu amply forewarned the scholarly community of a critical gap in the historiography of Sino-American relations. He surveyed the years that encompassed the 1911 Revolution and concluded that "except for the years 1906–1909, the period between 1906 and 1913 has been neglected in the history of American East Asian relations." Michael Hunt's pioneering study of America's diplomatic initiatives in Manchuria, *Frontier Defense and the Open Door*, has done much to fill this void with respect to the early years of the Taft administration's China policy. But America's response to the 1911 Revolution and its policies during the early years of the Republic, as Neu observed, remain largely neglected, or are treated parenthetically in connection with studies focusing primarily on the East Asian policy of Taft's successor, Woodrow Wilson.[5]

That this period should be neglected is unfortunate, for in several respects it represents a unique chapter in Sino-American relations. First, the number of actors involved was unusually large. Politicians, bureaucrats, editorialists, businessmen, and missionaries all played vital roles in shaping the American response to the revolution. American policy at this time was therefore multidimensional, involving political, cultural, and economic factors that alone make it a fascinating case study. Second, the revolution spanned two presidencies widely perceived to be different in their approaches to foreign affairs—the conservative, business-oriented Taft administration and the progressive, idealistic, democratic Wilson administration—thereby providing an ideal testing ground in which to examine the continuities and discontinuities of American foreign policy. Third, the revolution occurred during a critical transition period for the United States. Following the Spanish-American War of 1898 and the acquisition of the Philippines, the United States began a rapid transformation from a nation with few overseas commitments to the world's preeminent economic and political power, with an intensified interest in the maintenance of the international status quo. This process was not completed, however, until after World War I. The United States, therefore, had maximum flexibility in responding to the revolution: It could either support the Chinese Revolution as consistent with its own revolutionary heritage or oppose it as a threat to its not yet realized potential economic interests in East Asia. How the United States reacted during this transition period to a democratic revolution, ostensibly modeled upon the American Revolution, provides a clear preview of future American responses to less palatable revolutionary movements, including those in China itself and in Vietnam—responses that have been decidedly at odds with America's own revolutionary origins and harmful to the well-being of the republic.

A brief survey of the literature amply documents the need for a comprehensive study of both Taft's and Wilson's policies toward China during this critical period. Students of this era are familiar with Roy Curry's *Woodrow Wilson and Far Eastern Policy, 1913–1921*, Burton Beers's *Vain Endeavor: Robert Lansing's Attempts to End the American-Japanese Rivalry*, Charles Vevier's *The United States and China, 1906–1913: A Study in Finance and Diplomacy*, Tien-yi Li's *Woodrow Wilson's China Policy 1913–1917*, Madeleine Chi's *China Diplomacy, 1914–1918*, Noel Pugach's *Paul S. Reinsch: Open Door Diplomat in Action*, and Jerry Israel's *Progressivism and the Open Door: America and China, 1905–1921*. While these works all have merit and contribute to our understanding of Sino-American relations, they are very different in scope, focus, and interpretation from this study.

The differences can be broadly and rapidly sketched. First, Vevier's focus is on Taft's China policy, not Wilson's, while Curry, Li, Beers, Pugach, and Chi deal with Wilson's China policy but not Taft's. By compartmentalizing their studies in accordance with presidential administrations, these scholars have forfeited the opportunity to draw meaningful comparisons regarding the continuity of American foreign policy—something that we have specifically attempted to do.

Second, even though several of these studies touch upon many of the same events covered here, their focus is on China policy in general rather than on how the United States reacted to an allegedly democratic revolution, which happened to have occurred in China. Again, while we realize that a study of American China policy per se is important and we address it for that reason, we also believe that the broader issue of America's response to revolution must be incorporated into the analysis to gain a complete understanding of that policy, especially in light of the critical significance of the 1949 Communist Revolution for Sino-American relations. Third, all of these works are vastly different in scope from our study. Chi, Beers, and Curry devote considerable attention to the diplomacy of World War I and American-Japanese relations. Li and Pugach, the latter in a biography of Paul Reinsch, Wilson's minister to China, discuss Taft's policies only incidentally, preferring instead isolated studies of Wilson's China policy that involve them in several matters that are totally unrelated to the issues we discuss. Vevier deals primarily with Taft's pre-1911 economic diplomacy and not his policies during the 1911 Revolution. And Israel's thoughtful study, while spanning the administrations of Roosevelt, Taft, and Wilson, is not really a study of American foreign policy at all but rather an examination of Progressive Era attitudes toward China. Simply put, a reader of these books would find them only tangentially similar in focus and scope. Finally, these works offer significantly different interpretations of Sino-American relations during this period from those presented here, particularly in that they accept the myth of the special Sino-American relationship. A detailed look at the theses of these authors fully illustrates this point.

Monographic studies of Taft's China policy during the 1911 Revolution are virtually nonexistent, although the subject is sparsely treated in several general studies and articles and in works on Wilson.

Akira Iriye, in *Across the Pacific*, posits a strikingly revisionist view of Taft's China policy. When compared with Wilson, Taft is traditionally depicted as a materialist rather than an idealist in his conduct of foreign affairs, a president dedicated to advancing America's political and, most important, economic interests in China at the expense of China's sovereignty and of America's own democratic principles. Iriye's view of Taft is, however, quite different: "It is with the Taft administration that one may date the beginning of a moralistic diplomacy in East Asia. President Taft and Secretary Knox were more willing than their respective predecessors . . . to make a moral concern with China's destiny a basis of their policy. . . . The Taft-Knox diplomacy has sometimes been described as 'dollar diplomacy.' That epithet would apply to their East Asian policy only with respect to the means they employed. They resorted to financial tactics to achieve ends that were basically moral. . . . At a time when other Western countries were pursuing the usual power-oriented diplomacy, regarding Japan merely as another power, the United States tended to view it as an Asian imperialist, an object of moral concern." In Iriye's opinion, Wilson's moralistic, sympathetic China policy originated with Taft and grew to unprecedented heights, leading Wilson to repudiate the consortium of foreign banks as an "immoral imposition" upon China. Thus, "the climate of American opinion and Wilson's personal inclinations served to perpetuate a moralistic approach to East Asian problems instead of a return to the Rooseveltian emphasis on economics and security."[6]

Iriye's interpretation of Taft's China policy is, to say the least, surprising. Taft's successor, Woodrow Wilson, ostensibly repudiated Taft's policies precisely because they were not moral. Moreover, the common view of Taft as an instrument of Wall Street emphasizes the economic, not the moral, component of his policy. Yet, Iriye's views, perhaps because of his preeminence in the field of American–East Asian relations, are widely respected and represent the current historiographical trend, though one which has not until now been subjected to detailed scrutiny. No less an authority than John King Fairbank has uncritically repeated Iriye's views. Similarly, Charles Neu, in *American–East Asian Relations: A Survey*, concurred that the "president [Taft] and his secretary of state [Knox] felt an obligation to employ American power and prestige for humanity's benefit, particularly in . . . East Asia." Iriye and his adherents are incorrect in their analysis of Taft but there is no denying the significance of their thesis for, as Neu has written, "[i]f this is so, then the years 1909–1913 mark a major watershed in the history of American–East Asian relations, one which historians have only begun to comprehend."[7] We agree with Neu, but for different reasons, that historians have not perceived the significance of this era of Sino-American relations. That perception has often been blocked by acceptance of the notion of a special Sino-American relationship, a development lately given further encouragement by the Iriye analysis.

Unfortunately, the myth of a special Sino-American relationship also pervades scholarship on the Wilson administration. Perhaps the most authoritative work to date on this period is Tien-yi Li's *Woodrow Wilson's China Policy 1913–1917*. Indeed, Wilson's distinguished biographer, Arthur Link, relies heavily on Li's research and analysis of Wilson's China policy in his multivolume treatise on Wilson. Li's view of Wilson, while critical from a practical standpoint, is wholly consistent with the idea of a special relationship and a benign American policy toward China. According to Li, Wilson was "benevolently inclined toward China as an independent nation," out of a "profound sympathy for weak, oppressed and underdeveloped peoples." Morality and duty, rather than political or commercial advantage, were thus the guideposts of Wilson's China policy. He withdrew the United States from the international banking consortium because of "his sense of justice, his sympathy for the Chinese people, his respect for the independence and administrative integrity of a weak nation, his disapproval of the terms of the loan arrangement, and above all, his distaste for the use of finance as a tool of diplomacy." Similarly, Wilson recognized the new Republic of China because of his benevolent sympathy for China. While Li's analysis of Wilson's China policy is, we believe, wrong, he does recognize that Wilson supported Yuan Shikai over Yuan's more democratic rivals for power in China during the abortive 1913 Revolution and backed Yuan's attempt to elevate himself to emperor. Although these actions seemed to be at odds with Wilson's avowed dedication to the propagation of democratic principles, Li explains away this apparent inconsistency by claiming that Wilson did so "to strengthen China's internal unity and order without which democracy would be unable later to take root."[8]

In our view, Wilson's China policy was not so benign. He unilaterally withdrew from the consortium and recognized the Republic of China because by so doing he hoped to gain political and economic advantage for the United States in China. Or, as his secretary of state, William Jennings Bryan, put it, because the United States would not have the "controlling voice" if it continued to cooperate with the other powers. Also, regardless of Wilson's avowed devotion to Christian principle, morality, and democracy, his actions were clearly dictated by tangible, material objectives. Similarly, Wilson's support for Yuan over more democratic rivals was part and parcel of his attempt to advance independently American interests in that country and not part of a long-range plan to create the conditions in which democracy might flourish in China. What was wrong with Wilson's policy, therefore, was not the policy itself, although it was tactically flawed, as Li and others have correctly pointed out. It was the rhetoric in which he couched his true aims, a rhetoric which served to perpetuate the myth of a special relationship and to debase American democratic discourse. Thus, Li's observation that Wilson's China policy was "as impractical as it was morally praiseworthy" demonstrates that Li missed this fundamental point, one which we hope this study will correct.

Li's orthodox interpretation of Wilson's China policy has many adherents. As Arthur Link observed in *Wilson: The New Freedom*, "There is no reason to doubt that he [Wilson] was acting in a moral capacity to save China from the designs of scheming European and American imperialists" when he withdrew the United States from the consortium. Similarly, Roy Curry, in *Woodrow Wilson and Far Eastern Policy, 1913–1921*, sees Wilson as an idealist who sought in his foreign policy a "reign of practical justice and peace." In Curry's view, Wilson's China policy was designed to help China transform and uplift itself into a modern, independent, democratic state. It was for these reasons that Wilson withdrew from the consortium and recognized the Republic. In other words, Curry, unlike Li, ignores Wilson's support of Yuan's antidemocratic tendencies and views Wilson's China policy as moral, benevolent, and prodemocratic, not materialistic and self-seeking.[9]

Even more "realistic" scholars, such as Burton Beers, Noel Pugach, Jerry Israel, and Charles Vevier, have fallen prey to the allure of the Wilson rhetoric. For example, in *Vain Endeavor*, Beers correctly recognizes that the United States did not support Chinese sovereignty out of concern for China itself but rather to advance its own interests in East Asia. However, Beers claims that Wilson deviated from this realistic policy in a flight of idealistic fancy. "Wilson's purpose was clear. He hoped that China would develop along modern, democratic, and Christian lines. Moreover, he was convinced that the United States was morally obligated to assist in the task." Similarly, Jerry Israel, in *Progressivism and the Open Door*, departs from what is otherwise an astute analysis of American attitudes toward China by claiming that the 1911 Revolution had the sympathy of progressives everywhere, including Woodrow Wilson, who, Israel contends, was convinced of the need to preserve China's shaky republican government. In *The United States and China, 1906–1913*, Vevier, a disciple of Fred Harvey Harrington, and a critic of Taft's "shopkeeper diplomacy," accepts as well the myth of Wilson as "a good Christian moralist who recommended altruism to aid the weak and self-help to discipline the strong." Thus, even though Vevier correctly identifies the self-interested economic and political aspects of Taft's dollar diplomacy, he tacitly accepts Wilson's explanation that the United States withdrew from the consortium because the proposed Reorganization Loan offended China's administrative independence and was obnoxious to American principles. Finally, in *Paul S. Reinsch*, Pugach accurately perceived that the United States withdrew from the consortium because it had little leverage in that organization and mistakenly thought that it could go it alone in China, and also that America sought to cultivate Chinese friendship principally to gain advantage for itself. Pugach nonetheless paid lip service to Wilson's sincere desire to foster constitutional government and democracy in China.[10]

In addition to these monographs dealing specifically with Wilsonian diplomacy, several broad interpretive studies of Sino-American relations have also viewed Wilson's China policy as altruistic and benevolent. What is most ironic about these studies, however, is that except for their analyses of the Wilson administration, and, to a lesser degree, the Taft administration, they recognize the realistic, self-interested bent of America's historical China policy. For example, Warren Cohen, in his highly regarded *America's Response to China: An Interpretive History of Sino-American Relations*, goes to great pains to debunk the idea of a special relationship. Yet, in this same work, Cohen argues that both Taft and Wilson were sympathetic to the aspirations of Chinese nationalists; that Taft and his advisers "believed that in the pursuit of American interests . . . [they were] helping China"; that the United States "demonstrated its altruistic intentions"; that Wilson was "determined to offer the Chinese the disinterested assistance of the United States"; and that Wilson's China policy was based on friendship and good will. In other words, despite his general disavowal of the idea of a special relationship, Cohen believes that "Taft and Wilson actually contemplated such a [benevolent] role for the United States" and only abandoned it "when confronted with the reality of Japanese power."[11]

Perhaps even more surprising than Cohen's analysis is that contained in Michael Hunt's widely acclaimed *The Making of a Special Relationship: The United States and China to 1914*, which is entirely devoted to tracing the history of this relationship. He demonstrates convincingly that the United States consciously adopted a policy of cultivating China's goodwill as the only means available to it to make any effective inroads—political, commercial, or religious—into China, and that the only thing "special" about this relationship was the degree to which two distinctly different peoples became locked in conflict, the victims of their own misconceptions and myths.[12]

Despite Hunt's otherwise perceptive look at Sino-American relations, when he deals with Wilson he finds a president motivated not by economic or political considerations but rather by "the obligation of the United States to promote the modern trinity—democracy, the rule of law, and Christianity" in China. Hunt ignores Wilson's many domestic initiatives to promote foreign trade, such as amending the Federal Reserve Act to facilitate foreign branch banking, exempting U.S. export trade from the antitrust laws (the Webb-Pomerene and Edge acts), beefing up the export functions of the Department of Commerce and subsidizing the merchant marine, and, in China, making vigorous efforts to promote independent American loans and development activities as well as the president's subsequent decision to reconstitute the consortium. Yet Hunt claims that Wilson was not overly interested in promoting foreign markets. "By contrast [with Taft], China was to Wilson not a market but rather fertile soil where Americans might help self-government and Christianity take root." This view leads Hunt, as it has so many others, to argue that Wilson withdrew from the consortium because it violated China's integrity and impeded the exercise of benevolent American influence and that he recognized the Chinese Republic as a sign of encouragement and support to China in its struggle to establish democratic institutions. Hunt even claims that Wilson's democratic principles led eventually to disillusionment and tempered support for Yuan Shikai when Yuan outlawed the Guomindang and suppressed the 1913 Revolution. The impact of Hunt's otherwise skillful destruction of the myth of a special relationship is thus severely undermined by his failure to scrutinize critically the China policy of the one American president who, above all others, stands out as the leading exponent of the very type of rhetoric that gave life to the myth itself.[13]

As this brief survey shows, Burton Beers accurately summarized historiographical interpretations of Wilson's China policy when, in 1962, he wrote that "on one point historians have agreed: idealism figured prominently in the Wilson administration's approach to Far Eastern questions." Indeed, even such a noted realist as William Appleman Williams wrote that Wilson brought to his conduct of foreign affairs a "religious intensity and righteousness that was not apparent in earlier administrations and has not been matched since."[14]

In this work we will register a strong dissent to the prevailing view of Sino-American relations during China's early republican period, not because we wish to cast Wilson as a cynical hypocrite but because we believe that the perpetuation of the myth of a special relationship has had a negative impact on American society and a deleterious effect on Sino-American relations. As Varg noted, "The inversion of this myth, since 1949, into hostility toward China on the one hand and the denunciation of our policy on the other, has now entrapped us." When the Communists took power in China in 1949, the American people felt betrayed, a sentiment that can be understood only within the context of a special relationship. Harold Isaacs cogently explained this sense of betrayal: "Only as a flouted parent could the American feel that the Chinese, in their waywardness and delinquency, had strayed or allowed themselves to be led astray, that they failed to appreciate and be guided by paternal precept and example and had thus brought down upon themselves a wrathful fate." [15]

In this climate it was all the easier to lead the American people into a disaster in Vietnam that rivaled the disaster of the Athenian empire's Syracusan folly. George Kennan, a distinguished diplomat and author of one of the era's three most influential diplomatic history books, demonstrated, perhaps unwittingly, that the myth of the special relationship was still playing a vital role in public discourse on America's East Asian policy when he wrote in 1964, during the debate over America's involvement in the Vietnam War:

> At the heart of all our difficulties in the Far East lies a preposterous and almost incomprehensible fact. The great country of China, forming the heart of Asia, a country which for many years we befriended above all others and in defense of whose interests, in past, we fought the Pacific War, has fallen into the hands of a group of embittered fanatics . . . consumed with the ambition to extend to further areas of Asia the dictatorial authority they now wield over the Chinese people themselves . . . and now absolutely permeated with hatred toward ourselves, not only because their ideology pictures us as villains, but also because we, more than any other people, have had the strength and tenacity to stand in their path and to obstruct the expansion of their power. [16]

There is, then, ample justification for a reevaluation of the idea of a special relationship between the United States and China. Not only did the myth of a special relationship and the ensuing sense of betrayal brought on by the Communist victory in 1949 lead to over twenty years of unwarranted hostility between the United States and China; it contributed to the domestic turbulence of the McCarthy era over the "loss of China." It also helped propel America into the Vietnam War. And its effects are still with us, for the "normalization of relations" with China during the Nixon years did not resolve the problem. Rather, if anything, the United States once again went overboard in its enthusiasm for China both as an object of popular adulation and as a diplomatic and military counterweight to the Soviet Union. Predictably, the Reagan administration's support for Taiwan and the Chinese government's efforts to improve relations with the Soviet Union threaten to replace Nixon's overly optimistic "era of good feelings" with one of increased tensions between the two countries. Thus, unless the idea of a special relationship is abandoned once and for all, there will remain in Sino-American relations a needless element of instability carrying with it seriously adverse consequences for all concerned.

Our thesis is simply that there was no special Sino-American relationship in either a positive or a negative sense. The United States treated China much as it had treated other nations since the beginning of the American republic for reasons that were rooted in the exigencies of domestic politics. In a brief introductory chapter we will outline America's response to early challenges, both foreign and domestic, to the political and economic system established after the American Revolution. Our findings will indicate that, rather than being a proponent of revolutionary change, the United States sought to promote domestic and international stability so as to preserve and enhance America's political and economic power. In presenting our findings, we hope to set forth a conceptual framework that can give larger meaning to the principal focus of our study: America's response to the 1911 Chinese Revolution.

To fully appreciate America's response to the 1911 Revolution, one must begin not with the revolution itself but with a review of American China policy in the late nineteenth century. We will outline American China policy from the time of the Sino-Japanese War in 1894–95, when China appeared to be on the verge of dismemberment, through the issuance of the Open Door notes, the Boxer Rebellion, the American remission of the Boxer indemnity, the anti-American boycott over American immigration policies, the 1905 Manchu Reform movement (the beginning, according to Harold Isaacs, of America's "Age of Benevolence" toward China), and the early efforts of the Taft administration to secure an economic foothold for the United States in China in cooperation with the other Great Powers. In so doing, we will set the appropriate context for examining the events that followed: America's response to the outbreak of revolution in late 1911 and early 1912; the complex and lengthy financial negotiations conducted by an international banking consortium with the leaders of the new Republic; the question of diplomatic recognition of the Chinese Republic; Taft's policy of cooperating with the other powers in these latter two issues and Wilson's decision to break with his predecessor's policy and pursue an independent course in China; America's response to the abortive 1913 Revolution against President Yuan Shikai, whose dictatorial ambitions led to the revolt; the Japanese threat to the Chinese Republic as embodied in the infamous 21 Demands; and, finally, America's response to Yuan Shikai's efforts to reestablish the monarchy in China, a move which dispelled once and for all the democratic aura surrounding the 1911 Revolution.

In examining these several episodes we will find that not only the American government and business sectors opposed reform and revolution in China but that the editorialists and missionaries also were basically unsympathetic to the revolution and to the Chinese Republic. Taft, for example, initially preferred the Manchus to the republicans when the revolution broke out, and the United States stood ready to intervene and to crush the rebellion if it threatened American interests. Taft and his Wall Street partners also cooperated with the other powers in matters of international finance and diplomatic recognition, not to ameliorate the designs of the other powers on China but to ensure that the United States would share in whatever benefits cooperation might derive. Similarly, Wilson withdrew the United States from the international banking consortium and unilaterally recognized the Republic of China not because he was primarily concerned with Chinese sovereignty or because he felt Taft's policies were obnoxious to American principles but because he believed that the United States could achieve greater political and economic benefits by proceeding independently rather than in conjunction with the other powers in China. For the same reasons, Wilson supported Yuan Shikai in his efforts to crush democratic opposition in China in 1913 and to reestablish the monarchy in 1915–16. The propagation of democratic principles was secondary to the achievement of more tangible American objectives in East Asia. The nongovernmental sector, i.e., missionaries and editorialists, were equally self-interested and ethnocentric in their approach to China. If the revolution and the Republic led to the conversion and Americanization of China, that was well and good; but if the opposite should occur, it would have to be opposed. When confronted with the choice of supporting or opposing revolution and democracy in China, the United States chose opposition because the imperatives of domestic and international politics demanded it. China was not a special case after all.

Our thesis directly contradicts much of the historiography of this period. We hope that it will gain widespread acceptance, eclipse the myth of the special Sino-American relationship, promote clear democratic dialogue about U.S. relations with China, and contribute thereby to the stabilization of those relations.

Domestic Control and Overseas Expansion: America's Road to China

THROUGHOUT the course of American history, the nation's political elite, including presidents, cabinet secretaries, and Supreme Court justices, for example, have steadfastly pursued the preservation of both the national government and, whenever possible, the contemporary economic system upon which it was based. In their discourse, they have often boasted of an American revolutionary heritage characterized by liberty and democracy. In practice, however, they have frequently cast their lot with the established governments of the world and those who controlled them to thwart revolutionary change overseas, thereby preserving the concept of elite control. Their conservatism has been rooted in the fear that either failure to find foreign markets or the emergence abroad of attractive alternatives to the American political and economic system could lead to domestic unrest and loss of their political dominance.

The desire of the national leadership for domestic and international stability has been so great that often the United States has actively supported the colonial systems of nations with which it enjoyed or sought to enjoy profitable relations. As a result, this nation has, over the years, opposed the emergence of revolutionary and democratic movements as near as Haiti and Cuba and as far away as China.

Political control is, of course, a central problem for the leaders of any society. The issue is particularly critical when lines of communication are tenuous and vast distances make the extension of governmental control, especially of the military sort, very costly. Americans' own successful prerevolutionary experience as smugglers who defied British attempts to control the trade in the immensely popular Chinese leaf tea exemplified the difficulty of exerting governmental control on the distant American continent. The brazenness of American colonials in flaunting the mother country's tea laws, their frequent bribery of customs officials, and their resort to intimidation and violence of a personal and symbolic nature not only demoralized the customs service in the western sector of the British Empire but also led to a war from which the Americans emerged victorious after many years of desperate struggle.[1]

America's direct revolutionary experience has not been proof against the conservative impulse. The American Republic was barely established when the Washington administration adopted a policy designed to assist the French in putting down a slave rebellion in the French colony of Haiti. Northern merchants feared the loss of an important market; political leaders such as George Washington and Thomas Jefferson were concerned that the example of the Haitian slaves would spread to North America and ignite a slave uprising, which would incinerate southern society and destroy a vital part of the new nation's economy. Alexander Hamilton viewed the rebellion as "calamitous." The Congress shared his sentiment and appropriated sums totaling $726,000 to assist the French planters in putting down the revolt. The administration led by Washington's successor, the New England Federalist, John Adams, was also hostile to the Haitian revolution. Nonetheless, the Haitian slaves achieved political power in 1804.[2]

The American response to the Haitian Revolution was not an aberration. In the years between the American Revolution and the American Civil War, revolution shook the European continent. Major revolutions in France, Greece, and Hungary were aimed at overthrowing the monarchical system of government which offered the only real alternative to the American experiment in republicanism. For a few years the French Revolution was the premier issue in America. While some Americans offered eloquent support for the goals of the insurgents, and some served as privateers for France, more concrete assistance was not forthcoming. America's republican principles did not automatically translate into a prorevolutionary or prodemocratic foreign policy. In justifying America's refusal to go to the aid of the new revolutionary government in France, Alexander Hamilton pointed out the dangers of unthinking adherence to principles that "have a natural tendency to lead us aside from our true interests." [3] Indeed the U.S. government eventually engaged in an undeclared naval war with revolutionary France and, through the Alien and Sedition Acts, sought to repress pro-French republican and democratic sentiment.

The once-revolutionary leadership was equally willing to use armed force against its own citizenry to maintain the preeminence of the state when it found that the farmers of the western hinterland were flouting the new nation's authority by refusing to pay taxes on another popular beverage, whiskey. The disgruntled farmers had begun talking, as had the citizens of Boston years before, about breaking away from centralized political control headquartered not in London this time, but right at home. At the insistence of Alexander Hamilton, himself a former revolutionary officer, the young republic went even further in its response to this domestic threat than it had in seeking to quash the Haitian uprising; it mobilized thousands of soldiers and quickly crushed the so-called Whiskey Rebellion.

Despite the success of the national government in fending off the French and putting down the Whiskey Rebellion, the experience of the first generation of American leaders proved that state power was guaranteed to be effective only against scattered American Indians or unorganized citizens. Against an aroused mass of citizens, especially armed citizens, state power was apt to fail with dire consequences.

Even if armed force were effective in preserving state power against weak opposition, in the early days of the republic not all the threats facing the national government were susceptible to military solutions. Having come to America to escape religious tyranny and persecution in England, the former colonists were acutely aware of the power of organized religion to influence and indeed dominate secular matters. To prevent such a development in the United States, Thomas Jefferson suggested that a multiplicity of churches competing among themselves would divide the citizenry and prevent any one church from growing strong enough to challenge the state. To accomplish this goal, he justified severing official ties between church and state and encouraging multiplicity of churches.

Jefferson's prescription proved to be effective, and organized religion never did present a serious threat to the policies and programs adopted by the national government in the early nineteenth century. Harriet Martineau, a traveler and writer of that era, observed regarding the silence of the American clergy on the issue of slavery, "They who uphold a faith which shall move mountains . . . are the most timid class of society." She believed that in their hands religion was an opiate and that the clergy were in self-exile from the great moral questions of the time. She repeated the observation of a commentator who told her that the clergy were "looked upon by all grown men as a sort of people between men and women"; it was their function to deal with "weak members of society, women and superstitious men. By such they are called 'faithful guardians.'"[4]

Because the church no longer presented a danger to the ruling class, the American elite felt free to support and use the clergy as its servants in order to maintain the status quo. Orestes Brownson commented, "Our clergy are raised up, educated, fashioned, and sustained by wealthy employers. Not a few of our churches rest on Mammon for their foundation. The basement is a trader's shop."[5] The Presbyterian historian Robert Baird was of the belief that nineteenth-century America was as conservative as it was because of the clergy's efforts against religious and philosophical reform. In gratitude, the American leadership supported the missionary-benevolent societies and took part in the revivals of Charles G. Finney in the 1820s and Dwight Moody in the 1870s which were designed to impose order on society.[6]

Social control would be achieved from within through the internalization of a new set of moral guidelines designed to regulate individual behavior. The revival meeting was the chief instrument for propagating these new controls and individual guilt was to be the penalty for nonadherence. In his classic *Lectures on Revivals of Religion*, Finney, the century's best known and most influential revivalist, laid out an oratorical strategy of cultivating distress among his listeners and then, in a group context, of providing a sense of relief, of personal safety and salvation. "It is of great importance," he wrote, "that the sinner should be made to *feel his guilt*, and not left to the impression that he is *unfortunate*." Until the preacher can make the sinner blame and condemn himself or herself, Finney believed, "the gospel will never take effect."[7]

To control the populace through use of the clergy was an immense undertaking that required a considerable increase in the number of preachers available for such a task. While the national population grew by 88 percent between 1832 and 1854—growth that included a large number of staunchly Roman Catholic immigrants—the number of evangelical clergy grew by 175 percent.[8] Contrary to their expectations, however, these new preachers were not greeted warmly by the citizenry. Society still was composed basically of proud farmers who were reluctant to support the clergy with their hard-earned money.

The populace appeared to have little use for organized religion; successful campaigns to disestablish religion in various states occurred, and opposition to the spread of religious institutions grew throughout the country.[9] Rather than proving to be an effective instrument for controlling the population, the program to expand the number of clergy appeared to backfire as the financial burden of supporting the clergy sparked popular resentment. A dangerous surplus of potential agitators, ambitious young men trained to lead but politically and socially frustrated, had been created. There was, however, a solution available that would make the clergy more effective at controlling the people at home and make the surplus clergy useful in assisting America to extend its overseas markets and influence. Thus, with considerable eagerness the American leadership financed the journey abroad of surplus clergy as missionaries intent on implanting American ideals in places such as the Ottoman Empire, India, and, especially, China. Having disposed of these surplus preachers through the establishment of overseas missions, their patrons hoped that those who remained at home would meet with more success in their appointed task of controlling the domestic populace by rallying enthusiasm behind non-threatening activities in distant lands.[10]

Despite the clergy's efforts to perfect ways of reaching and controlling individuals in the United States, new and different tensions began to emerge that threatened the very survival of the nation. Their resolution required not moral suasion but direct action by the national leadership such as had been taken to quell the Whiskey Rebellion. The divergent regional interests of the states jeopardized the precarious national unity, which could only be preserved by continued cultivation and control of regional interests that often were replete with international dimensions. Thus, the national leadership felt compelled to gain control of the Mississippi River in order to retain the allegiance of the West, to fight England in order to quell the spirit of secession in the mercantile Northeast, and to acquire the Floridas from Spain to pacify southerners eager for new land and worried by fears of slaves escaping along the southern borders.

While these actions helped mollify regional interests and thereby preserved the national leadership's political control, they did not alleviate all strain on the system. In particular, the integration of the slave subsystem into the American state system, which had led to the acquisition of the Floridas, emerged as the overriding issue in American foreign policy as well as in domestic policy from the conclusion of the War of 1812 until the Civil War. No sooner had Spain and the

United States ratified the cession of the Floridas to the United States than southern firebrand John C. Calhoun began agitating for the annexation of Cuba, which he believed was a haven for runaway slaves and a potential seedbed of black revolution. Secretary of State John Quincy Adams, though more patient than Calhoun and less concerned with southern regional interests, shared his conviction that the United States ought to acquire Cuba. "Cuba," he wrote, "almost in sight of our shores, from a multitude of considerations has become an object of transcendent importance to the political and commercial interest of our Union. . . . It is scarcely possible to resist the conviction that the annexation of Cuba to our federal republic will be indispensable to the continuance and integrity of the Union itself." Adams's successor as secretary of state, Henry Clay, invoked the diplomatic assistance of the European powers to stifle a projected Mexican-Colombian expedition to liberate Cuba from Spain. Unable to take the island without inducing social unrest and also provoking Great Britain, the Caribbean's foremost power, perhaps to the point of war, the United States acquiesced in the continuation of Spanish rule in Cuba.[11]

Slavery continued to be the American state's prime political problem, the immediate source of disequilibrium and possible dissolution. The slave system was breaking down along its southeastern and southwestern borders. Runaway slaves were disappearing into the wilderness of Florida to join local Indians; still others were fleeing into Mexican-held Texas, where slavery was outlawed. Although the Seminole War in the 1830s stabilized the Florida frontier and made it safe for the slaveowners, the situation along the Texas border took a more dangerous turn. After land-hungry slaveowners moved into Texas and established a republic there, France and England maneuvered to shore up the Republic of Texas as a buffer against American expansion. The meddling of abolitionist England alarmed southerners, who, fearing the emergence of a nonslave Texas on their borders, demanded the annexation of Texas. Northern antislavery leaders managed to beat back their demands but at the cost of great strain on the national state. To alleviate that strain, the national political leadership promoted the acquisition of Texas for reasons of state, or, as they termed it, "manifest destiny." They successfully annexed Texas and involved the nation in a victorious war with Mexico.

The acquisition of Texas left the South unsatisfied. Southern leaders wanted an active northern commitment to the preservation of slavery and to a policy of low tariffs which facilitated their trade with England. When this commitment was not forthcoming and the South sought to leave the Union, the national leadership, as it had with the Whiskey Rebellion, did what it had to do in order to maintain political control: it led the rest of the nation into war for the integrity of the Union, industrial development, and economic independence from England. From both a national and a northern point of view, the war was successful. As a region, it was years before the South was able to make strong positive demands upon the state system. In the meantime, the North was able to develop its industry behind tariff walls high enough to discourage English competition.

Victory in the Civil War gave the state system only a brief respite from intense political pressure. In the depression-racked generation after the war, profound changes in the American economy created severe tensions between the agrarian and industrial sectors. Farmers were becoming alienated from the system of finance capitalism then taking shape. Industrial workers shared their discontent. These tensions again forced the national leadership to develop a strategy that would ease political tensions between the agrarian and industrial sectors and that would reconcile both sectors to finance capitalism and the political system upon which it was based.

The alienation of the agrarian sector was a severe test for the leadership of the nation. Since the American economy was still dependent upon foreign markets for disposal of its agricultural surplus, the national leadership had to deal with the agrarian sector's international interests. The Panic of 1873 was an unpleasant reminder to the nation's leaders that overproduction could be alleviated only by expanding international trade, or so it seemed.[12] But that was a difficult task with worldwide dimensions. Intense competition from farmers in Russia, Argentina, Canada, and Australia threatened American farmers, especially those with small and medium-sized farms. Successful commercial agriculture required greater and greater amounts of capital, land, and machinery. Small farmers reacted by forming producers' and buyers' cooperatives to achieve greater economic strength. When those efforts proved insufficient to make them competitive, they capitalized on their numbers. With their ballots, they took control of local and state governments and legislated reforms opposed to finance capitalism. Frustrated by limited results at those levels of power, they made a strong but futile bid to gain national electoral power in 1896 by supporting the presidential candidacy of William Jennings Bryan.

The higher level of international competition that drove so many in the agrarian sector to bankruptcy and despair was also operating in the industrial sector, with similar results. Just as the railroads drew farmers into national and international competition, so they put craftsmen and small manufacturers into direct competition with larger industrial units around the world. Innovation, cost-cutting, and amalgamation were the alternatives to ruin in such a market. Giant corporations emerged in each field and attempted to reduce competition by fixing prices and market shares. Government assisted in this process by establishing regulatory commissions that were to enjoin anticompetitive practices but that in fact limited competition and guaranteed minimum profits.

American political leaders began to conceive of the United States, with its agrarian insurgency and labor unrest, as a hostile and forbidding nation that was about to reject the legitimacy of their rule. The attachment of those same leaders to democracy nearly vanished. In 1893, Grover Cleveland wrote, "Our revolutionary fathers . . . went too far with their notions of popular government. Democracy is now the enemy of law and order." [13] Some of the nation's leaders appeared to be on the verge of panic. Theodore Roosevelt shrilly preached to his peers that they must eschew effeteness for the strenuous life, the life of the warrior. President Cleveland dispatched federal troops to quell labor agitation against wage cuts and dangerous working conditions in mines, mills, and railroads.

Having pacified the labor force but still in the midst of a political struggle with the agrarian populists, the Cleveland administration forged ahead with its industrial program. The program included repression of labor, a steep protective tariff, and the construction of a navy that could be used to open up and defend foreign markets for American investment and industrial and agricultural exports that the domestic economy purportedly could not absorb. But by the mid-1890s, the national leadership was looking out on a world bristling with European power and seething with indigenous independence movements in such places as Cuba, the Philippines, and Africa. The promise of American life, and with it the legitimacy of its political order, seemed doomed unless foreign markets could be penetrated and American domestic unrest thereby ultimately quelled. Under these circumstances, leaders who did not hesitate to use military force against their own citizens could not be expected to refrain from using it to open up markets in Cuba, the Philippines, or China.

The crescendo of domestic unrest in the early and mid-1890s was accentuated by an economic panic in 1893. Every actual and potential foreign market assumed added importance. Among the principal overseas markets eyed by the United States was Cuba, which by the 1880s absorbed an estimated one-fourth of American tonnage involved in foreign trade. In 1893, Cuba ranked third in exports to the United States and fifth as a U.S. export market.[14] American manipulation of the tariff structure in 1894 brought ruin to the mainstay of Cuba's economy, the sugar industry, which exported three-fourths of its production to the United States. Rebellion against Spain flared on the island, and Cuban-American trade fell even further. Also imperiled by the fighting were investments totaling $45 million in sugar plantations and mines, including mines producing manganese needed to manufacture naval armor.[15]

While national and especially northern economic interests were threatened by the Cuban revolution, critical southern regional interests were also deeply involved. Secretary of State Olney feared that white and black republics would emerge in Cuba if Spanish rule were overthrown and that there would be a fight to the death in a race war. Such a manifestation of black political power so close to the racially tense American South could only be unsettling. Olney communicated to President Cleveland his belief that the establishment of a Cuban republic had to be avoided at all costs since blacks would be an influential force in such a government and would be anything but docile. "The negro elements," he noted, "are acquiring a taste for blood and incendiarism which will be difficult if not impossible to eradicate for many years to come."[16] Consequently, the Cleveland administration vigilantly attempted to cut off the flow of arms and supplies to the revolutionaries while it sold supplies to the Spanish forces in Cuba. It also pressed the Spanish government to permit loyal Cubans to establish an autonomous government under Spanish dominion. Spanish leaders were initially unsympathetic to a compromise and almost lost the island to the revolutionaries before the United States intervened to protect its own economic and political interests.

When war with Spain over Cuba broke out in 1898, the United States was able to seize the Philippines, the scene of another potentially successful revolt against Spanish rule. The process of seizure began with the victory by Dewey over the Spanish naval forces in Manila Bay. Convinced of the military value of Manila as a coaling station and naval base to protect American interests in China, the American leadership refused to allow the Filipinos to capture Manila and ordered American forces to seize the city. To secure the city, the U.S. government soon launched a war to take Luzon and the entire archipelago.

The long and bloody war that pitted America's battle-hardened

Indian fighters against the Filipinos had a profound political dimension in Asia. The Filipinos had nearly become the first Asians to throw off white rule, and they fought as stubbornly against the Americans as they had against the Spanish. The Japanese, whose narrow victory over the Russians in 1905 would send shock waves throughout the world, had an interest in the defeat of the Occidentals and sent advisers to work with the Filipinos; a Japanese arms shipment that might have influenced the outcome of the struggle against the Americans was lost at sea in a typhoon.

Despite strong domestic opposition, the American leadership believed that it had several compelling reasons to press on with the guerrilla war in the Philippines. Defeat there would threaten the entire Western colonial position in Asia and would call into question the legitimacy of American claims to full standing in the ranks of the Western powers. More important, defeat would undo the schemes of those who wanted the archipelago as a base for American penetration of China, a market that they believed was essential to American economic survival amidst strong international competition.

Most important, coming so soon after the 1890 census confirmed the closing of the continental frontier and after the depths of a long depression, defeat in the Philippines and a retreat from the China market would have threatened the very legitimacy of the American political order. That legitimacy was based on individual and mass confidence that the nation had a frontier that offered boundless opportunities for those willing and able to put Europe behind them and withstand minimal dangers. Brooks Adams, the brooding spirit of the leadership group, was acutely sensitive to the ties between political legitimacy and access to the China market. He wrote that if continental European competitors seized the East Asian markets, they would close them to the United States and then "the pressure caused by the stoppage of the current which has so long run westward might shake American society to its foundation, and would probably make the scale of life to which our people are habituated impossible." [17] According to Adams, the choice for the nation was to "expand, cost what it may, or to resign itself to . . . a relatively stationary period." [18]

Adams correctly perceived that popular confidence was brittle. Small, temporary setbacks such as had occurred at Cherry Valley, the Alamo, and the Little Big Horn had dampened confidence in the government and in the future of society. A major setback in the Philippines would obliterate the notion of an economic frontier in a China pacified by American power. The United States would be left with only Hawaii, a few small islands in an empty sea, as a western frontier, instead of a China market that had grown at a dazzling fivefold rate in the 1890s. Political confidence and legitimacy are not built upon such reversals and losses.

Thus by the 1890s the record of the American government was one of consistent foreign intervention by military assistance, purchase, or outright conquest along its frontier for the purpose of stabilizing domestic power relationships. The national political leadership believed that stability depended on the ordinary people's ignorance of more democratic ways of organizing society or, failing that, on their certainty that the national government would maintain the status quo by force of law or arms. Political leaders also believed that stability depended on the government's ability to channel abroad goods and produce not profitably marketable at home. Furthermore, in the 1840s a long era had begun of increasingly bitter Protestant-Catholic tension in which religious zealotry became a threat to domestic peace. The same leaders therefore committed themselves to keeping open distant missionary fields where the overzealous could spend their energies at least partly for the benefit of the domestic status quo by spreading American ways and a taste for American exports. China, as a potentially large market and as a vast mission field, was appropriately a key concern in such calculations. Control over events in China, therefore, assumed increasing importance as tensions mounted in the United States in the late nineteenth century. America's efforts to assert itself in China at this time, however, ran afoul of a vigorous attempt by the Chinese to reform their nation and rid it of the foreign influence and domination that had taken root in the 1840s.

1

America's Response to China's Prerevolutionary Reforms

A s American political leaders came to believe that their fate was tied to China's willingness and ability to absorb American goods and missionaries, they began to pay more and more attention to internal conditions in China and to the nature of foreign competition in that market. At best, domestic conditions in China were fluid and foreign competition aggressive. Under such circumstances, securing the China market would be difficult. The Japanese and European powers were both willing and able to use military force to secure their share of the market. Moreover, the Sino-Japanese War of 1894–95 illustrated dramatically China's inability to resist foreign aggression. Yet China's poor showing in that war served to arouse American contempt rather than sympathy. As the future minister to China, William Rockhill noted that "a good thrashing will not hurt China in the least. . . . It is the only tonic which seems to suit her."[1] Suggestions that the United States come to China's assistance were dismissed as impertinent: "Its [i.e., intervention's] only effect would be to preserve from destruction a dynasty which stands for all that is odious, reactionary, cruel and detestable in the government of mankind. Defeat will mean the liberation of many millions . . . from the bonds of ignorance, tyranny and barbarity. . . . For an American President and Secretary of State to undertake to rescue China from the Japanese was an offense against international justice."[2] The other major powers were

13

quick to exploit a China weakened by defeat. Spheres of foreign influence rapidly expanded in China. Russia and Japan extended their power in Manchuria; in 1897, Germany seized Jiaozhou; in 1898, Great Britain proclaimed its dominance in the Chang Jiang (Yangtze River) Valley; and France began making considerable inroads in southern China. The Chinese, cognizant of these and other maneuvers and still smarting over their humiliation at the hands of the Japanese in 1894–95, began to seek ways of strengthening their government and its military arm in order to regain control of their country.

Clearly, something had to be done if the United States was not to be excluded completely from the China market. As early as 1898, Minister to China Edwin Conger recommended to Secretary of State John Hay that the United States obtain control of a naval base on the China coast "from which we can potently assert our rights and effectively wield our influence."[3] In November 1900, Hay authorized Conger to attempt to secure Sansha Bay in Fujian province for an American naval station.[4] Although Japanese opposition doomed this effort, American opinion leaders were ever mindful of the importance of enhancing the U.S. military presence in China. For example, Senator Albert Beveridge in his book, *The Russian Advance*, admonished his reading audience to remember that the China market could not be taken by "polite notes or banquet speeches" but would have to be secured by "ships, commercial agents, modern methods, the expenditure of money, and the resourceful vigilance of a firm and comprehensive business policy."[5]

The United States, despite its ostensible disavowal of territorial ambitions in China, was not above suspicion. As Chang Zhidong, a leading reformer and governor-general of Hunan and Hubei remarked, the intentions of American merchants in coming to China were "deceitful in the extreme."[6] Given this attitude, Charles Denby, U.S. minister to China, was well aware that "[t]he foreigner in China holds his position by force alone. . . . We must recognize the fact that kindness to this people goes for little."[7]

With the United States too weak to oppose the Europeans and the Japanese by military force, the secretary of state, John Hay, deftly attempted to play them off one against the other by issuing two "Open Door Notes." These espoused the principles of territorial integrity and commercial equality in the hope that the other powers would not divide China among themselves or raise discriminatory trade barriers in their spheres of influence against Americans. These notes also had the advantage of justifying American participation in any new privileges obtained by the other powers while at the same time constituting an apparent U.S. commitment to China's territorial integrity. Significantly, however, Hay did not even bother to inform the Chinese that the United States was adopting such an "Open Door" policy.[8] China was to be preserved as a viable commercial and political entity not for the direct benefit of the Chinese but rather for that of the United States. As Alfred Hippisley, a British subject, wrote to the actual author of the Open Door notes, William Rockhill, "Steps taken to assure the integrity of China are not taken out of pure altruism but to maintain trade and avoid international conflicts." The Chinese also were not completely unaware of these motivations. Thus, in 1902, an anonymous Chinese author was able to comment perceptively that "[d]ismemberment and spheres of influence belonged to political aggression . . . while preservation and Open Door policies constitute economic aggression."[9]

No sooner had the United States reached an understanding with the other imperialistic nations regarding the preservation of an economic and political balance of power in China than a great wave of militant xenophobia, known in the West as the Boxer Rebellion, swept over northern China. The Boxers made little secret of their intention of purging all sorts of foreign influence, especially religion, from China. This sudden outburst of antiforeignism deeply disturbed the American press, which demanded a forceful response to the disorder on the new frontier. The *New York Tribune* described the struggle against the Boxers as the "duty of civilization toward barbarism, the duty of law and order toward riot and anarchy. It was the duty of the United States to impose an orderly government on China without the consent of the coolies and Boxers who are thus to be governed." In a similar vein, the *Independent* called for the American occupation of Beijing and the establishment of an international protectorate over China.[10] Always sensitive to its political duty to police the frontier, the federal government dispatched troops from the Philippines to assist in putting down the native uprising in consort with the forces of the other Great Powers, which had a similar stake in preserving the status quo in China.

The American missionary community was in the forefront, demanding vengeance against the pagan transgressors. The Christian men and women who comprised this community had journeyed to China partly because there were too few opportunities to pursue their vocation in the United States. But when they arrived in China they found themselves presented with both great opportunity and challenge. Only with the assistance of their government were they able to establish their outposts in China. Indeed, had it not been for the diplomatic and military pressure of the Western powers, the ruling Manchu dynasty would have excluded the missionaries from what was the world's greatest market of potential converts. Once in China, the missionaries found the Chinese to be "proud," resistant to their message of damnation and guilt. The Chinese, firmly rooted in a stable social setting and culture every bit as ethnocentric as the American, were generally impervious to techniques that had been only marginally successful in the United States. While the missionaries stayed in the cities and larger towns, as they had in the United States, they also found it necessary to embark on a wide range of activities, such as providing much-needed education and medical care, in the hope that these activities would win over the Chinese.

In many respects, the missionaries' benevolent activities were both useful and beneficial to the Chinese. Firm in this conviction, the missionaries had few doubts about the sacred and altruistic nature of their work. Yet these men and women who journeyed thousands of miles to imbue the Chinese with Western religious ideas were more concerned with their own success than with the fate of China. Despite their innumerable works of charity, they tended to view the Chinese and Chinese affairs in the light of Western needs.

As the Boxer Rebellion threatened the very existence of the missionary community in China, it was hardly surprising that the missionaries should be among the leading advocates of revenge against the rebellious Chinese. That such an attitude was at odds with the Christian message which the missionaries were trying to bring to China did not go unnoticed, however, even in the United States. So harsh was the missionary response to the Boxers that a counter-reaction developed in the United States. Distinguished Americans such as Mark Twain attacked the non-Christian spirit of the China missionaries and argued that the United States had no business being so involved in China's internal affairs in the first place. In the resulting polemics, however, neither the missionaries nor their critics came to grips with the grievances that had led the Chinese to resist the presence of foreigners in their midst.[11]

The turmoil in the United States over the missionary reaction to the Boxer Rebellion amply demonstrated that the missionaries were able to generate a good deal of publicity in their homeland. As the largest group of Americans present in China, they were privy to the largest amount of information concerning developments in that country. Moreover, they were able to parlay their role as keepers of the status quo into special access to those who wielded political power. Presidents from Theodore Roosevelt to Woodrow Wilson all were steady churchgoers who sought out the missionary view of events in China. Similarly, even the great financial moguls of the time maintained close contact with the missionary community.[12]

The missionaries were not the only American interest group that had a vital stake in China. Just as the missionaries viewed China as a potentially great market for converts, the financial community eyed China as an economic market that might yield extraordinary profit. Similarly, as the Christian leanings of the nation's leaders created a commonality of interest between the government and the missionary community, the absence of a central bank to finance government activity caused the nation's leaders to establish an alliance with the financiers. For example, both Grover Cleveland and Theodore Roosevelt had found it necessary during their terms of office to call upon the services of J. Pierpont Morgan to preserve the government from bankruptcy. The situation was not all one-sided, however. These alliances were particularly useful to the U.S. government. The cultural inroads made by the missionaries and the economic inroads made by the financiers were both necessary prerequisites for the successful establishment of American political power and influence in China.

Morgan himself shared the propensity of the nation's political leaders for control. He had made great fortunes for himself and his partners in the House of Morgan by combining America's railroads and steel companies into great trusts, by refunding part of the Mexican national debt, and by underwriting one-fifth of the cost of Britain's Boer War. The Morgan formula for successful industrial development contained two ingredients: absolute control of the venture through hand-picked managers, and a favorable business climate. When these conditions were not met, Morgan put his money elsewhere, as in the case of the American China Development Company. This enterprise was begun by Standard Oil interests to run a railroad from Hankou to Guangzhou (Canton) and Sichuan but later was sold to Morgan's client, King Leopold of Belgium, who, in turn, sold control of it to Morgan. When the Chinese government protested what seemed to be increased Belgian railroad activity in China, and when the Chinese began boycotting American goods in response to the Chinese Exclusion Acts, Morgan returned the railroad concession to the Chinese government in exchange for an indemnity.[13]

The anti-American boycott was aimed not at a friendly power but at one that had participated in the suppression of the Boxers and in the exaction of a huge indemnity from the Chinese government. Although some Europeans and Americans welcomed the boycott as signaling a movement toward democracy in China, inspired by America's objectionable immigration policies, the U.S. government was prepared to use force to put down the boycott.

The immigration ban, which was the subject of the boycott, sought to exclude Chinese from entering the United States. This ban, which had begun as a temporary measure in 1882, was renewed for another ten years in 1892 and was made permanent in 1902. It was a response to the economic requirements of American workingmen concerned with the influx of cheap Chinese labor and also to the racism that pervaded American society. As the U.S. commissioner-general of immigration observed in 1906, the exclusion laws were directed "to a people who, according to all the recognized authorities are different in a sense of moral obligation . . . and who in their political views hold caste in higher esteem than law."[14] Similarly, Charles Denby, former minister to China, warned of the dangers of a liberal immigration policy which would permit the "yellow peril" to "attack our institutions, our customs, and habits, and overwhelm them."[15]

The boycott originated in Shanghai where the Chinese merchants decided to strike back at the American ban on Chinese immigration into the United States. As G. E. Morrison, China correspondent for the London *Times*, noted, "The Chinese have awakened to a consciousness of nationality. Outrages on Cantonese who have emigrated to the Pacific coast are no longer resented only by the people of Kwangtung. They make all Chinese indignant."[16]

Although it was aimed only at American immigration laws, the boycott caused American policymakers to fear not only for the profits of U.S. businesses dealing with China but also for the grip that the powers had on China through the declining Manchus. Willard Straight, at the time a U.S. consular official actively engaged in the promotion of American economic interests in China and later J. P. Morgan's representative in that country, was especially chagrined by the boycott and asserted that the Chinese had no right to endanger American trade. He called upon his government to accede "to the clamoring of the merchants who have lost thousands of dollars because of the interruption of their trade with the Orient and attempt to force the Chinese Government to remove their embargo on our exports." He alluded darkly to the students who were spurring on the boycott as revolutionaries who would bring down the Manchus and with them the status quo of concessions to foreigners and extraterritoriality:

> Instead of being the perhaps overzealous servants of a stable ad-
> ministration, the returned students are hot-headed leaders of in-
> cipient rebellion. Fresh from Tokyo having acquired a great deal
> of illy [sic] digested knowledge, the irresponsible majority con-
> sider themselves Oriental Washingtons, Garibaldis, and Crom-
> wells. They cry for representative government, a constitution, the
> abolition of extra-territoriality, the cancellation of all conces-
> sions to foreigners . . . and scorn the saner plans proposed by
> more cautious and better balanced men who would make haste
> slowly. . . . The results are apt to be disastrous, for they preach
> revolution and would have overthrown the existing government
> [and] like Marat and Robespierre guillotine the Tartar royalists
> who surround the Throne.[17]

Likeminded American officials in Washington also took a hard line against the boycott. Secretary of State Elihu Root warned the Chinese minister in Washington of the dangers of permitting the continued development of the anti-American movement. President Theodore Roosevelt, who felt that the presence of Chinese in the United States "would be ruinous to the white race," warned Beijing that "[t]he American Government would hold the Chinese Government directly responsible for any loss our interests sustain or may hereafter have to bear through the manifest failure . . . of the Imperial Government to stop the present organized movement against us." To back up his threat, Roosevelt instructed his minister to China, William Rockhill, "to take a stiff tone with the Chinese" and ordered troops to the Philippines where they waited for orders to sail to China to suppress the boycott.[18] Willard Straight enthusiastically applauded Roosevelt's hard line, stating:

> Force is the only effective means of persuading the Chinese Gov-
> ernment to take action to suppress the boycott.
>   Christian powers may regret the necessities that have obliged
> them to employ the sword as the unanswerable argument but it
> must be admitted that force alone has been effective in compel-
> ling action where procrastination has been the rule. There may
> be no moral right to justify insistence that relations should be
> amicable where one party has no intercourse but since the West

has broken down Oriental barriers and by right of might obtained the dominating position it now occupies, we as Americans
must follow the recognized procedure if we wish to obtain actual
results.[19]

The only opposition in America to Roosevelt's policy was of a tactical nature. Anti-administration spokesmen feared that the exclusion
laws were damaging America's trade and prestige in China and hence
were counterproductive. No major segment of American society ever
questioned the moral issues involved or recognized the boycott as a
legitimate diplomatic device.

The Chinese boycott of American goods ultimately lost its momentum and collapsed, but not before it had reduced America's prestige in China to its lowest level in history. The American leadership
cast about for ways to restore American stature in China. Rockhill
urged his superiors to remit a portion of the Boxer indemnity for the
education of Chinese students in the United States. Education would
promote political stability and economic progress, and the eventual
rise to prominence of American-educated leaders in Beijing would
give the United States unprecedented influence. As Walter Hines Page,
a vice-presidential candidate and later American minister to Great
Britain, declared, "[I]f we desire the good will, the trade and intellectual influence in China, there is no other way to get these things quite
so directly as by welcoming and training the men who a few decades
hence will exert a strong influence in governmental, educational, financial and industrial ways." F. M. Huntington-Wilson, one of the
foremost advocates of dollar diplomacy and a key figure in the future
Taft administration, put the matter quite baldly when he commented
to Root that the remission "should be used to make China do some
of the things we want. Otherwise I fear her gratitude will be quite
empty."[20] Such were the motivations behind one of America's most
ambitious philanthropic endeavors in China.

While American leaders were pushing ahead with their program
to develop a new generation of pliant Chinese officials, they continued
to deal with the Manchu government which had weathered both the
Boxer debacle and the anti-American boycott and which now was attempting to institute a reform program. A prior attempt at reform had
been launched in 1898 under the aegis of the great Chinese intellectual Kang Yuwei. Kang's motivation in promoting reform did not reflect an alienation from traditional Chinese culture. However, something had to be done or "China will soon perish. . . . Unless we

change the old institutions entirely . . . we cannot make ourselves strong."[21] Despite the imminent threat of partition, his efforts were doomed to failure by the opposition of the Empress Dowager Ci Xi who, in the judgment of the *Baptist Missionary Union Magazine*, had prevented the reformers from "precipitating turmoil and disorder which would be a more effectual check to progress than her more conservative view."[22] However, in 1905, in a dramatic reversal of policy, Ci Xi embarked on a series of reforms similar to those which she had so recently opposed. Her reform measures were aimed at transforming China's educational, social, political, and military institutions. Indeed, on September 6, 1906, the empress took the unprecedented step of endorsing the principle of constitutional government.[23] Although the proposed reforms marked a significant departure from past policies, the transition to constitutional government was to be a gradual one, with supreme authority remaining in the hands of the crown.[24]

The Manchus' endorsement of constitutionalism did not represent a sudden conversion to democratic principles. The Russo-Japanese War of 1904–5, which was fought to determine which country would dominate Manchuria, starkly demonstrated China's inability to protect its own territorial integrity. This further heightened the vulnerability of the Manchus to their domestic foes, who maintained that the Manchus were responsible for China's semicolonial status. Japan's defeat of Russia also was interpreted as a victory for constitutional monarchy over autocracy.[25] The Manchus therefore chose to promote constitutional government to buttress their sagging authority and to convince both foreign powers and the Chinese people of their commitment to reform. In this respect, the reform movement did not constitute a genuine effort to promote democracy.[26]

Despite the self-serving motives of the Manchus, the reform movement nonetheless had a significant impact on Chinese society. The abolition of the traditional examination system represented a severe blow to the existing power alignment by eliminating the dividing line between the upper and lower classes. As one observer remarked regarding this step, "The consequences for China's social order, educational system, and administrative structure were so direct and concrete that they meant imminent doom for traditional institutions."[27] Similarly, the encouragement of overseas study gave rise to a group of foreign-educated students who were to become the most radical proponents of Chinese nationalism. The reform movement also stimulated participation by the gentry in provincial assemblies, which eventually became the leading forums advocating anti-imperialism and thorough institutional reform.[28] The military reforms that were designed to strengthen China's defense also permitted the alienation of the one institution that stood between the dynasty and its domestic opponents. Yet, for all its accomplishments, the Manchu reform movement further weakened the domestic viability of the monarchy by raising expectations that the dynasty could not meet.

A few American leaders applauded the new reforms. William Jennings Bryan, the Democratic Party leader and the party's link to the democratic and reform tendencies of the populist movement, enthusiastically remarked, "The sleeping giantess, whose drowsy eyes have so long shut out the rays of the morning sun, is showing unmistakable signs of awakening. There was a vitality among her people which even 2,000 years of political apathy could not exhaust."[29] W. A. P. Martin, the famous missionary, noted that "China is the theatre of the greatest movement now taking place on the face of the globe."[30] The editor of *World Today* found the abolition of the traditional examination system to be most significant: "In thus summarily abolishing the ancient system of education it undermines the strongest fortification of China's conservatism and isolation. It throws the door open for western learning. . . . It is a long step toward the emancipation of the people and it will be hailed with satisfaction by friends of civilization throughout the world. It marks the dawning of the day in the great Empire of the East."[31] William Rockhill, one of the foremost China scholars of his day and minister to China under Theodore Roosevelt, also praised the reform movement, at least in its initial stages, as likely to strengthen the central government and promote internal order, basic prerequisites of a thriving international trade. For this reason, he argued, it was in the interest of the United States to encourage the reform movement.[32]

But most of the leadership had strong reservations about political change in China. The editor of the *Washington Post* shuddered at the prospect of a constitutional government in China and wondered whether a people who had never changed their religion or invented a new god in three thousand years wasn't almost beyond the pale of modern progress, for it certainly was not fit to perform the functions of a modern civilized government.[33]

Within the American government, men of influence were similarly pessimistic about the Manchu reform movement. As one State Department official noted, "The inertia of China is disheartening, but what can you expect of a jellyfish."[34] Even Rockhill ultimately despaired over the prospects of the reform movement. Remarking on the new provincial assemblies formed in 1908, he asserted that the whole scheme was "no other than a perpetuation of the existing system under a thin veil of constitutional guarantees." Rockhill was of the belief that China lacked statesmen and was "quite unable to manage her international affairs without strong support and constant pressure from without." A close associate of William Howard Taft, Congressman John Wiley of Alabama commented on his return from the Orient that the "Chinese remain always the same incomprehensible, unfathomable, unchanging, unchangeable, unassimilating and inscrutable people. . . . Of all the Orientals, no race is so alien. There is no kinship or common feeling possible between the Anglo-Saxon and Chinese."[35]

Disillusionment with the reform movement only served to increase America's interest in China. Under the Taft administration, which came to office in 1909, China and access to its markets assumed unprecedented importance in the thinking of the American leadership. As Roosevelt's secretary of war, Taft had expressed his conviction that a growing United States would need China to absorb an expanding agricultural and industrial surplus. When the former governor-general of the Philippines and secretary of war assumed the presidency, one of his first actions was to promote American financial involvement in China. To that end, he chose Philander Knox, a corporate lawyer and director of two Mellon-controlled banks, as secretary of state and cast about for a business-oriented person to replace the distinguished yet scholarly William Rockhill as American minister to China.[36] Of his decision to replace Rockhill, Taft wrote:

> Rockhill has not the slightest interest in American trade or in promoting it. He is pessimistic and not optimistic in his views of what can be done, and he is not a man of strength and force of action such as we need at Peking. . . . I regard the position at Peking as the most important diplomatic position that I have to fill and it is necessary to send there a man of business force and perception and ability to withstand the aggressions of the Japanese, the English, and the Russians. China is very friendly toward us, and . . . anxious to encourage American trade and investment capital, because she does not mistrust our motives. The opportunities it seems to me therefore, for the development of the Oriental trade are great if only we can have a man on the ground who realizes the necessity and has the force and pluck and experience to take advantage of the opportunity.[37]

Taft's first choice as minister to China was the wealthy Chicago industrialist Charles Crane. Crane, however, never made it to Beijing. As the result of a series of indiscreet comments by Crane to the press, Taft withdrew his nomination. Although the actual reasons for this decision remain obscure, indications are that Crane opposed Taft's desire to work closely with the other major powers, particularly the Japanese, in Chinese financial matters. In addition to being out-spokenly anti-Japanese and thus a threat to Taft's policy of cooper-ating with the other Great Powers to promote American economic interests in China, Crane appeared to reflect the American manufac-turing sector's distrust of the Wall Street banking community, which was to play such a critical role in Taft's China policy. Indeed, Crane went so far as to describe the consortium of American banks that Taft had established to promote American economic penetration of China as "the new form of hold-up which the State Department has recently been so successfully engaged in of forcing money on China." Whatever the reason for Crane's political demise, Taft's next choice was clearly a man of strong business orientation. In 1909, Taft sent William J. Calhoun, a corporate lawyer and former head of J. P. Morgan's creation, U.S. Steel, to represent the United States in China for the next four years.[38]

Taft and his colleagues within his administration wholeheartedly endorsed the views of Brooks Adams, Albert Beveridge, and others that it was absolutely essential for the political and economic well-being of the United States to adopt a comprehensive national business policy to assist in the penetration of foreign markets. The implementation of such a policy was made more urgent by the decline of American exports to China from $8 million in 1908 to $6 million in 1909. Whereas 4 percent of U.S. exports had gone to China prior to Taft's inauguration, the figure had declined to 1 percent by 1910. At the same time, Amer-ica's Japanese rivals were doubling their trade with China. Something had to be done to reverse this trend, so Taft and Knox became the champions of "dollar diplomacy." As a State Department official noted, "Today diplomacy works for trade, and the Foreign Offices of the world are powerful engines for the promotion of the commerce of each coun-try."[39] Thus, dollar diplomacy entailed the protection and promotion of American markets in China by invigorating the U.S. diplomatic and consular service, building up the merchant marine, encouraging busi-ness to engage in overseas ventures, appointing financial advisers to foreign governments, and organizing financial instruments of national policy. If the U.S. government could stimulate the flow of American capital to China through this policy, the China trade would prosper: "The Department has in view the general extension of American influence in China so that when the commercial interests and exporters of the United States turn their attention more vigorously toward securing the markets of the Orient, they will find those of China open to their products and the Chinese public favorably disposed toward American enterprise."[40]

The means by which Taft sought to promote American economic interests in China were almost as important as the goal itself. Paradoxically, while the drive to break the great trusts was gaining momentum in the United States, and Taft was acquiring something of a reputation as a trustbuster in the process, he also was seeking to create an international monopoly to deal with the financially desperate Chinese. Such a policy was enthusiastically endorsed by many of his top advisers. Henry Stimson, future secretary of state, in an address to the New York Republican Club, described a large amount of economic concentration as "necessary and beneficial."[41] Similarly, F. M. Huntington-Wilson argued that "the efficiency of combination may be availed of with large benefit and no possible detriment to the nation . . . in the foreign field."[42] Secretary Knox shared these sentiments, especially with respect to China, remarking that "the policy of mutual cooperation and division of profits as opposed to the old system of single efforts versus combined opposition would hasten the time when China would be seamed with wealth-producing and opportunity-giving railways."[43]

Because American financiers had been funneling their own relatively limited capital elsewhere, the United States had been unable to compete with the other powers for a major share of the Chinese financial market. By 1909, the danger of complete exclusion from that market appeared possible as an international syndicate composed of British, French, and German banking interests entered into an agreement with the viceroy of Huguang to finance railway construction. Knox viewed this development as especially ominous because he believed that investment in railway development was the means by which the United States would increase its trade and influence in China.[44] To Taft and his advisers, the United States seemed to be facing a financial crisis similar to the political and commercial crisis some years before, which had led to the issuance of the Open Door Notes. Abandoning any hope of independent American financial activity in

China, Taft and Knox exerted every pressure to gain admittance to the international consortium.

In June 1909, Knox brought together the premier Wall Street financial houses to persuade them to participate in the proposed railway loan should the United States gain admission to the international consortium. While many of the bankers were reluctant to become involved in this venture, J. P. Morgan, Wall Street's dominant figure, agreed to Knox's pleadings lest he jeopardize his firm's position as banker to the U.S. government. Considerable pressure also was brought to bear upon the Chinese. Unless China agreed to U.S. participation, the excess portion of the Boxer indemnity would not be returned and American friendship toward China would be forfeit. These threats forced the Chinese to capitulate and, in June, Beijing agreed to delay final approval of the Huguang loan pending American participation, which was forthcoming in July.[45] The American banking firms chosen to participate in the consortium were J. P. Morgan & Company, Kuhn, Loeb and Company, the National City Bank, and the First National Bank, all of New York City.[46] Indeed, despite the entreaties of a number of other investors who wished to participate in the China business, the State Department steadfastly defended the exclusive nature of the American group.[47]

On November 10, 1910, the London Agreement was signed which, in effect, extended the Huguang railway agreement to encompass all future major loans to China. As Straight explained to Huntington-Wilson, the American group signed this agreement because there was a limited market for financial securities in the United States and because "neither the American Group nor any other association of American financiers can compete against European banks for Chinese loans. That being the case, it was necessary to avoid competition by associating itself with its most powerful competitors."[48] At American insistence, the institution of an international trust designed to eliminate competition in the financial market of China had been accomplished with the United States as a full-fledged partner. It was testimony to the increasing influence and power of the United States in Chinese affairs.

For the United States, the consortium represented the financial counterpart of the Open Door. The Taft administration and the New York financiers hoped that this cooperative venture would provide the United States with more profit and influence than it presently could achieve independently. Cooperation rather than confrontation with the other powers via the consortium was the price the United States would have to pay if American interests in China were to be safeguarded.[49] To assure the profitability of the joint enterprise, the U.S. government, as well as the governments of the other nations represented in the consortium, exerted considerable pressure on their nationals to maintain a solid and monopolistic posture toward China. This pressure also was to be brought to bear upon the "unenlightened" Chinese who otherwise would create "a financial plague spot to the injury of the general [U.S.] interest."[50]

Association with the other powers did not force the United States to abandon a conciliatory policy toward the Chinese in financial matters, for such a policy never existed. Indeed, America's hard-line posture toward the Chinese predated its entry into the consortium. For example, in December 1909, the Chinese awarded the American group a loan contract for national currency reform. Knox insisted, however, that an American adviser be appointed to oversee the loan.[51] Though the Chinese vigorously resisted this demand, the American position on the issue was adamant. As one consular official remarked, "Conciliation is the worst argument to employ in dealing with [China]."[52] Because the majority of Chinese officials could not be trusted to carry out currency reform honestly and professionally, Straight recommended to J. P. Morgan that ample security and stringent guarantees be obtained prior to any loan, lest the money be "diverted to the pockets of officials or wasted in accordance with the whims of a half-baked National Assembly."[53] Although circumstances eventually forced Knox to modify his demands, American behavior during the negotiations made the Chinese wary of America's "malicious designs" in China. The entry of the United States into the consortium, a "bankers' ring" whose purpose was to monopolize international loans to China, further heightened this anti-American sentiment and contributed to the growth of Chinese nationalism.[54]

Notwithstanding the glum predictions of American opinion makers and the shift in American strategy toward matters of high finance in China, the Manchu reform movement gained momentum. As it did so, it stirred up American fears of Chinese nationalism. The Manchus were finding it very difficult to resist the vociferous demands of many Chinese that the transition period to genuine constitutional government be accelerated. To American political leaders and opinion makers, these ostensibly democratic demands seemed dangerously tinged with nationalism.

Taft's minister to China, William J. Calhoun, particularly feared the trend toward democracy symbolized by the provincial and national assemblies. Realizing that a government that truly expressed the will of the Chinese people would threaten foreign dominance, Calhoun praised Prince Qing for opposing rapid reform and immediate convocation of a genuine parliament. Calhoun hoped that the Manchus would be able to continue to exert a restraining influence and thwart the "agitators" who were demanding too much power. Of the National Assembly, Calhoun noted apprehensively, "Already there appears to be a disposition to discuss foreign affairs. The fact is that no controlling force had appeared competent to restrain its deliberations, a sign which may be indicative of future troubles." The China expert of the American legation, Chargé d'Affaires Henry Fletcher, kept a watchful eye on the provincial assemblies, where antiforeignism was most pronounced.[55]

American leaders became particularly anxious when the Manchus were unable to suppress nationalistic sentiment in the Chinese deliberative bodies. Willard Straight was dismayed that the government was so weak that it had been forced to acquiesce in the demands of the "young scatterbrains" for an early convocation of the National Assembly. Straight particularly feared that "[t]hese Voxes [*sic*] Populi . . . will above all things wish to mix in finance and that is the quarter from which we must expect much trouble."

Calhoun believed that the Manchus' inability to control the assemblies was the result of a "conspicuous dearth in China of men of authority and force." Calhoun's peers shared his sentiments and attributed the state of affairs to the absence of the Chinese general Yuan Shikai from the political scene in Beijing. Walter Kirton, editor of the *National Review*, confided to Secretary of State Philander Knox that "[w]hile generally speaking, no man is indispensable yet in the case of Yuan and following the apparently immutable law regarding China and the Chinese, the dictum is reversed. He alone of all officials of high rank possesses the status, grip, and capacity to get work done." Though Yuan had the reputation of a reformer, his efforts had centered largely upon military, not political, matters. Americans viewed him as a person who could restore order to China without fostering social reforms or democracy.[56]

Events in China were rapidly coming to a head. The nationalistic and democratic forces that had been so instrumental in forcing the Manchus to initiate reform were becoming completely alienated from the dynasty. The threat from these forces was not just to the dynasty, however, but to all the foreign powers, including the United States, that had a stake in the status quo. Thus, fear of democratization and nationalism, support of authoritarian rule, and devotion to the cause of the militarist Yuan pervaded America's ruling circles and presaged the dogged resistance to the Chinese Revolution of 1911 that suffused the ranks of American officialdom, the business sector, and even the missionary community. The result was that American ideals of liberty and democracy fell victim to the proponents of institutionalized power, profit, and control.

2

The Initial American Reaction to the 1911 Revolution

THE PRECARIOUS balance between state and local power in China was lost in 1911 when the Manchu dynasty was overthrown and replaced by a republic. Historically, the central government had ruled that vast country through an unwritten understanding with powerful local gentry that legitimatized their exploitation of the peasantry. The most talented gentry were invited to share in the choicest spoils of government, and, in return, they supported the ruling dynasty. Both sides understood that exploitation had to be kept to a bearable and predictable level or the peasantry would rise up and exact a terrible vengeance. Hence, imperial and local elites watched each other for signs of overindulgence and extravagance that would endanger the entire ruling system.[1]

In the eyes of the Chinese elite, since the Opium War of 1839–42, the Manchus—whose fortunes had first begun to decline as early as the late eighteenth century—had not kept their side of the bargain. For over half a century, foreign encroachment gradually had been transforming and undermining China's political, economic, and social stability. The so-called treaty system instituted following Chinese defeat in the Opium War brought foreign settlements, spheres of influence, tariff restrictions, extraterritoriality, economic exploitation, and missionary proselytization to China and vividly illustrated that nation's weakness vis-à-vis the West. The Manchus had failed to keep out foreign goods; as a result, the peasant handicraft industry, which had generated revenue for the local elite and which had been necessary for the smooth functioning of a balanced local economy, was in distress. Equally disastrous from the perspective of the local elite, the Manchus had permitted the foreigners to send in missionaries and establish schools which, by teaching Western subjects, began to supersede the traditionalist schools dominated by the elite. Still worse, the missionaries built up local followings protected by foreign treaties or the threat of foreign intervention, to the detriment of the elite's power and prestige. And even worse, the Manchus insisted on trying to build up a centralized military force paid for by a rapidly expanding system of taxes imposed on the ordinary necessities of life. The enraged peasants directed their murderous anger at the elite who collected the taxes for the Manchus, and their frequent antitax riots drove many gentry to the cities, leaving the countryside unattended.[2]

By the early twentieth century, the Manchus' inability to reverse foreign encroachments on the nation's economic and political sovereignty came to overshadow all other issues in Chinese politics.[3] A consensus had emerged among the Chinese elite concerning the necessity for reform and modernization to meet the imperialist threat. While the conservative elements of Chinese society hoped to accomplish this modernization through existing institutions, a growing number of Chinese intelligentsia felt that this goal could be achieved only by overthrowing the ineffectual Manchus.

China's integrity could be preserved only by instituting wide-ranging reforms, such as modernizing the military, abolishing the traditional examination system, establishing constitutional government, and promoting Western learning. These reforms were designed to make China strong enough to defend itself against the onslaught of the powers. Although the early reformers still preferred "Chinese learning for the fundamental principles, Western learning for practical application,"[4] widespread recognition of the need to reform boded ill for the Manchus. Foreign encroachment would have to be reversed if the dynasty were to be preserved.

Following the Boxer Rebellion, China had to choose between wholesale transformation or national extinction. As a Japanese diplomat observed shortly before the Manchus launched their reform movement in 1905, "Nationalistic thought in connection with foreign rights has permeated the entire land of China, and all classes of people have been affected by the currents of the new thought."[5] The watchword for the new China would be "recovery of sovereign rights." Fear of partition gave the rights-recovery movement an aggressive territorial character. Efforts were made to reassert Chinese authority in Bhutan, Nepal, Burma, Indochina, Mongolia, and Manchuria.[6] The Chinese were indignant over the loss of sovereign rights within China as well. Extraterritoriality was bitterly resented and even "good" institutions such as the Imperial Maritime Customs Service were targeted for takeover by the Chinese authorities. Anti-imperialism also focused on foreign investment which threatened to deprive China of control over its natural resources and economy. Drives were launched to recover China's foreign-controlled railroads, and officials contemplating granting further concessions to secure foreign loans were subjected to popular protest. The British Foreign Office took the position that "It is undoubtedly true that the Chinese government and people are showing increasing signs of resentment at what they consider the harsh and unreasonable conditions imposed by the foreign financial interests in China . . . against the tightening grip of foreign financiers on the nation's purse strings."[7]

Imperialism was not the only problem the Manchus faced as they entered the twentieth century. A population explosion in the nineteenth century had exacerbated China's chronic economic woes.[8] The first decade of the new century also brought an uncommon number of natural disasters which further contributed to the Manchus' difficulties. Economic failures in the major cities and food shortages in the countryside occurred in 1910 and 1911. Resentment over high taxes levied to finance the reform program fed the discontent of the populace. The nation was facing both a political and a financial crisis.[9]

In addition to their numerous foreign and domestic difficulties, the Manchus became the subject of vicious racial propaganda which struck a responsive chord among the Han Chinese. On August 20, 1905, a united revolutionary organization known as the Tongmenghui was formed, dedicated to the overthrow of the Manchus. While the Tongmenghui, the "anti-dynastic society of the upper class," shared the nationalistic sentiment then pervading the country, it chose to attack not the powers but the Manchus, whose weakness permitted the exploitation of China.[10] Sun Yat-sen, the leading figure in this organization, bitterly attacked the Manchus for excluding Han Chinese from key positions of authority and otherwise discriminating against the Chinese. The Manchus were castigated as an inferior race guilty of perpetrating a gigantic hoax by posing as reformers intent on saving China. Hu Hanmin asserted that "the Manchu government is evil because it is the evil race which usurped our government, and their evils are not confined to a few political measures but are rooted in the nature of the race and can neither be eliminated nor reformed."[11]

The advantages of such a racially motivated strategy were several. This racial propaganda enabled the revolutionaries to establish working ties with the secret societies, which were historically anti-Manchu. It also enabled rebel spokesmen, such as Sun Yat-sen, to appeal to foreign audiences for support without revealing their anti-imperialist goals. Along with the several real internal and external threats facing China, these racial attacks further weakened the Manchus' hold on the throne.

Despite some modest successes during the rights recovery movement, the dismal record of the Manchus in coping with the powers made them highly vulnerable to their domestic critics. These critics argued that the Manchus had so weakened China that it had lost the ability to defend itself. Rather than opposing foreign encroachment, the Manchus, their critics argued, preferred to grant concessions to the powers to maintain themselves on the throne, even at the expense of China's sovereignty. Instead of applauding the Manchu reform program, opponents of the regime viewed it as a confession of weakness. For example, Wang Jingwei dismissed the dynasty's endorsement of constitutionalism as "the inevitable result of a minority race controlling a majority race."[12] The reforms were not aimed at strengthening China but were designed to limit regional power by enhancing the authority of the central government and thereby preserving the Manchus' domestic political control.

Although the Tongmenghui's strong advocacy of republicanism was largely responsible for the ultimate establishment of that form of government, the Manchus would not have fallen without the cooperation of the military. Since China's defeat at the hands of Japan in 1894–95, modernization of the army had been an explicit policy of the Chinese government. The Manchu reforms accelerated efforts to modernize the nation's armed forces. No longer was military service viewed with distaste by China's upper classes. The abolition of the examination system and the encouragement of overseas study led eventually to the emergence of a new scholar/officer class strongly imbued with nationalistic fervor. The influx of young nationalists and radical students into the army also influenced the attitudes of the urban poor and destitute peasantry who constituted the rank and file. Within a relatively short period of time, the social composition of the army had been transformed.[13]

This "New Army" was keenly aware of the dire social, economic, and political conditions facing the country. The nationalistic bent of the military fostered anti-Manchu sentiment among the young officer class, which was dissatisfied with the dynasty's inability to meet both foreign challenges and internal problems. Infiltration of the armed forces by revolutionary elements made the loyalty of the royal troops suspect and the increasing literacy of the common soldier made him more susceptible to revolutionary propaganda. In addition to this growing nationalism, other factors contributed to the alienation of the military. The government found itself unable to pay its troops on a regular basis. This, coupled with traditional corruption among the officers, maltreatment of enlisted men, personnel cutbacks, and diminished prospects for advancement further alienated the military from the dynasty it was pledged to support. The disaffected troops blamed the Manchus for these conditions.[14]

If the Manchus were to turn back the tide of imperialism and defuse revolutionary sentiment throughout the country, it would be necessary to create a loyal, modern army. Yet, the central authority needed to accomplish this task simply was not present during the last years of Manchu rule. As late as 1908, despite the initiation of the reform movement, Manchus continued to occupy a disproportionate number of high government offices, to the detriment of the Han Chinese. Failure to expand the scope of political participation fostered provincial autonomy, which made centralization impossible. Thus, as a result of weak central leadership and the growing financial and political independence of the provinces, the New Army, especially in the south, rather than becoming an instrument of Beijing, developed a territorial character whose ties to the central government were only as strong as its conviction that the dynasty was adequately pursuing nationalistic goals. When this conviction weakened in 1911, New Army units defected to the revolution.

As military loyalty to the dynasty eroded, the Manchus also found their hold over the reformist elements of Chinese society weakening. When the Manchus abolished the traditional examination system, they lost one of their principal tools for regulating and controlling the local gentry. According to one observer, "by this act the door to the past was closed to the younger generation once and for all."[15]

The socially dominant gentry class had been in the forefront, advocating the establishment of provincial assemblies and local self-governing bodies in order to formalize its political power, which had been threatened by the abolition of the traditional examination system. On August 27, 1908, the Manchus announced a nine-year program designed to pave the way for the establishment of a constitutional monarchy. Local self-governing bodies were sanctioned and in 1909–10 provincial assemblies and a Provisional National Assembly were formed. These bodies, which were intended to serve as substitutes for the traditional examination system, also provided the constitutionalists with legally recognized forums. The elections that ensued, however, did not meet Western standards for democracy. Suffrage was greatly limited and bribery and apathy prevalent. According to a contemporary observer, "These elections excited no popular enthusiasm and [only] a small proportion of those qualified to vote actually cast ballots. The official influence in the choice of assembly members was very strong . . . amounting almost to the appointment of the members by officials."[16] Those elected came primarily from the gentry class, which eventually dominated these bodies.

Although the provincial assemblies reflected particularistic interests, they, too, were not immune to the anti-imperialist sentiment sweeping the country. The gentry and the local merchants who joined them in dominating these assemblies resented foreigners' usurpation of their economic prerogatives. Provincialism was beginning to emerge as a dominant force in Chinese politics due to the inability of the central government to stem foreign encroachment. The Manchus were becoming increasingly unable to control their own creations. By failing to satisfy the ever-growing demand that the balance of power with the West be redressed while at the same time raising expectations that this would be done, the Manchus lost even more of their legitimacy. [17]

While the Manchus were as apathetic as the people regarding the establishment of parliamentary rule, the constitutionalists felt that China's critical condition demanded an early convening of Parliament. The constitutionalists argued that only a parliament could achieve the national unity necessary to save the nation, stave off rebellion, and force the Manchus to behave responsibly. However, the formation of a Manchu-dominated royal cabinet on May 8, 1910, frustrated the reformist elite who were becoming convinced that the Manchus would never willingly share genuine political power. Although on November 4, 1910, the preparation period for constitutional rule was reduced by three years, the dynasty continued to resist demands for the appointment of a cabinet responsible to the National Assembly. Similarly, frustration was building on the local level, where provincial assemblies, already resentful of government overtaxation and interference, also were being denied real power. Manchu inaction was undermining support for moderate reform. According to Liang Qichao, "The longer [the present government] lasts, the more power of evolution we lose." [18]

Local resentment came to a head in May 1911, when Beijing declared that China's railway trunk lines were to be placed under the direct control of the central government. On May 20, 1911, Sheng Xuanhuai, the minister of posts and communications, contracted for a foreign loan of six million taels to complete the Beijing-Hankou and Guangzhou-Hankou railway lines. This loan had been negotiated without consulting the provinces. A storm of protest erupted in Hubei, Hunan, Guangdong, and Sichuan as local gentry shareholders and provincial assemblymen argued that the imperial government was mortgaging the country's economy to the foreign powers. A railway protection movement was launched, demanding submission of the loan agreement to the national and provincial assemblies. Peasants and urban workers, fearful that the loan would mean higher taxes, as well as nationalistic students supported the protest. On September 7, 1911, the central government had to intervene militarily in Sichuan to put down a virtual rebellion. To the provinces, nationalization of the railways meant further political and financial control by the central government. To the assemblymen, such control was detrimental to the development of provincial autonomy and constitutional rule. To the nationalists, the loan was just another instance of Manchu inability to resist foreign encroachment. Disaffection within the army and the alienation of the reformist elite placed the Manchus in dire straits. Foreign pressure on China was also mounting. On January 11, 1911, the revolutionary leader Huang Xing wrote:

> Japan has annexed Korea and has reached an agreement with Russia respecting Manchuria and Mongolia. Britain, seeing China's weakness, has sent troops to Tibet and the Yunnan-Burma border. It is only a matter of days until Western China is lost. The Germans are in Shantung and the French in Yunnan. The U.S.A. has not occupied any of our lands and has not done us any harm but they are monopolizing foreign loans. . . . The Manchu government, however, remains in a drunken state. Unaware of the dangers (sugar-coated in sweet gestures), it welcomes the American policy while tacitly consenting to the demands of other powers. . . . China's present condition is that if it is not conquered by partition it will be lost through invisible financial control by foreign powers. [19]

Huang was correct in his perception that the foreign threat to China was increasing. Before the revolution erupted, for example, while the Manchus were struggling to maintain their grip on China, President William Howard Taft and his circle of trusted advisers were casting about for ways to increase American power and influence in China, to avoid being shut out altogether by European and Japanese imperialists. Taft and his circle were unabashed Anglo-Saxon supremacists who approached the challenge confident in their belief that while their future was precarious, it still was the most promising in the world.

As Theodore Roosevelt's proconsul in the Philippines, Taft had learned at firsthand the problems and potential of an Anglo-Saxon empire in Asia. Given a choice between using the carrot or the stick, Taft was inclined to offer the carrot, or dollars for developmental purposes. He believed that military power was a far less effective instrument than economic power, and consequently he hoped that financial support for the Manchus would best serve American interests in China. The Manchus were a known entity that had proved to be quite responsive to foreign powers. President Taft had, in fact, once complimented the prince regent on the Manchu government's support for the principles of the Open Door.[20]

President Taft and his secretary of state, Philander Knox, were so committed to their strategy of using the Manchus to attain American ends in China that they were not prepared to accept field reports that emphasized Manchu weakness.[21] American Chargé d'Affaires Henry Fletcher, a former Rough Rider in the Spanish-American War, soldier in the Philippines, career diplomat, and China expert, was one source of such reports. He wrote Washington that the Manchus were on the verge of bankruptcy and that an infusion of more foreign capital into the country would only heighten the pervasive spirit of hostility toward the central government. He noted that this spirit was so strong that the Manchus had begun to buy back many of the concessions they had granted to attract foreign capital. Elsewhere in China, other American diplomats compared the atmosphere to that preceding the Boxer Rebellion. They observed, however, that this time the Manchus might not be able to deflect popular discontent from themselves to the foreigners.[22]

Revolutionary propaganda notwithstanding, some foreigners feared that Chinese unrest would not strike the Manchus alone. In Nanjing, for example, antiforeign agitation contributed to the prevailing state of anxiety and caused the powers to make general military preparations in case of actual hostilities. The commander of the U.S. Asiatic Fleet, Rear Admiral John Hubbard, not only agreed with his colleagues in the diplomatic corps that the situation was worsening, he believed that revolution was imminent. To safeguard against the potential threat to American lives and property, Hubbard requested the assignment of more gunboats and cruisers to the Asiatic Fleet. These reinforcements, he argued, would also serve a broader policy: "While the really tangible American interests in China are relatively, and even actually, exceedingly small, it is supposed that there exists a certain looking ahead to future possibilities which might preclude any idea of abandoning the fate of China entirely to other foreign Powers, and this being so, it would seem we should be getting into readiness to assert, if necessary, whatever claims we may think our due." [23]

Despite the incisiveness of earlier field reports, the reluctance of top administration officials to accept such pessimistic findings soon altered the perceptions of American diplomats stationed in China. When the Manchus inaugurated the constitutional assembly in 1911, the American embassy staff breathed a sigh of relief. Surely, this device would alleviate dissatisfaction directed at the Manchu regime. In Guangzhou, originally believed by American officials to be the most potentially explosive trouble spot in the country, Consul Bergholz claimed that a serious uprising was impossible. Bergholz hedged a bit, however, by reporting that should the impossible happen, the Chinese were so enamored of the United States that there would be no threat to American interests in China. [24]

Earlier predictions that revolution was imminent proved accurate on October 9, 1911, when a bomb accidentally exploded in the Russian concession in Hankou. The next day, the authorities obtained a list of rebel infiltrators in the area. Prompt rebel action was required if the bombers were not to be apprehended, and on the evening of October 10, the army in the Hankou area, which had been systematically infiltrated by the rebels, unfurled the revolutionary banner and began the struggle to unseat the dynasty that had ruled China for over two hundred years. The army, which as recently as April 1911 had stood by the imperial government in quelling an uprising in Guangzhou, deserted the throne. Widespread disaffection in the army encouraged the provincial assemblies, merchants, gentry, and chambers of commerce to join the revolt. [25] Four days after the outbreak of the uprising, Sir John Jordan, the British minister and dean of the diplomatic corps in Beijing, reported that the revolutionary movement "has enlisted a measure of sympathy amongst the Chinese which the Manchu dynasty can no longer claim to command."[26] The Hubei provincial assembly quickly aligned itself with the rebels and by October 12, Hanyang and Hankou had fallen. Collaboration between the New Army and the provincial assemblies permitted the revolution to make rapid strides.

On October 13, the minister of war was ordered to lead a southern expeditionary force to suppress the revolution in Hubei. Yuan Shikai, who had been in forced retirement since 1909, was almost immediately recalled to active duty by the Manchus. On October 14, he was appointed viceroy of Huguang in the hope of strengthening the loyalty of the northern troops, and in November he was named prime minister. Yuan's return to power greatly encouraged those who hoped the Manchus would be able to turn back the revolutionary tide. As a result, officials in Washington initially gave little credence to reports that questioned the Manchus' staying power. Secretary of State Knox and Willard Straight persisted in the belief that the revolution posed little danger to the status quo and would be quickly suppressed by the Manchus.[27] Circumstances soon called into question Knox's assurances that the Manchus would put down the rebellion and restore order to China.

During the remainder of October and November, the revolutionary tide spread across most of central and southern China. By early November, with fifteen provinces having declared their independence of Beijing, the acting military attaché of the British legation described the position of the imperial government as "almost desperate." With the forces at their disposal, the Manchus "could not possibly hope to bring the remaining provinces into line."[28] As E. T. Williams, the new American chargé and a man widely known for his scholarly assessments of the Chinese situation, reported, "the present Manchu dynasty is face to face with the greatest crisis in its history. Unless a reconciliation can be effected there is at hand either a division of the Empire or the entire overthrow of the Manchus."[29]

Predictably, the rapidly deteriorating situation in China began to endanger foreign lives and property holdings. Attempts by rebels to use the foreign concessions as cover in the Wuhan area seriously threatened the lives of American residents, including many missionaries. Furthermore, the widespread disintegration of authority exposed the foreign community, especially in Wuhan, the center of revolutionary activity, to the hazards of anarchy.[30] Antimissionary violence had been a distinguishing feature of Manchu-era lawlessness. The murder of eight members of the English Baptist Mission in Hankou by an unruly mob underscored this characteristic.[31]

The murder of the Baptist missionaries prompted a series of moves by the foreign powers. The major powers communicated to Yuan their fear of an antiforeign uprising in the provinces. Minister Calhoun advised all American nationals to congregate at ports readily accessible to foreign warships. He reported to Knox that "[t]he condition of the Empire is . . . one of considerable disorder. . . . Armed bands that seem to acknowledge allegiance to no authority are plundering the countryside."[32] Knox urged Taft to order the fleet to render assistance in the event that the Chinese could not control the rebellion. Taft thereupon diverted five armored cruisers of the Pacific Fleet from Hawaii to China.[33]

As the U.S. Navy rapidly concentrated all its available vessels on the Chang Jiang, the United States quickly became the leading naval power in Chinese waters. The American fleet at the mouth of the Chang Jiang was larger than any other foreign force assembled.[34] The Americans also joined the other powers in sending reinforcements upriver to Wuhan to safeguard the foreign community there, and 2,400 troops arrived from the Philippines as additional ground support.[35]

This massive influx of American power evoked congressional criticism that it infringed upon Chinese sovereignty. Knox brushed aside the criticism, however, with the claim that the United States was only acting in accordance with the Boxer Protocol.[36] In fact, the United States stood poised with the other powers, ready to crush the revolution should it threaten American interests in China.

The Chinese revolutionaries acted quickly to minimize the threat represented by the sudden increase of foreign forces in China and in its territorial waters. They knew that the slaughter of foreigners would discredit the revolution in the eyes of the world and provide a pretext for foreign intervention. To prevent such an occurrence, the Revolutionary Committee issued a proclamation designed to alleviate the fears and anxieties of the foreign community. The manifesto explicitly stated that anyone who harmed a foreigner would be immediately decapitated.[37]

The revolutionaries soon learned that, despite their assurances, the foreigners remained concerned for the safety of their nationals in China. The *San Francisco Examiner*, for example, took note of the "China for the Chinese" slogan of the revolutionaries and, while admitting that the revolutionary leaders had shown extraordinary consideration to foreigners, expressed doubts that they could for long

control the common people: "But can the leaders permanently maintain authority over every mob in China? It is gravely doubtful. Once
let the crowd of excited Chinese break away from the control of their
wise leaders, once let them start pillaging and killing among the non-
Chinese, and the fire is set which is not easily put out, even by the
wisest and most temperate leaders." For these reasons, the *Examiner*
advocated an extended occupation of China in the event that foreign
troops were required to enter the country to put down antiforeign
activity.[38]

The *Examiner* was correct in its perception that a strong current
of antiforeignism permeated the revolution. The Chinese nationalists
who were leading the opposition to the Manchus had as their ultimate goal the complete recovery of China's sovereign rights. As Huang
Xing wrote some years later, "Although the purpose of the revolution
was declared to be the overthrow of the Manchus, the real aim in fact
was to save the country [from foreign aggression]." But "the foreigners
had better not know this; otherwise their anger will be kindled. . . . We
must keep our mouths shut and not say a word."[39] Even Sun Yat-sen,
whose assiduous cultivation of Western support over the years made
him appear anything but antiforeign, secretly hoped that the revolution would make China sufficiently strong that the powers would be
unable "to carve us up like a melon."[40]

The leaders of the anti-Manchu forces diligently attempted to
conceal their true motives, to forestall intervention by the powers. By
maintaining extensive contacts with foreign consuls in the areas under
their control, they were able to continue to promise foreign governments that lives and property would be respected and, most important, that once they achieved sovereign authority they would honor
all treaties, loans, and indemnities. The special attention showered
upon American diplomats particularly impressed American public
opinion. The *Christian Science Monitor* traced this special attention
to the intellectual influence of American educational institutions at
home and in China and to the funds raised by Chinese in the United
States on behalf of the revolutionaries.[41]

The revolutionaries were especially effective in cultivating public
opinion in the United States and, as they hoped, made antirevolutionary intervention politically difficult for American leaders to undertake. At the time of the outbreak in Wuhan, Sun Yat-sen, China's best
known revolutionary, was on a speaking tour of the United States successfully promoting the rebel cause before American audiences. While
Sun's Western orientation and Christian upbringing made him a most

effective spokesman, he also benefitted from the assistance of the National Chinese Association, which represented 80 percent of all North American Chinese and which strove constantly to create a favorable impression of the Chinese revolutionaries. As its spokesman Wong Foon Chuck told the *Washington Post*, if the powers did not intervene, the revolutionaries would "take China out of the darkness that has enshrouded it for centuries and make it one of the enlightened nations of the world." [42]

In speaking to foreigners, the Chinese revolutionaries sought to exploit the universal human tendency to accept a new development if it is described in familiar and appealing terms. This tactic was most successful in the United States, where the rebel propagandists emphasized parallels between the Chinese and American revolutions. Thus, Sun Fo, Sun Yat-sen's son, stated the goals of the revolution: "We expect to establish a modern republic with two houses of Congress, much the same as you have in the United States. Men and women who can read and write will be permitted to vote. Martial law will prevail for a time, if we are successful, after which a President and a cabinet will be popularly chosen." [43]

In their greatest public relations coup, the revolutionaries succeeded in painting a picture of the struggle against the Manchus as an important part of a great universal movement against monarchy and oligarchy which was rooted in the American political experience. The insurgents' claims enabled them to exploit the popular self-conception of America as the mother of democracy and republicanism. As the *Atlanta Constitution* noted, the success of the revolution would have a scarcely imaginable effect upon the world struggle against monarchy and oligarchy in the Orient. [44]

The insurgents also worked to convince foreigners that they had the ability to manage and develop China once they gained power. The revolutionaries' ability to create a viable and progressive republican government in China, despite the nation's many political and economic difficulties, was, in fact, the dominant theme of revolutionary propaganda. The insurgents pledged the establishment of a progressive and honestly administered tax system and promised to develop China's great internal resources. They projected the development of hydropower and a large and efficient railway system funded by foreign loans transacted in a responsible, businesslike fashion. [45] These formidable tasks, especially the establishment of a republic, would not be accomplished overnight. According to Sun Yat-sen, political, social, and economic justice would be established in successive stages spanning a nine-year period during which China would have a military government to pave the way for such an evolution.[46] In the meantime, the new China would honor all treaty commitments and protect foreigners from harm during the revolution. Sun wanted to appeal to republican sentiments in the United States without appearing to be unduly naïve or optimistic regarding the prospects for democratic development. At the same time he wanted to alleviate fears that revolution threatened foreign interests in China.

This propaganda, which promised so much to so many in the West, counteracted much of the skepticism that had initially greeted the revolution. Credit for this feat was due largely to Sun Yat-sen, the man most intimately connected in the minds of the Western public with the republican cause in China. Sun had won the British press to his side and this swayed the strongly influential *New York Times*. Sun's work in the United States was also responsible for arousing support for the republican cause. As the *Boston Herald* noted of his years of fund-raising and propagandizing in Europe and the United States, "Sun Yat-sen has shown during the last twenty years that he has ideas of his own, as well as the energy and patience which have been necessary to start them on the road to realization."

Although the *Herald* recognized the "colossal" nature of the undertaking, with Sun at the helm the revolution "must not by any means be regarded as foredoomed to failure."[47] The *Christian Science Monitor* found Sun's Christianity his most attractive asset: "He has been trained by a Christian father convert to a high esteem for the faith of the Occident, and [by] his own career of consecration to the cause of his countrymen, his endurance of perils and daring of assassination with a penalty on his head, he has shown the result of an inner moral discipline that Jesus as well as Confucius has shaped. If he is confirmed by a national assembly as President of the Republic, and if the China of the future is to be molded largely by his views, then the outlook for the Christian missions, schools, and ideals in the vast nation is brighter than it would be under any other man."[48]

Perhaps the revolutionaries' most potent propaganda weapon was the Manchu dynasty itself. The imperial family was seen as effete, corrupt, vacillating, and oppressive. By comparison, the opposition appeared to be a progressive force struggling against reactionary remnants of the old order. The dynasty simply could not and did not compete in currying favor with the insurgents in the antimonarchical and staunchly republican United States.

Public opinion had mistakenly, yet consciously, assumed that the

Chinese Revolution was a re-creation of the American Revolution and that the rebels were intent on implanting American ideals and institutions into the Chinese body politic, and thus in no way threatened American interests in China.

Many missionaries succumbed to the racial propaganda of the rebels which pictured the Manchus as the primary obstacle to "progress" in China. Although nationalism and anti-imperialism motivated the rebels in opposing the dynasty, the missionaries seemed oblivious to the logical consequences of the rebels' nationalism. For example, one of the prime reasons for the revolution was the failure of the dynasty to assert the nation's sovereignty in the face of foreign intrusion into China. Nevertheless, one Methodist Episcopal missionary wrote that he and his colleagues wished "the revolutionary party success, for there seems to be little hope of the old government ever doing much for the improvement of conditions."[49] The missionaries singled out the Manchus as the reason for their own minimal success and viewed the revolution as the turning point of Christian fortunes in China. As one missionary wrote: "We have been in the midst of a marvelous Revolution. For China, the change from a monarchy with its entrenchment behind the shelters of tradition and experience to a Twentieth Century Republic has been so tremendous that description must be inadequate, and any forecast as to all that may be involved quite presumptuous. If the transformation proves to be as permanent and as radical as the ideals of the new leaders, the results will soon be manifest to the world."[50]

Although the revolutionary break with tradition evoked a generally favorable response from the missionaries, many of them still harbored a good deal of anxiety about the future course of events. Was China yet ready for a republic and, more specifically, were there not several dangers attendant on change brought about by revolution?

Bishop James Bashford of the Methodist Episcopal Church, a recognized friend of China and a man who had ready access to America's business and political leaders, was not overenthusiastic about the revolution. Although Bashford admitted the need for change in China, he felt that peaceful "evolution" would serve both China and the missionaries far better than revolution. Bashford was quite content with the progress that China had made under the prince regent and regretted that these efforts had not prevented revolution. With many colleagues he felt the Manchus were being made scapegoats and worried that ambition and fear would result in a national hysteria, driving individual Chinese even further along the revolutionary path. He was also greatly concerned that the long-term presence of disorder would dissipate any opportunities that might otherwise result from the changes then sweeping China. George Newell echoed the same concern from Fujian Province where the local missionaries were reported to be pleased that the "decadent" Manchus had been replaced but worried over the inexperience of the young progressives in charge of the province.[51]

The missionaries who feared revolution also felt that China was not yet ready for a republican form of government. Having failed for so long to convert the Chinese to their religious viewpoint, these missionaries were convinced that the Chinese were still captives of the old ways and would be equally resistant to American political ideas. They believed that only a few Chinese had leadership ability and that not even one Chinese in a thousand understood what a republic was. For these reasons, democracy in China would have to be severely limited. One popularly held notion was that Yuan Shikai should be left to run the affairs of state under nominal monarchical rule. Victor Eastman of the American Board of Commissioners for Foreign Missions (ABCFM) prayed that the rebels would behave rationally and would stop short of demanding a republic and settle for a constitutional monarchy.[52]

These pessimistic evaluations of Chinese potential did not discourage the missionaries. Rather, they reaffirmed the sense of mission that had originally brought the Americans to China. For the missionaries believed that only a radical change of heart, a conversion to Christianity, would save China from a group of revolutionary leaders "just as corrupt as the old school . . . a new set of thieves instead of the experienced ones."[53] As Bashford noted, "the crisis in China is revealing to the world the absolute necessity of civilization resting upon the word of God in order to be enduring."[54]

Fear of physical violence lurked behind fear of political change. Antiforeign and antimissionary sentiments evoked memories of the Boxer Rebellion and created deep-seated anxiety within the missionary community whenever a disturbance occurred in China. The missionaries feared that revolution would loosen the bonds of authority and that famine-stricken Chinese might attack the foreigners or, worst of all in Bashford's mind, that it would bring forth a "socialistic" form of government.[55]

There were objective grounds for the missionaries' fears. Several schools, including Fuzhou Christian University, were forced to close because the students were so concerned with revolution. The young people had found that Western learning brought them great public attention. Formerly docile women students, offered a voice in their own affairs for the first time, were especially zealous and active in revolutionary affairs and startled their missionary mentors with a vibrant disregard for traditional authority. The missionaries perceived as their responsibility the restoration of respect for authority: "It is impossible to conceive from without what wise and constant direction and guidance are needed to prevent our students from making shipwrecks of their lives on the rocks of their new liberty and independence. The line between liberty and license is seldom visible to the young man or woman taking the first eager steps out of bondage of any kind." In south China the agitation was particularly intense. Guangzhou, birthplace of Sun Yat-sen, had been swept up in the turmoil. Financial bankruptcy and looting quickly followed the revolutionaries' abolition of taxes, a move designed only to gain political support. Popular expectations of better days were raised to great heights and then dashed. English missionaries were murdered in Hankou.[56]

As noted above, the widespread disorder throughout the empire and the rapid disintegration of traditional authority prompted a State Department warning to American nationals, particularly the missionaries, that they should evacuate the interior and congregate in ports readily accessible to foreign warships. Calhoun felt that, although imperial and rebel authorities had been providing protection, continued fighting would expose the missionaries to unacceptable risks.[57]

Despite the danger, most American missionaries preferred to remain at their posts. Arthur Judson Brown, head of the Presbyterian mission in China, which had no posts in the zone of hostilities, was in the forefront of the movement to keep the missionaries in the field during the revolution. He claimed that the missionaries had too huge a stake in China and too great a responsibility to their congregations to vacate their stations. He wanted the missionaries to look after their mission property and assist the distressed and wounded, the women and children. Although willing to accede to the evacuation of foreign women and children to port cities should the situation worsen, he remained convinced that since both sides in the conflict remembered China's humiliation by the foreign powers after the Boxer uprising and feared the threat of foreign military intervention, such a development was unlikely.[58]

Although some of the missionaries did abandon their stations, the majority remained on the job. As one missionary said, "If the foreigner went, the property would doubtless be destroyed." Moreover, the missionaries hoped to ingratiate themselves with the Chinese by remaining at their posts and thus to improve their reputation among the residents.[59]

To Bashford, the reluctance of the missionaries to evacuate their posts posed a grave dilemma. American consular officials disclaimed any responsibility for the safety of the missionaries remaining in the interior. Yet, if the United States persisted in this attitude and refused to punish any wrongs done to the missionaries, the "bad elements" in China would be greatly encouraged and would terrorize the missionaries and their Chinese congregants. If, however, the United States actively intervened to punish the transgressors, there was a danger of provoking a nationalistic backlash against the missionaries. Unable to resolve the conflicting considerations, Bashford merely told his Methodist colleagues to use their own discretion whether to leave their posts.[60]

The missionaries who remained in the interior had no hesitation about seeking military protection against violence. Thus, when presented with the opportunity to disassociate themselves from foreign military forces in China, the missionaries resorted to the old device of calling in the gunboats to keep the Chinese in line. Several missionaries requested and received the presence of American gunboats and soldiers. Congregationalist missionary Henry Martin, reported that he "felt safer if foreign soldiers were nearby."[61]

Despite the missionaries' preference for a strong American military presence, it was fear of the Chinese masses and of the other powers, not the spell of idealism and enlightened self-interest that the insurgents had cast on American opinion leaders, that stayed the American talons. While the Taft administration prepared to intervene in China, American leaders calculated again the risks and benefits involved in intervention. Minister Calhoun and his colleagues sent warnings from Beijing that foreign lives and property were still safe and that foreign intervention would touch off a wave of xenophobia that would especially endanger foreigners in rebel-held territory. Antiforeign sentiment was so great, the British consul in Chongqing reported, that if any power intervened, "the resentment of the people will be so great that I doubt if any one person will leave this port alive."[62] Secretary of State Knox hesitantly began to caution against any move that might inflame the Chinese against local foreigners. The president and his cabinet also were not receiving encouragement from the other powers to intervene. They could only interpret this as a refusal to support intervention.[63]

In their assessment of the other powers' interests and intentions, the Americans were partly accurate. The British, for example, felt that intervention would pose too great a risk to their own interests in China. Sir John Jordan informed Foreign Minister Sir Edward Grey that, as the rebels held territory containing 75 percent of the foreign population and commerce in China, any move to thwart the rebellion would greatly endanger British subjects and trade. In addition, it was quite clear to London that the populations of the British colonies of Hong Kong and Singapore were sympathetic to the revolution and would cause trouble if Britain attempted to influence the outcome of the struggle. With Britain, the mightiest of the powers, unwilling to intervene or to countenance intervention by others, the American leadership would have to restrain itself for the time being.[64]

As the weeks passed into months, Washington finally began to realize that the revolution presented the most serious threat to the Manchu dynasty since the Taiping Rebellion. Yuan's four-year absence from the Beiyang Army had eroded that body's reliability as a military instrument that could be used against the rebels. Equally important, the desperate economic problems besetting the Manchus precluded financing a major military effort. The fall of Nanjing on December 2 and the unwillingness of the Southern Expeditionary Force to fight further undermined the position of the throne. Meanwhile, the rebels continued military preparations for a march on Beijing.[65] So great was the resentment against the Manchus, Knox wrote to Taft, that either the dynasty would fall or the country would split asunder. J. K. Ohl, correspondent of the *New York Herald* and a man considered to be one of the most astute foreign journalists in China, also believed that the nation would split into two or three states and, in the process, endanger the entire treaty port system as well as the foreign missions and railway investments. If this proved to be the case, then, in Ohl's view, it would be necessary for the foreign powers to intervene.[66]

There were foreign observers who resisted such pessimistic assessments concerning the Manchus' fate. Willard Straight, for example, confided to Charles Norton, vice-president of the First National Bank of New York, his belief that Yuan Shikai would be able to retrieve the situation for the dynasty if he received the powers he sought in order to reorganize the cabinet and the government. Straight told Morgan partner H. P. Davison that if the Manchus took such a step, the revolutionaries would lose their nerve and "mount on the [Manchu] Band Wagon." The United States, therefore, should come to Yuan's aid, "irrespective of our wobbling British friends."[67]

Straight had little sympathy for the Manchus but believed the revolutionaries to be "infinitely worse." Commenting to Frank McKnight about the rebel minister of foreign affairs, Wu Tingfang, Straight cried out, "When it comes to a choice between the most reactionary Manchu, and that ass, Wu Ting Fang, I should prefer the Manchu every time." China was, in Straight's words, "verily a nation of skunks." And he confided to McKnight his scorn for the roseate view of the rebels held by many journalists and missionaries. Straight was more than a little skeptical that the rebels would find a panacea for all China's ills in "an orgy of hot-air and republican nonsense." As for the vast majority of the Chinese masses, Straight described them to Jacob Schiff as apolitical people who wanted only to earn their livings in peace and who accordingly accepted the "principle enunciated by the nearest man with a gun," rebel or Manchu.[68]

Ex-diplomat Straight managed to find one positive aspect to the rebellion: "Progressive" albeit antirepublican figures, such as Yuan Shikai and Tang Shaoyi, would be able to take advantage of the unrest to seize power from the corrupt and inefficient Manchus. At that point, the foreign financial community would find it profitable to offer loans to the central government to enable it to suppress the revolution. In the unlikely event that the revolutionaries won, the resultant instability would, he believed, destroy America's trade prospects. As he wrote to a business associate, Frank McKnight, "If a Republic is established, there will be chaos, constant disturbance, and but little satisfactory business for the honest bankers unless the foreign powers actively intervene."[69]

Wall Street readily accepted Straight's warnings that unless Yuan received financial aid to suppress the rebels, chaos would result. In London, too, the bankers shuddered at the thought of a Chinese republic. Yet they could not make a loan to Yuan without securing the consent of the respective governments. To that end, the financiers sent the State Department a memorandum that couched their interests in general terms, stating that "[t]he prolongation of the present disorders in China will only inflict increasing injury to foreign trade and not only the Groups, but the general commercial interests will suffer. It is this fact rather than their desire to successfully negotiate the loan now under consideration that has induced the representatives to approach [the government] in this manner."[70]

The financiers were willing to gamble their compatriots' lives and fortunes for future profits. They knew that a loan to Yuan might provoke an antiforeign reaction among the rebels, but they were confident that should the rebels win, they could retrieve their own investments, albeit at some cost. Although a rebel victory did not promise much future profit, a Yuan victory did. There was no alternative but to support "the one man competent to force the disaffected provinces to recognize anew the authority of the throne."[71] As Straight wrote during the first weeks of the armed struggle, "Yuan is the right horse to back. If he wins, he will use the Group to finance the reorganization which he hopes to undertake. If he is killed, we can still enforce our claim despite rebel disclaimers."[72]

Several other powers shared the American and British financiers' fear of republican rule in China. Germany, through its financial representatives in the loan consortium, let it be known that it was ready to undertake joint action to uphold monarchical rule in China. Japan, the nation most violently opposed to the establishment of a republic in China, raised the spectre of disorder and severe damage to foreign interests. It used the leverage of its alliance with England, which required the two nations to cooperate with each other to safeguard their interests in China, to press that nation and the other powers to urge China "to abandon all futile attempts at the establishment of a Republic." Viscount Uchida attempted to put more pressure on Britain by informing the British government that, through inquiries in the United States, the Japanese had learned "that the American Government . . . recognized the futility and danger of a republic for China."[73]

Only Great Britain stood against aid to the tottering Manchus. Although Sir Edward Grey agreed that a republic was not suited to China's needs, Britain refused to permit the bankers to lend financial support to the faltering dynasty. The refusal provoked a strong reaction from the other powers. Sir John Jordan reported that "[t]he American, German, and French representatives urged strongly the necessity of coming at once to the assistance of Yuan Shi-k'ai and dwelt upon the moral support which financial aid would bring him in bringing the revolutionaries to a reasonable compromise."[74]

The British statesmen would not be moved. As leaders of a global empire severely tested by Germany, and dependent on the wealth of its worldwide commerce for the resources to meet the challenge from across the North Sea, they were unwilling to invite rebel attacks on their missionary and trading outposts in the Chang Jiang valley. Since British mercantile interests were keeping great pressure on Grey to avoid any action that could lead to a boycott of English goods in that fertile valley, Britain had very little room to maneuver.[75]

British opposition to the loan was decisive, and on November 8, 1911, the group formally decided to refuse any loan application for the present time. But the State Department, at the urging of Minister Calhoun, refused to rule out the possibility that financial aid to Yuan might be forthcoming at some future date, if it was deemed necessary to safeguard American interests in China.[76]

The decision by the group to maintain strict neutrality seriously undermined Yuan's ability to deal summarily with the rebels and thus disappointed Willard Straight. The American banker correctly attributed his nation's inaction not to altruism but to military weakness, which forced the United States to follow Great Britain's lead. He wished to see a greater American military presence in Asia and the willingness to use it actively. "I do not mean to advocate war by any means," he wrote to H. P. Davison. "I only wish we were strong enough to talk, and that we were not the discredited bluffers as we are."[77]

Stymied by the British refusal to provide financial aid to Yuan, let alone to intervene militarily, the Taft administration faced a continuing dilemma: How could it influence China's civil conflict without overtly supporting the discredited Manchu government? Reports from Chargé Williams in Beijing predicted that China would split into a monarchical north and a republican south. Such a development seemed to portend massive political changes. From Tokyo the American minister reported that monarchical circles in Japan were already expressing serious reservations about the possible establishment of a republic in nearby China. Willard Straight expressed fear that the existence of a republican government in China would undermine colonial rule in the Philippines and India.[78]

Even had republicanism not been an issue, continuing internal strife in China was sufficient to encourage Russia and Japan to effectively detach Manchuria and Outer Mongolia and Britain to solidify its position in Tibet. Wary of the consequences of republican rule to its position in China, the United States, within two months of the outbreak of the revolution, began to urge the adoption of a constitutional monarchy. According to Minister Calhoun, such a government would suit both China and the United States:

> Undoubtedly, a limited monarchy seems most likely to meet
> the present needs of the Chinese, their provincial jealousies, and
> their unfamiliarity with the principles of self-government make

them most unlikely to succeed in establishing a stable government without some such tie as would be supplied by a line of he-
reditary rulers. . . . The thing most to be feared in the attempt to
establish republican government in China is that after the Manchus are removed, the common hatred of whom forms the bonds
of union among the seceding provinces, there will be no sentiment to bind them together.[79]

In other words, Calhoun expressed concern that republican seizure of
all or part of China would revive the danger that the powers would
establish exclusive spheres of influence, thereby undermining the
Open Door policy which was designed to give the United States an
equal footing in China with its foreign rivals.[80]

In hope of preventing the partition of China, the United States,
with support from Germany, recommended that the powers renew
their pledges to maintain China's integrity. The failure of this gambit
caused the Navy Department to envisage a savage battle among the
Great Powers over China's remains. The navy urged Taft to join in the
plunder before there was nothing left for the United States. It recommended that the United States concentrate its efforts on the Yangtze
River and seize Ningbo "to the southward of Shanghai, such a base
being a vital necessity if we are to compete successfully with the rival
Powers." [81]

To adopt the Navy's recommendations was tantamount to recognition of China's dismemberment and Taft, who had served in the war-
torn Philippines as president of the United States–Philippine Commission from 1900 to 1904, was reluctant to involve the United States
in another Asian war. He declined, not out of solicitude for the fate of
the Chinese but because he realized that the United States would have
to pay an extremely high price for any conquests in China. Not only
would the policy threaten relations with other imperial powers and
possibly trigger a costly war with one or more of them, but the Chinese might make a campaign of colonial conquest a very expensive
enterprise, as the Filipinos had some years before.

Attempting to resolve this quandary, Taft secured a signed agreement binding the six major powers not to intervene militarily without
the consent of the majority of the signatories. By thus heading off an
outright power struggle over China, Taft managed to preserve America's position in East Asia. He accomplished this, however, at the expense of the Chinese republicans, whose successes in cultivating American public opinion had been for nothing.[82]

America's conservative posture called for a policy of strict neutrality between Manchus and revolutionists, but increasingly the Taft administration found such a policy quite uncomfortable. Despite the rebels' attempt to avoid all unpleasant incidents with the foreign powers, the ferocity of the fighting eventually began to endanger American interests. To an alarming extent, the revolutionists were losing control of their more exuberant followers. From Hankou, Consul Roger Greene reported that American shipping was in constant danger on China's inland waterways and that, although the rebels always promptly apologized for any untoward incidents, their lack of effective organization and discipline prevented the complete elimination of such episodes. The U.S. Navy also complained that the activities of the insurgents were threatening the considerable facilities, located throughout China, of the Standard Oil Company. Finally, Wu Ting-fang, minister of foreign affairs for the rebels, warned that any foreign ships suspected of carrying contraband would be boarded. Since the United States had not recognized the belligerency of the rebels, this statement greatly upset Admiral Murdock as well as American consular officials throughout China, who viewed it as a threat to the powers' privileged position in China.[83]

These events demanded a reassessment of the earlier policy of non-interference in the civil conflict. As early as October 23, the American military attaché had pointed out that the grave financial situation resulting from the strains of the revolution created the risk of eventual anarchy. At a meeting of the six ministers in Beijing, there was general agreement that the situation was rapidly deteriorating. It seemed likely to the ministers that because of the reduction in customs receipts, there would be no balance for indemnities and that the lack of revenue would increase the likelihood of mutiny among the troops.[84]

Minister Calhoun reported that if a settlement were not reached at the proposed Shanghai Peace Conference, the foreign powers would soon face a crisis. Calhoun urged Secretary Knox not to await passively the outcome of the conference but rather to endorse a loan to Yuan to enable him to bring stability to the nation. Calhoun's fear of increasing brigandage in the countryside was greater than his fear of alienating the rebels or endangering the foreigners in rebel-held China. He believed that the rebels lacked the leadership and organization to foster peace and stability but that Yuan stood at the head of a force of recognized prowess and that, with prompt outside support, he could return the nation to normalcy. Continued neutrality and delay in offering support to Yuan would mean disaster because both sides would soon be bankrupt and the armies would have to resort to pillaging merely to subsist.[85]

As the situation of the Manchus deteriorated, foreign support for a loan grew, as did rebel objections to such a breach of neutrality. Wu Tingfang stated that such a loan would obstruct the effort being made by his people to secure "freedom for themselves and the opening of this great country to unrestricted trade and commerce with foreign nations."[86] Wu insisted that the Chinese Republic would not recognize such a loan and he pleaded with the State Department to restrain the financiers from sending funds to the Manchus. Finally, however, it was the open threat of a boycott of foreign goods that prevented the powers from tendering financial support to Yuan.[87]

Despite the desire of the powers to influence the outcome of the revolution, there appeared to be no safe way of departing from the policy of strict neutrality. The powers put pressure on both sides to stop fighting. In December 1911, Sir John Jordan warned Yuan that Britain would be most upset should the conflict not soon come to a halt. Similarly, in areas under rebel control, British consular officials stressed to the revolutionaries the necessity of arriving at a peaceful settlement. Yuan, who was having difficulty paying his troops and buying military equipment, realized that both his own and the Manchus' positions were quite precarious. A negotiated settlement with the rebels offered the only hope of salvaging some of his newly restored power. The rebels also desired a quick end to the fighting. If order were not restored, the powers would intervene and crush the revolution. To forestall this eventuality, a central government had to be organized that could bring peace to the country and conduct its foreign relations. The inability of the revolutionary government to raise money to continue the struggle further contributed to its desire to end the fighting as quickly as possible. As a result of these internal and external pressures, an armistice was arranged on December 3, 1911. Yuan selected Tang Shaoyi to represent him at the peace conference in Shanghai, while the republicans chose as their delegate Wu Tingfang.[88]

At a meeting in Beijing, the six ministers concluded that pressure should be brought to bear on the conferees to achieve a quick settlement of their differences. On December 18, the United States issued a formal communiqué conveying to both parties its interest in a speedy resolution of the conflict:

> The United States considers that the continuation of the present struggle in China seriously affects not only the country

itself but also the material interests and security of foreigners. While maintaining the attitude of strict neutrality adopted by it up to the present time, the American Government considers that it is its duty, in an unofficial manner to call to the attention of the two delegations the necessity of arriving as soon as possible at an understanding capable of putting an end to the present conflict, being persuaded that this attitude represents the desire of both parties in question.

There were also rumors that American and other foreign officials had privately warned the conferees that, should a settlement not be reached, the powers might intervene militarily to safeguard their interests.[89]

Attention quickly focused on Yuan as the one man who could achieve the dynasty's abdication and at the same time "retain national unity and keep the powers at bay."[90] The nationalists' desire to free China from foreign domination could be achieved only if foreign intervention could be avoided, to give China sufficient time to strengthen itself. For this reason, Sun Yat-sen decided to throw his support to Yuan who, on December 1, 1911, declared that "my most important concern is the preservation of China. I rely on patriots of all parties to sacrifice some of their policies in order to cooperate with me in achieving this goal. Only by so doing can China escape partition or disintegration and the lamentable consequences. For the sake of our country, we must establish a strong government at once."[91] The next day, representatives of the revolutionary provinces gathering in Wuhan endorsed Yuan for the presidency. Support for Yuan was conditional, however, on his adoption of republicanism. Just as the rebels wanted to recruit Yuan because they believed him to be the one person who could avert foreign intervention, Yuan, realizing that the Manchus were finished, actively sought an accommodation with the opposition to maintain his own political position. To increase his leverage with both factions, however, Yuan was rumored to have tendered huge sums of money to rebel leaders, such as Sun Yat-sen, Wu Tingfang, and others, while at the same time encouraging troops under Manchu control to mutiny, thereby further weakening the dynasty's grip on the throne.[92]

There seemed little doubt that the Manchus' days were numbered. Their fate was genuinely sealed when Tang Shaoyi, the imperial delegate, defected to the republican cause. This development was very unpleasant news to the State Department, which preferred a limited monarchy in China under Yuan's control. To compound the discomfort of the powers, on December 29, 1911, the rebels elected as provisional president of the republic Sun Yat-sen, a man whom the powers felt lacked the political clout to ensure China's stability.[93]

The rebels moved quickly to secure foreign support for the republic which they were so determined to establish. Sun issued a manifesto promising to respect all treaties, foreign loans, indemnities, and concessions made by the Manchus prior to the revolution. He also promised many domestic reforms and pledged that "all persons and property of any foreign nations within the jurisdiction of the Republic of China will be respected and protected."[94]

Although the rebels were clearly adamant in their determination to establish a republic, the Manchus were still on the throne and the powers were backing Yuan. To unite the country and avoid a long and costly civil war, the revolutionists, led by Sun and Huang Xing, decided by late December 1911 to offer Yuan the presidency of the new republic. In exchange, Yuan agreed to secure the abdication of the Manchu dynasty. With the de facto desertion of the army, the Manchu cause was lost, and on February 12, 1912, an imperial edict invested Yuan with full power to organize a provisional republican government that would unite the country. That same day, Yuan wrote Sun Yat-sen that "[n]ever again shall we allow monarchical government in China."[95] On February 14, Sun tendered his resignation as provisional president and urged the election of Yuan. The *Washington Post* praised Sun for this act, referring to it as an "example of purity of purpose and self-sacrifice . . . unparalleled in history."[96] On the next day, the republican leaders unanimously elected Yuan provisional president of the republic. Yuan's oath of office committed him to "enhancing the republican spirit, to cleansing the marring stains of despotism, and to assiduously maintaining the constitution."[97]

Despite Yuan's election as president, the rebels still hoped to retain some control over him. Leaders such as Song Zhiaoren, Huang Xing, and Sun Yat-sen favored moving the capital to their stronghold of Nanjing. Situating the capital in Nanjing would constitute a symbolic acknowledgment of the revolutionary origins of the new regime and place Yuan at a military disadvantage vis-á-vis the southern leaders. With the support of the powers, who claimed that such a move would violate the Boxer protocol, Yuan refused to abandon his power base in the north. The revolutionists, deserted by their gentry and military allies, were forced to capitulate to Yuan's demands. Sun Yat-sen and Huang Xing subsequently endorsed Yuan's dominant political position and, in return, were given authority over industrial matters. Indeed, Sun praised Yuan as "a man of strong shoulders, energetic;

such a man is hard to find. And he is not a megalomaniac." Republican rule had been instituted throughout China.[98]

American opinion divided over these developments. While the State Department was anxious, the American press was euphoric. Editors were convinced that China had established a republic on the American model. For example, the *Boston Globe* observed that "[t]he world will no longer be astonished by the spectacle of a great Asiatic republic. . . . The leaders of the revolution and their followers have shown a constancy and a devotion to their cause, a steadiness of purpose and a self-control probably unequalled in the history of such convulsions." Similarly, the *Washington Post* optimistically noted that "[r]evolutions do not turn backwards, even in China," and the *Boston Herald* was greatly carried away in its enthusiasm for the new Republic, applauding "the devotion to the ideals of liberty, justice, and fair play which has characterized the Oriental Cromwells and Washingtons." The contradictory aspects of American public opinion seemed to be reconciled. No longer was there fear that the republican movement would turn into another Boxer Rebellion. The danger that revolutionary change would create chaos seemed to be an idle worry. Despite earlier doubts, it now seemed that China could change, and at the same time remain stable. Sun Yat-sen seemed a wonder worker.[99]

The elevation of Yuan Shikai to the presidency of the new Republic comforted those who feared that a truly democratic regime would reflect the antiforeign sentiment that had inspired the revolution. Yuan was not one to embrace republicanism enthusiastically and his apparent liberalism was quite superficial. As Yuan said to the British minister, John Jordan, "a republic meant a [lot] of useless talking and very little work." Nor was Yuan inclined to allow the mobilization of popular anti-imperialist sentiment. While he was not reluctant to use force to suppress his domestic opposition, he would not countenance its use against the powers. Thus, the powers recognized that while Yuan was "more of an opportunist than a statesman, more of an intriguer than a leader" and that he was "not overscrupulous, and when occasion requires . . . can strike swiftly and mercilessly," they appreciated the benefits that would inure to their position from his authoritarianism.[100]

Fear of violence and disorder also had convinced many missionaries of the need for a strong authority figure who would control the unruly masses. The missionaries joined with most other foreigners in China in the belief that Yuan Shikai was the man best suited to this task. When Yuan returned to Beijing at the behest of the faltering

Manchus, the missionaries were buoyed by the belief that he would bring order out of chaos. After he forcefully suppressed one of the many disturbances plaguing China, the missionaries enthusiastically applauded. Even when his troops got out of control and mutinied early in 1912, Henry Martin of the ABCFM reported that "[t]he members of the American Board Mission have expressed to President Yuan their deep sympathy and full trust."[101]

As the turbulence subsided, optimism replaced the fear of violence that had made the missionaries so amenable to authoritarian measures and so pessimistic about the Chinese. The missionaries now claimed that though the rebels were anti-Manchu, they were not anti-foreign. Lewis Hodous of the ABCFM rejoiced that the government had "passed into the hands of young progressive men of the nation. Many of them had been trained in mission schools or have travelled abroad. Their attitude toward the missionary is one of good will, confidence and cordial appreciation." Houdons believed that an intellectual change was sweeping the vast multitude and that old social customs and religious ideas were being discarded.[102]

Clearly, the missionaries could take comfort from such an interpretation of events. They did not want China to retain any of the ancient heritage that had shown itself so impervious to Christian proselytization. Once the imperial system of government had been eliminated, the traditional political order and culture would rapidly disintegrate. The revolution, wrote one elated missionary couple, had "happily shorn the dynasty of its powers to cripple the development of a virile people." Never again would the Manchus "chill China's hot yearnings after freedom, nor stand in the way . . . of an unfettered choice of the truth as presented in the Gospel."[103]

With some exaggeration, the missionaries claimed that the revolution was produced and controlled by Christian influence and thought. The *Missionary Review of the World* exclaimed that while Christianity was not exclusively responsible for the revolution, "the truths of the Bible had greatly influenced the actual agents of change." Another missionary journal credited the American missions with having accomplished the "impossible" in convincing the Chinese people to establish "a government like that of America." Arthur Brown, of the Presbyterian mission, believed that "the ideas brought to the vast mass of humanity by the missionaries have in their logical outworking caused . . . that ferment in men's minds upon which the world is now looking." The missionaries' exaggerations aside, they were justified in their belief that they had contributed something positive to the course of events and to the downfall of the sterile Confucian order. There seems no basis, however, for Bashford's claim that the presence of the missionaries was a major reason why the revolution was relatively nonviolent.[104]

Missionaries were elated over the large number of Christians, especially Sun Yat-sen, who occupied leading positions within the revolutionary movement. The election of Christians as provisional president and vice-president prompted one missionary to proclaim that the establishment of a republic "is God's doing and marvelous in our eyes."[105] Some missionaries who initially had felt that a monarchy was better suited to China's needs than a republic later supported the rebels merely because of Sun's presence in the republican ranks. One missionary, who felt that Sun would be China's Constantine and would make Christianity the state religion, consoled himself upon Sun's resignation as provisional president with the delusion that Sun would be the power behind the throne and would use this power to the direct benefit of the missions.[106]

The missionaries' growing confidence in the revolutionary leadership did not extend to the masses of China, however. As there were only relatively few Christians in China, the missionaries could not give Christianity credit for the revolution without distinguishing between the small Christian elite and the pagan masses. For this reason, many missionaries shied away from advocating democracy for China because it would remove power from the Christian minority.[107]

Because they perceived the revolution as both Christian-influenced and -dominated, the missionaries anticipated great new opportunities for spreading their faith in China. Bashford noted, "Christianity . . . has an opportunity to furnish the molds into which a new civilization of one-fourth of the human race may be cast." He urged his religious colleagues "to put forth every effort to aid the Chinese people in remoulding their institutions and shaping their destiny."[108] In the missionaries' view, political revolution would also spark a "religious revolution with all the attendant opportunities."[109] For years the missionaries had been seriously handicapped by the lack of religious liberty and tolerance in China. This situation had to be changed if the missionaries were to capitalize on the perceived opportunities created by the revolution. The missionaries were not sure, however, that Yuan would remedy the condition, so to gain his favor they encouraged the Chinese Christians to meet in Beijing to celebrate the establishment of a republic in China. Following the meeting, Yuan received a delegation of Christians to discuss the problem of religious liberty in China.

Yuan did not disappoint the supplicants and pledged religious liberty throughout the land.[110]

Yuan's pledge of religious liberty stirred the emotions of missionaries across China. Henry Martin referred to Yuan's proclamation as a "great day for world-wide Christianity when one-third of the people of the world are relieved of religious repression and the new leaders . . . express their approval of the principles of Christianity and bid the Church godspeed in its endeavors to establish a kingdom of righteousness." Opportunities for the spread of Christianity—and for the missionaries—would be even greater than anticipated with what the churchpeople felt was an official endorsement of their work. The opportunity to guide and mold "the destinies of an awakened and enquiring people" had finally arrived. With the Chinese government no longer opposed to Christianity, the number of converts would multiply. Dr. Barton, foreign secretary of ABCFM, recommended doubling the number of missionaries in China within the year, and members of the Methodist missionary force called for increased efforts to meet the challenges of "moulding one of the world's greatest peoples and winning a nation for Christ. We are now only beginning to see the vast meaning for Christ in the changes that befell the Government and to feel the import of the mighty forces which are heaving under the surface and ever thrusting out some new projection of the Kingdom of God."[111]

During the first few months of the republic, even cautious missionaries such as Bashford found support for a roseate view of missionary prospects. Following a meeting with General Song, the new military commander of Fujian Province, who told Bashford that he could expect hundreds of thousands of converts under the new republican regime, the bishop exclaimed that he had "never been more surprised than at the longing with which the Chinese turn to us for help and instruction in regard to the true God and the true way of life in the crisis which is upon them."[112]

The optimism of stalwarts such as Bashford was contagious. Methodist headquarters responded by urging him to use his new leverage to shape the infant republic's policies, including its criminal code. As one member of the Methodist hierarchy commented, "I cannot bear to think of its adoption without having the contents, . . . at least in some measure, shaped by the hands that have been trained in the school of Christ."[113] The missionaries now believed that the revolution's effect on the country was pervasive, reaching into the most remote provinces and effecting not only political change but significant "psychological changes in the people themselves." As one missionary summed up the situation, "From the crown of his head to the sole of his feet the old 'giant' is tingling with new life." [114]

Events would demonstrate that the euphoria of the press and the missionaries lacked a solid foundation. Before China's first experiment in republican government had run its course, American public opinion, as reflected in the press and by the American missionaries, would find common ground with an American government whose primary concern was the achievement of concrete political and economic goals rather than the growth of democracy in China.

3

U.S. Policy and the Six-Power
Consortium Loan Negotiations

B Y 1911, China stood on the verge of bankruptcy with the foreign
powers its principal creditors. Under the Manchus, the national
debt had risen to £150 million, with no end in sight. The magnitude
of this debt, plus the failure of the liberal Tianjing-Pukou Loan Agreement in 1908, caused the foreign banking community to require strict
control of the Chinese economy as a precondition of further loans to
China. The consortium established a mechanism for financial cooperation among the powers that could prevent competition and establish
a monopoly in the China loan business, and facilitate foreign attempts
to gain control of the Chinese economy. Indeed, American entry into
the foreign loan consortium in 1909 served only to tighten the monopolistic noose around China's economy. As Huntington-Wilson declared, regarding foreign domination of China's financial affairs, "As
well leave the slum to manage its own sanitation and thus infest the
whole city, as to allow an unenlightened government . . . to create or
maintain a financial plague spot to the injury of the general interest."[1]

A Manchu dynasty financially dependent on foreigners could
never achieve political emancipation for China. The formation of the
foreign loan consortium was a reminder to the Chinese that their political and financial fortunes had become inextricably intertwined
with those of the Great Powers. As a result of this situation, when the
Revolution of 1911 struck, it was apparent not only that the Manchus

were in jeopardy but that foreign economic and political privileges were imperiled as well. For this reason, the forces of economic imperialism would prove to be the greatest challenge to China's developing nationalism.

As the powers watched the Manchus—in whom they had invested so much capital—struggle to maintain the throne, they began to recalculate their own position. While the status quo was preferable, the foreigners did not want to risk offending the revolutionaries. The possibility always existed that the insurgents might win and make good on their foreign minister's threat to repudiate wartime financial obligations incurred by the Manchus. Nor were the powers anxious to test the rebels' threat to treat a loan to the Manchus as a hostile act. The British, in particular, were concerned that overt assistance to the Manchus would jeopardize the substantial British economic holdings in the rebel-dominated Chang Jiang valley. It also would create unrest in their colonies of Hong Kong and Singapore, where sympathy for the revolutionaries ran high. Under the circumstances, neutrality seemed the safest course.[2]

The foreigners also feared that additional foreign indebtedness would topple the precarious Chinese economic system. The British government expressed to the American government its concern that even if a new Chinese government honored loans made during the revolution, the increased debt obligations would likely bankrupt the country. J. P. Morgan & Company concurred in the British assessment and instructed Willard Straight, its representative in Beijing, to dispense with any thought of a loan to the Manchus because such an advance would have a devastating effect on other American investments and would seriously disrupt China's credit.[3]

The United States, despite its preference for maintaining the status quo, decided on a policy of formal neutrality and cooperation with the other big powers. Knox believed that this policy would better serve American interests than a high risk involvement in China's civil struggle. Within a month after the outbreak of fighting, the secretary of state detailed the guidelines of American policy: Any loan should be part of a general plan endorsed by the powers to help China to meet her international obligations and to perform the ordinary administrative tasks of government. Such a loan mainly would provide income to meet China's foreign debts and could not be used to advance the political fortunes of a single faction. Knox also stressed the importance of foreign supervision of any loan earmarked to eliminate China's foreign debt. The secretary refused, however, to implement this policy unilaterally. Any action in China would have to be the result of a broad international understanding involving those nations with the largest stakes in the Far East.[4]

As a consequence of American inaction, the financiers, led by the British, met in Paris and resolved that until their representatives in Beijing could assure them that a responsible Chinese government was in power, they would neither receive loan applications from any Chinese faction nor make any payments or advances under the terms of the Huguang Agreement or the Currency Reform Loan Agreement. The financiers also agreed that they would not issue the Currency Loan as planned on April 14, 1912, unless the Chinese agreed to stiffer terms, including lower bond prices and further guarantees concerning the control of loan expenditures. Diplomatic assistance would be sought to secure China's consent to these more stringent demands.[5]

The financiers' inflexibility worked to the disadvantage of the Manchus. Early in the course of the struggle, the Chinese Foreign Office realized that the nation would not be able to meet all its financial obligations. Yet, despite the recommendation of the resident diplomatic corps that loan payments be suspended, the bankers insisted that there could be no relaxation of terms. As a consequence, the government was unable to meet the October installment of the Boxer indemnity. To prevent precipitous foreign action as a result of this default, the Chinese Foreign Office quickly assured Sir John Jordan, dean of the Beijing diplomatic corps, that the delay occasioned by the revolutionary disturbances would not happen again. Although the rebels also sought to reassure the powers that the struggling Republic of China was well aware of its financial obligations and would fulfill them to the letter, the burden of actually doing so seriously weakened the Manchus, who required a financial respite to meet the challenge of the revolution.[6]

The difficulties of the situation doomed Chinese efforts at reassurance, as the powers moved quickly to safeguard their interests against future such interruptions. The Imperial Maritime Customs Service, prior to 1911, had only audited and supervised the collection of customs, but it now extended its grip over China's fiscal affairs. When revolutionary provinces tried to claim all locally collected customs revenue as their own, to hire troops and purchase munitions, Sir John Jordan recommended foreign control of all customs revenue emanating from both rebel- and government-held ports. The foreign inspector general, on Jordan's recommendation, ordered foreign commissioners to assume all actual collection duties and to deposit the proceeds in foreign banks. On January 1, 1912, the International Commission of Bankers was established to manage the payment of customs revenue toward the foreign debt. Representatives of the Hong Kong–Shanghai Bank, the Deutsche-Asiatische Bank, and the Russo-Asiatic Bank—the financial institutions most interested in the service of the outstanding loans and the indemnity—made up the commission that was to schedule the debt repayment. No longer could these funds be used to meet internal needs but henceforth would be exclusively applied to China's foreign obligations. The powers also moved to take complete control of the Shanghai Mixed Court by unilaterally removing all its operations beyond Chinese government authority. Greatly exaggerated indemnification claims for foreign losses arising from the revolution were pressed upon the government. As the inspector general of the Maritime Customs Service wrote, "the Powers ought to treat China with severity, it is their only chance for forcing the Chinese with setting things in order."[7]

These actions by the foreign powers and financiers to protect their own interests worked fortuitously to the advantage of the rebels. To eliminate the possibility of foreign intervention, the rebels, despite isolated attempts by certain provincial officials to appropriate this source of funds, formally adopted a hands-off policy regarding customs revenue. The imperial government, which had previously availed itself of customs revenues, now found itself deprived of resources that it needed desperately to suppress the rebellion.

The combination of official neutrality and confiscation of customs revenues further weakened the Manchus and greatly alarmed Minister Calhoun, who counseled Washington that "the consequences of such inaction may be more disastrous than those which might possibly result should the Four Groups now be permitted to come to the assistance of Yuan Shih-k'ai." Calhoun warned that if Yuan did not achieve widespread support for a constitutional monarchy, China would dissolve into petty and antagonistic factions, a chaotic situation that could be retrieved only by administrative and military intervention. Discarding caution as well as republican sympathies, the American minister recommended that the United States render immediate financial assistance to the struggling monarchists.[8]

The American banking group, consisting of J. P. Morgan & Company, Kuhn, Loeb and Company, National City Bank, and First National Bank, was a receptive audience for such advice as Calhoun's. The group's Beijing representative, the irrepressible diplomat-turned-financier Willard Straight, had been urging it for weeks to support

Yuan. Although Straight mourned the passing of the Manchus, he was grateful that the revolution had brought to the fore Yuan and Tang Shaoyi, two authoritarians who favored the development of China by foreign, and particularly American, capital. Straight had argued that only Yuan could bring stability to the nation. The alternative was chaos and, ultimately, foreign intervention. Under the circumstances, Straight recommended that the group should give Yuan the financial assistance necessary for him to secure complete control. Otherwise, China would dissolve as a nation or Yuan would turn for support to America's rivals under terms so onerous that either China would be financially ruined or the United States would be excluded from participation in future economic ventures.[9]

The American financiers took Straight's warnings seriously. The group already had perceived indications of Yuan's displeasure at the lack of assistance. Moreover, Yuan was enhancing his bargaining position by simultaneously negotiating with the international consortium's rivals. He was, for example, engaged in discussions with the British and Chinese Corporation and with Salmon & Company. In fact, only the personal intervention of Secretary Knox prevented Salmon & Company from advancing Yuan £2 million in violation of the government's policy of international cooperation. Ultimately, Yuan's need for funds led to the eventuality which Straight and his fellow financiers so feared. On November 30, 1911, the Chinese signed the so-called Cottu loan sponsored by one of the consortium's competitors. This loan undermined the consortium's bargaining position to such a degree that it had to employ all its resources to force the loan's cancellation. If the financiers were not able to eliminate such competition, prospects for future profits would be sharply diminished.[10]

The threat of international competition was not the only factor that jeopardized the bankers' position. When the revolutionaries abolished the internal commerce tax, which was pledged as security for the Huguang Loan Agreement of May 1911, the financiers realized that a policy of neutrality could lead to the ascendancy of Chinese leaders hostile to their interests. Still, the American financiers hesitated, waiting for a concert of powers to support Yuan, who would establish a climate favorable to new business opportunities. Yuan, they thought, would oppose new loans on onerous terms that might jeopardize either existing long-term loans or the proposed Reorganization Loan. Secretary Knox shared their caution and waited on Britain. But though the British government was willing to take the risk to extend temporary financial assistance to the Chinese government, there was trepidation in British banking circles that such a move would make compromise more difficult and alienate the hitherto friendly revolutionaries.[11]

The State Department finally opted for a compromise solution. While it did not condone a departure from strict neutrality, it agreed to support a small, internationally backed loan intended solely to bolster administrative and police functions. At last, with British support and American acquiescence, the consortium floated Yuan a small loan. Predictably, the provisional revolutionary government refused to recognize the loan, warning that the loan would touch off antiforeign riots.[12]

When the prince regent abdicated, the movement among the bankers to support Yuan against the revolutionaries gained added momentum. Straight informed J. P. Morgan that with the imperial government bankrupt, Yuan would not be able to hold the country together without financial support. In response, the American financiers authorized Straight to negotiate a three million tael loan, secured by the railroads of north China. But before the transaction was completed, J. P. Morgan insisted on international support and government approval, and because the American government refused to take an initiative on the matter, the proposed loan failed to materialize.[13]

The conditions in China that had prompted the Morgan loan initiative eventually galvanized the British, who began to advocate some form of financial assistance merely to keep China afloat. E. C. Greenfell of Morgan, Greenfell & Company suggested, however, that any loan should contain a guarantee of existing obligations, create a new source of security for further borrowing, and recommend the placement of capable foreigners in the areas of finance, industry, and railways. Assistant Secretary of State Huntington-Wilson concurred with Greenfell's suggestions.[14]

Economists for the consortium felt that the provisional government that had succeeded the prince regent required at least two million taels to sustain itself. Such a loan could be made at 6 percent, secured by a mortgage on the Chinese Merchants Steam Navigation Company, a holding valued at over seven million taels. The attractions of such a deal were many. Not only would there be a handsome profit, but the loan would lead to a pleasant business relationship with the new Chinese leaders. Moreover, the British feared that if the consortium did not provide the money, a competitor surely would. In addition, as a result of its alliance with imperial Japan (which feared that the institution of republican rule in nearby China would threaten its own system of government), Great Britain favored the establishment of a constitutional monarchy in China. An emergency advance to the Chinese government would primarily benefit Yuan, a man of monarchical rather than republican tendencies.[15]

Across the Atlantic, American business and governmental circles were coming together behind the concept of an emergency loan. The financiers took the position that the Chinese state could not continue to function without a short-term loan. The State Department endorsed the idea of an emergency loan under two conditions: It would have to be made to a government headed by Yuan, and it would have to be without prejudice to the ultimate participation of Russia and Japan—for only if the loan were fully internationalized would the U.S. government support it.[16]

This government policy proved to be a stumbling block. J. P. Morgan & Company felt that Russia and Japan, on the basis of their economic weakness, and despite their great political stakes in China, did not merit equal participation in the China loan business. Great Britain, however, could not oppose the demands of two badly needed allies against Germany that they participate in any loan to China on an equal basis with other lenders. The Chinese, who desperately needed money, feared to accept a loan that involved two nations well known for their desire to dismember China. Behind the pressure put on him by the British for an armistice, when he appeared to hold a military advantage over the insurgents, Yuan saw Japanese and Russian designs for a chaotic and weak China. Willard Straight accepted the validity of Yuan's claim that the British were undermining him to placate their allies.[17]

The Chinese fear that Japan and Russia would use participation in a loan arrangement to further territorial ambitions in China was well grounded, as the concurrent discussions over the Currency Loan demonstrated. Just before the revolution, the consortium had been negotiating a Currency Loan with the Manchus that would have actively involved the bankers in the economic development of Manchuria, an area of special interest to both Russia and Japan. Article XVI of the proposed agreement, for example, dealt with colonization and reclamation of land, agricultural and mining developments, and all industrial enterprises within Manchuria. The Russians and Japanese sought assiduously to eliminate the article. The Russians claimed that the consortium was attempting to establish a financial and, ultimately, a political monopoly in Manchuria. Similarly, the Japanese protested that no self-denying declaration could blunt the effect of creating an obvious financial, industrial, and commercial preference in favor of the consortium. If Article XVI became a reality, the preeminence of the Russian and Japanese positions in Manchuria would be greatly diminished.[18]

When the consortium finally sought Russian and Japanese participation in the Currency Loan, those two powers demanded the elimination of Article XVI and a detailed statement of the actual projects to be carried out under the loan agreement. Count Isvolsky, the Russian ambassador to France, further demanded that any future Chinese loans negotiated for territory north of the Great Wall, in Manchuria or Mongolia, be on the basis of 60 percent for Russia and Japan and 40 percent for the consortium. Russia and Japan also insisted on equal participation in loans dealing with political matters outside their spheres of influence, while for other loans they asked only for 10 to 15 percent participation.[19]

The disruption caused in China by the revolution made the demands of the Russians and Japanese seem irresistible to the consortium. To the bankers, China was now broken, an easier victim than ever before. Old China hands, such as Willard Straight, came to believe that the preservation of the crumbling Manchu empire was impossible. The outlying areas of the empire, especially those already under foreign influence, seemed beyond the grasp of any potential Chinese government. Under the circumstances, Straight believed it advisable to reach an understanding with Russia and Japan regarding their positions in Manchuria and Mongolia. Recognition of Russian and Japanese predominance in those areas was the price that the United States would have to pay if it wished to preserve both the Currency Loan and future business opportunities in China proper.[20]

American business and government officials welcomed Straight's assurance that such a compromise would exclude potential competitors from the Chinese financial market. Just before the organization of the provisional government, Minister Calhoun had informed Secretary Knox that Argentina, Russia, and Japan were forming plans to enter the China market. Calhoun agreed that an international understanding was necessary to prevent the growth of harmful competition. Similarly, the British felt that "[t]he only remedy for the disastrous competition will be the admission of Japan and Russia to the four-Power combine." Thus, the originally unwelcome presence of Russia and Japan now presented an opportunity for the consortium to further consolidate its financial monopoly at China's expense by inviting those powers to join the consortium.[21]

Unsuccessful in its earlier attempts to neutralize Russian and Japanese influence in Manchuria, the United States was neither willing nor able to oppose Russian or Japanese participation in China's fiscal affairs. The international power alignment had made Britain and France dependent upon Russia and Japan, to maintain parity with the growing strength of Germany. Because Britain and France would not allow the United States to oppose their allies' ambitions, Assistant Secretary of State Huntington-Wilson, who "preferred to follow any lead given by Great Britain," fully endorsed the participation of Russia and Japan in all China loans. Naturally, this solidification of the Triple Entente was opposed by Germany, whose representatives were of the opinion that the introduction of these two avaricious powers into the negotiations would make a settlement with the Chinese more difficult to achieve.[22]

Although Russian and Japanese participation in loans to China was desirable from a political standpoint, there were some differences of opinion in the financial community. Because Russia and Japan desired participation for political rather than economic reasons, J. P. Morgan felt that the two nations should receive a proportionately smaller share of the business than the original partners. The American bankers also thought that the admission of Russia and Japan as full members of the consortium could seriously prejudice their own interests by alienating Chinese public sentiment. Nonetheless, Morgan was willing to enter into a broad obligation on all future business, especially in matters relating to the territory south of the Great Wall. Morgan's British associates did not share these American concerns and felt that complete equality was the way to gain full Russian and Japanese cooperation. If the consortium did not accord Russia and Japan equal treatment, the two nations would achieve it later through strength, on terms unfavorable to the original members of the consortium. The British argued that since Russia and Japan were interested primarily in political matters, their participation would not hamper unduly the financial aspects of the partnership.[23]

The exacerbation of the fiscal crisis in China demanded the prompt resolution of the problem of Russian and Japanese participation, for without immediate financial assistance the new provisional government would collapse. The financiers were particularly anxious to extend and to prop up the faltering government, even at the expense of relaxing the conditions of the loan. However, unless the loan contained "adequate guarantees for proper and useful expenditure of the proceeds," as well as foreign-supervised security for repayment, the British government would withhold its support from the transaction.[24] Great Britain also announced that it would veto any financial aid until the group agreed to accept Russia and Japan as equal partners. The British minister to the United States, James Bryce, informed the State Department that the exclusion of Russia and Japan would prompt a return to the days of "unprofitable competition" in China.[25]

Following the British lead, Assistant Secretary of State Huntington-Wilson stated that Russia and Japan should be admitted to the consortium as equal partners and offered the opportunity to share in future Chinese loans. Once the United States endorsed Britain's wishes, Germany was forced to drop its opposition to Russian and Japanese participation. Finally, even Yuan Shikai and Tang Shaoyi went on record in favor of broad internationalization of all future loans. Yuan, however, continued to oppose the recognition of special spheres of influence in Manchuria and Mongolia. He hoped that the consortium would restrain the ambitions of Russia and Japan.[26]

Once they had achieved this consensus, the British lifted their prohibition against financial aid and, on February 28, 1912, the consortium advanced two million taels to the Chinese provisional government. Along with the money, the Chinese government accepted a new set of international political circumstances that posed a heightened threat to the territorial integrity of the nation. The governments behind the consortium were now committed to reaching a modus vivendi regarding the territorial ambitions of Russia and Japan. As a result, they were closer to achieving a financial monopoly over China than ever before.[27]

The quest for a monopolistic bargaining position was a vital element in the group's negotiating strategy. The object of these negotiations was to be the so-called Reorganization Loan, originally valued at £60 million but later reduced to the still sizable amount of £25 million. This loan was designed to enable China to meet its accumulated foreign obligations, to provide a fund for indemnities for damages suffered by foreigners during the revolution, to finance the reorganization of the salt tax, to pay for troop demobilization, and to underwrite certain specified administrative expenses of the central government. From the Chinese perspective, outside funding was needed not only to meet expenses but also for Yuan to effectively centralize political power in his hands. From the bankers' perspective, if the consortium could effectuate the desired monopoly, then it could exploit

China's desperate need for funds and impose harsh as well as profitable requirements that the Chinese would be in no position to resist. The British succinctly summed up the purpose of this strategy:

> From the outset of the negotiations in connection with the Chinese Reorganization Loan, His Majesty's Government have kept before them certain main objects to be secured, viz., the avoidance of unprofitable competition, adequate security for the payment of capital and interest, discretionary power over the purposes of the loan, and control over the proceeds of the loan in order to prevent leakage and to secure that they shall be economically expended and exclusively devoted to the purposes which have received the approval of the Governments interested.[28]

American bankers and government officials heartily supported this policy which bode so ill for the Chinese. The United States recognized early the danger that free competition would pose to the economic success of the fragile financial coalition that was negotiating the Chinese loan. To preserve the consortium's monopolistic position, the State Department exerted considerable pressure to prevent American nationals from becoming involved in dealings outside the consortium. As Knox told the German ambassador, "The present was an occasion where there might be invoked with peculiar appropriateness the principle of lending governments deterring their nationals from making loans not approved as to their broad policy by their own governments in consultation with the other interested powers." Assistant Secretary of State Huntington-Wilson vainly attempted to distinguish between giving the consortium the exclusive right to deal with China, and giving it a monopoly, claiming that any legitimate lender could join the consortium if it accepted the general ground rules.[29]

From the Chinese point of view, this distinction did not create more reasonable financial alternatives to the consortium's demands. By denying the Chinese the opportunity to play off one financier against another, the consortium would be able to force Chinese acceptance of its terms. With the active support and encouragement of their respective governments, the international bankers hoped to force the Chinese to surrender any future options that might be open to them. While the preliminary payments were being made, and until the Reorganization Loan was successfully issued, the Chinese provisional government would be required to bind itself and its successors not to negotiate any loan except through the medium of the consortium.[30]

The consortium hoped to attain its monopolistic objective by being designated China's fiscal agent. This would give it exclusive control of the markets for Chinese bonds during the term of the contract and would relieve it of the necessity to renegotiate the specifics of each subsequent loan. Assistant Secretary of State Huntington-Wilson registered no objection to the proposed fiscal agency but felt that the matter should be left primarily to the consortium and China to work out. With tacit approval from their government, the American bankers quickly gave their strong support to the concept of a fiscal agency which, as Jordan realized, offered "the prospect . . . of obtaining a more or less permanent control of Chinese finances." The security-conscious British group did not share the American group's enthusiasm for a fiscal agency, however. The British felt that it would be inexpedient to coerce China into accepting proposals that might incite antiforeign outbursts throughout the country. For, naturally, any plan that conferred upon foreigners considerable administrative authority over China's finances was likely to receive an extremely unpopular reception. Moreover, to gain acceptance of the plan, the consortium would have to overcome not only strong popular sentiment but the personal ambitions of President Yuan, who was jealous of his newly claimed power and did not relish surrendering his financial prerogatives to a group of foreign bankers. To allay British fears, McKnight recommended that the banks obtain commitments from their respective governments to intervene militarily, to crush any antiforeign outbursts that might follow the conclusion of the loan.[31]

Despite his earlier reluctance to place China at the mercy of the bankers, in March 1912, Yuan desperately needed funds to keep his government afloat and to pay his troops. To avert the impending crisis, Yuan, in exchange for an advance of two million taels, gave the consortium a firm option on a comprehensive loan, for general reorganization purposes already under discussion, provided that the consortium would extend the loan on "terms equally advantageous with those otherwise obtainable."[32]

Yuan's apparently reasonable proposal did not contain the degree of security that the consortium desired. The financiers did not want Yuan to have the option of deserting them if a better deal should come along. For, if the Chinese retained the freedom of action that Yuan wanted, the profitability of the loan would diminish and, in the consortium's opinion, sizable advances would be foolhardy.

Yuan realized full well that a consortium monopoly would make the united groups of bankers all the more difficult to deal with and unwilling to compromise. So he sought out financial competitors who would undermine the consortium's position. The accuracy of his judgment was proved by the consortium's anger and shock when he announced the procurement, from an independent Anglo-Belgian syndicate, of a £1 million loan at 5 percent, with another £10 million to follow. Furthermore, the loan was free of the requirements of strict control by foreigners that the Chinese found so loathsome. The consortium bankers bitterly attacked the Belgian loan. It was a violation of both the letter and the spirit of the March 9, 1912, contract between themselves and the Chinese government, which covered the first advance of the Reorganization Loan and purportedly gave the consortium an exclusive option on all future Chinese loans.[33]

The major powers shared the bankers' dim view of the Belgian loan because it seriously undermined future foreign control of the Chinese Republic. Great Britain, which strongly opposed foreign loans made outside the consortium, was determined to quash Chinese attempts to escape the grasp of the international banking cartel. "We ought not let this opportunity pass for impressing on the Chinese Government that the time for borrowing money on their own terms has gone past."[34] Huntington-Wilson ordered Calhoun to express America's similar displeasure with China's shortsightedness, and he recommended a renewed effort to gain China's acceptance of the fiscal agency plan, so that the Chinese would be compelled to guarantee the consortium fair treatment in the loan business. Huntington-Wilson, of course, defined "fair treatment" to preclude any subsequent loan that might conflict with the consortium's "legitimate interests" or might weaken the security of the large Reorganization Loan. The United States still felt that the financiers should retain a monopoly. As Huntington-Wilson wrote Calhoun on March 18: "It may be worth considering whether the Chinese Government should not at the same time be requested also to engage with the respective governments not to negotiate any large loan except with the combined banking groups and their associates, or with the corresponding groups of the same nationalities and upon the same broad principles of internationalization."[35]

Tang Shaoyi bore the brunt of foreign criticism of the Belgian loan. As the man who negotiated the loan, Tang was a natural target for the angry bankers. Yet, very early in the negotiations, he had informed the American government that his government wanted free competition in the loan business. Tang emphasized that China did not want to be bullied by a group of greedy capitalists but wanted to be free to act in its own best interests.[36]

Under extreme pressure from the National Assembly to save China from the consortium's monopoly and to foster free competition, Tang temporarily accomplished his goal. He justified his action to the consortium by stating that the failure of the consortium to respond to China's fiscal plight had prompted him to seek other sources of funds. Furthermore, China was free to seek funds from sources other than the consortium and would grant no group a monopoly. In response to the American claim that China had acted in bad faith and had broken a previous contract, Tang asserted that the consortium had itself breached the agreement by failing to keep up the payment of advances during riots that had recently broken out in Beijing. Not satisfied with Tang's explanation, Calhoun accused revolutionary leaders such as Sun Yat-sen and every member of the National Assembly of receiving large bribes in exchange for their approval of the Belgian loan. The countercharges heightened the distrust between the consortium and the Chinese.[37]

The consortium immediately urged that their governments exert pressure on the Chinese to disavow the Belgian loan. Charles Addis, representing the British group, suggested that either the Chinese repudiate the Belgian loan or forfeit future advances from the consortium. J. P. Morgan & Company advocated military pressure to secure Chinese acquiescence to the consortium's demands. Calhoun agreed that the governments should act to prevent such "foolish borrowing" that would lead to bankruptcy and foreign intervention. Following the advice of Calhoun and Willard Straight, the respective governments made it impossible for any independent group to negotiate loan agreements, especially agreements lacking stiff controls on the Chinese. The powers also pressured the czar to withdraw the Russo-Asiatic Bank from the Belgian syndicate. Attracted more by the prospect of bending the other powers to its plans for Manchuria, Mongolia, and Turkestan than by the possibilities inherent in Great Power competition in China, the Russian government acceded to the demands of the powers and withdrew the Russo-Asiatic Bank from the Belgian syndicate. Once this occurred, the Belgian syndicate was unable to provide China with the necessary funds and the Chinese had no alternative but to cancel the remainder of the Belgian loan.[38]

Russian participation in the Belgian loan syndicate underscored the necessity of working out the particulars of Russo-Japanese participation in the consortium. Negotiations intensified as the Russians and Japanese demanded protection for their special interests in Manchuria, Mongolia, and Turkestan. Only if these special interests were protected would the Russians and Japanese participate in the Reorganization Loan. In the opinion of Morgan, Greenfell & Company, the Russians and Japanese hoped to secure general approval of a formula that would enable them to determine arbitrarily the extent and character of all their rights in these territories that were not defined explicitly by treaty. Secretary Knox was fearful that refusal of their demands would drive Russia and Japan away and cause France and Britain to leave the consortium in pursuit of better ties with their anti-German allies. He informed J. P. Morgan that the State Department had no objection to a proposed declaration that the consortium "would not agree to any of the proceeds of the loan being used in Manchuria, Mongolia or Chinese Turkestan for any purpose which might be prejudicial to the special interests of Russia and Japan." Although, retrospectively, Knox defined "special interests" as referring only to rights based on treaties or conventions with China, the language of the proposal indicated American acquiescence in Russian and Japanese designs on Chinese territory.[39]

Once the American attitude toward Russia and Japan was made known, the bankers were free to conclude an agreement among themselves. Each bank was to have equal shares, as well as equal rights, in the Reorganization Loan and in any financial, industrial, commercial, or political benefits that might flow therefrom. The bankers also agreed to maintain their close ties with their respective governments and to restrict the loan to the general needs of the Chinese state, forbidding its use for "special undertakings in any of the provinces of China, especially not in Manchuria, Mongolia, and Chinese Turkestan."[40]

The desire to maintain a highly profitable financial monopoly in China prevented the State Department from realizing that the entry of Japan and Russia into the consortium would increase the difficulty of dealing with the Chinese. The United States was well aware that Russian and Japanese participation in the consortium would politicize the loan question. Government officials also were aware that the two nations would join the consortium only on their own terms. Yet, if the United States opposed this abandonment of Chinese interests, the consortium and, with it, American policy in East Asia would disintegrate. France and Britain would withdraw from the group before they would oppose the interests of their vitally important ally, Russia. The State Department therefore refused to abandon its policy of international cooperation and on June 20, 1912, it entered into an agreement that secured the position of Russia and Japan within the consortium.[41]

The new agreement did not mention the question of Russian and Japanese special rights in Manchuria. Sir Edward Grey, however, explained that this was tantamount to acceptance of Russian and Japanese demands. Britain would not oppose Russia and Japan in Manchuria and Mongolia, as long as the two nations did not oppose the Open Door for British commerce in China itself. Secretary of State Knox also tacitly endorsed a Russian or Japanese veto over any business that might be unfavorable to their special interests in China. Knox justified this commitment to China's two most dangerous enemies by claiming that it was necessary to prevent further, more exorbitant demands. It now remained for the Chinese to extricate themselves from a worsening economic and political situation and to preserve at least some semblance of independence.[42]

4

Chinese Nationalism and the Fight for Economic Independence

THE establishment of a financial monopoly in the China market allowed the financiers to pay greater attention to questions of security for their investment. While external conditions were increasingly favorable to high profits, internal conditions threatened heavy losses. To protect its possible financial investment, the United States adopted an extremely hard-line approach to the loan negotiations and to the matter of financial control, both of which threatened to endanger Sino-American relations.

Fundamentally, most high American officials had an unfavorable opinion of the Chinese and their state system. Minister Calhoun, for example, believed that the Chinese were "notoriously improvident and inefficient in all public financial matters" and were given to bribery and embezzlement. "The everlasting 'squeeze' poisons the life of the people, perverts public effort, diminishes the public revenues and corrupts the public administration," he wrote. "The Chinese are like children in financial matters—they want to do silly things like build bridges across the Yangtze as memorials to the Revolution." Even were the Chinese mature, Calhoun felt, the decrepit nature of the Chinese revenue system would likely render security devised for the loan ineffectual. E. T. Williams, the well-respected China expert of the American legation in Beijing, enumerated the reasons for this decrepitude, including the failure of the provinces to remit revenue to the central government, popular resistance to tax collection, rioting by soldiers, and dependence on the meager proceeds of the customs revenue.[1]

What most concerned foreign observers, such as Williams, was the fragmentation of the governmental system and the rise of anarchy. Communities were policing themselves and remitted no taxes to provincial or national authorities. Some local officials abolished taxes while others instituted new and heavy taxes. The central government was not likely to develop regular and reliable income sources for the foreseeable future. "Where there was confusion under the Empire," Williams reported, "there is complete chaos under the Republic."[2]

Possessing very minimal authority over the provinces, the new regime actually functioned in only an advisory and symbolic capacity. Furthermore, young and inexperienced officials were far too prominent in the administration to give the new government the substantive leadership that it required.[3] To foreign observers it appeared to be only a matter of time before the situation once again went out of control.

In early March, the Chinese troops stationed in Beijing mutinied. Indiscriminate gunfire and looting caused great alarm in the foreign community and presaged a general deterioration of conditions throughout China. Because of this growing anarchy, the threat of foreign military intervention once more was becoming a reality. As a result of the Boxer protocol, there were already several thousand foreign troops stationed in northern China to protect the railways.[4] Now there appeared to be a need for a more substantial foreign military presence in China.

The United States particularly felt that additional troops were needed to safeguard its interests. When the American legation in Beijing was shelled and reports began to circulate that British missionaries and Christians were being slaughtered in Shandong, Calhoun suggested that military occupation of the railways was necessary to ensure the safety of the foreign community. In response to this crisis, the United States sent an additional regiment of troops from the Philippines to northern China. Clearly, the formation of a coalition government had not brought peace and stability to China.[5]

Although rumors persisted that Yuan had instigated the riots to pressure the powers into rendering much-needed financial assistance, the powers found no solid evidence to support this hypothesis of planned chaos. Rather than blame Yuan, the powers attributed the continuing anarchy to the institution of republican rule in a land suited only to autocracy. Consul James Clifford McNally, in Qingdao, persuaded Secretary Knox that the sudden transformation from totalitarian rule to the loosely knit coalition government had thrown the people of China into a state of utter confusion.[6] Beyond the fear of chaos, there was trepidation that the new Chinese government would adopt a hostile attitude toward foreign interests in China: "China has in the past been greatly humiliated. The new government seemingly demands the treatment accorded to other nations. They want the right to borrow funds from whom they please and the best available conditions, rights recognized in other countries, and failing to obtain this measure of international justice, they will no doubt fight to the end."[7]

In the eyes of American officials, the prestige of the new Chinese Republic had ebbed to its lowest point since its inception. Calhoun felt that the new administration was incapable of engaging in constructive tasks and that this inability was permitting the provinces to drift beyond any semblance of unified control. In the north, resentment toward the Cantonese-led experiment in self-government was especially great. Northern Chinese resorted to passive resistance by refusing to remit taxes to the coalition government. In Gansu, Turkestan, Mongolia, and Tibet there actually was armed opposition to the central government. With the task of removing the Manchus accomplished, interest in building a republic waned in areas outside the south.[8]

In addition to the obvious difficulties created by provincial separatism and China's lack of political unity, there was evidence that the new coalition government itself was unstable. With the president in Beijing and the cabinet and assembly in Nanjing fighting each other for preeminence within the government, the outlook was bleak.[9] Lacking both cohesion and popular support, the government was powerless to halt the disorder, rioting, and anarchy plaguing the country. The promises of the revolution remained unfulfilled. To American policymakers, the failure of the new regime was rooted in two factors: lack of competent leadership and the inappropriateness of republican government in China. Regarding the latter, the United States had utter disdain for China's ability to manage its own affairs:

> The centralized system of government such as existed under the Manchu regimes, Chinese character considered, is the only form of government that will hold the Chinese. The republican form of government is as foreign to the Chinese people and as opposite to their peculiar makeup as earth is from heaven. They are wholly

unfitted both by superstitious beliefs and dense ignorance on the one hand, and provincial and sectional hatreds on the other. They are not endowed with the intellect to enjoy the blessings of a free government, the principles of which are wholly unknown to the great majority of the people.[10]

When Premier Tang Shaoyi departed from the government, the crisis in leadership worsened. In American diplomatic circles, Tang was highly regarded as a man of both experience and ability—two qualities sorely required in the Chinese government.[11] Unfortunately, Sun Yat-sen and the young members of his party, the Tongmenghui, seemed incapable of filling the void left by Tang's departure. So long had they been away from their native land, plotting revolutionary intrigue, that they had lost touch with China's real problems.[12] As Minister Calhoun wrote, "Many of them are but slightly acquainted with their own country and some scarcely able to read its literature. Too many are disposed to sneer at the traditions and customs of their own people and do not understand the problems they are seeking to solve."[13] Because these men did not inspire confidence within the foreign community, it would be foolhardy to allow them to borrow money indiscriminately and without adequate supervision. Calhoun held out little hope that Sun Yat-sen could take "hold of the situation or command the varied and conflicting interests which will become active."[14]

Minister Calhoun continually fretted over the lack of strong, vigorous leadership in China. He complained that "the country is like a ship without a rudder or a sail without a compass or chart, that is slowly drifting towards the rocks." With the treasury depleted and the collection of native revenues suspended, the economic situation seemed desperate. The question was, who could extract China from this quagmire? Sun Yat-sen and his followers were never considered even potential candidates for this task. If anything, China needed less, not more, democracy at this time. As the Chicago lawyer-turned-diplomat pointed out, "In the remote villages the unbroken silence of centuries still broods over the people . . . [who] . . . as a whole, have no conception of what a republic is or what the duties and responsibilities of citizenship are. To establish a republic upon such an uncertain foundation is like building a house upon the shifting sands."[15]

A nation fragmented into myriad pieces, and with weak political leadership, did not present an attractive business opportunity to foreign bankers. Nor could the economic resources of such a nation be systematically exploited. The consortium members had no confidence that the "extravagant, inefficient and . . . corrupt" Chinese government could rescue China from economic disaster. Only by supervising the process of reorganization down to the most minute detail could the financiers remedy China's fiscal and political woes. Only the extent of the supervision necessary to achieve political stability and financial profitability remained a subject for discussion. As Charles Eliot, president emeritus of Harvard University, advised Yuan, China could establish its credit in the world financial market only by instituting "methods of taxation that have approved themselves to Western economists and statesmen" and by spending her revenue "honestly and effectively on objects and in methods which have proved good in Western administrations." Foreign advisers vested with ample authority were an absolute prerequisite in this regard.[16] Possible measures being considered ranged from simply general control of China's finances and the revision of its tax system to the establishment of a fiscal agency that would regulate absolutely the investment and expenditure of funds. The lack of a viable legal system in China, to which a lender could appeal to enforce his rights under a contract, also argued for strict controls on the Chinese economy. As Calhoun pointed out, the only true security available to the bankers was the guarantee of the central government and "for its enforcement, he [the creditor] depends upon the diplomatic intervention of his own government, which, in the last resort, may be evinced by armed force."[17]

The consortium clearly preferred very strict fiscal controls. Morgan, Greenfell and Company, a dominant influence in the banking community, wanted control to last until China had rehabilitated itself fiscally. This control also should provide for the general supervision of China's finances so that the consortium could implement a drastic reform of the tax system. These conditions meant that the control exercised by the consortium would extend far beyond the revenue pledged for a specific loan and would have to last until such time as China convinced the foreign governments and financiers that it was capable of building up a "stable, strong and efficient administration." China would become a de facto financial protectorate of the international banking consortium. The State Department welcomed this development. According to Lewis Einstein, a high-level policymaking official of the department, "The so-called bankers' ring is . . . not China's natural enemy . . . but her natural friend aiming only to bring about those guarantees of security which however distasteful to her pride will be beneficial to the national credit."[18]

China had to either surrender its sovereignty to the foreign powers or accept fiscal impotency. The existence of the financial monopoly had left China with few alternatives to solving its financial woes, however. The American government was fully cognizant of China's predicament because it had worked to put China there. Minister Calhoun justified the monopoly by maintaining that without it the banking community would shy away from the desperate and unpromising fiscal condition of the new republic.[19]

The complex bargaining and negotiating between the bankers and the Chinese thus represented an attempt by the former to impose terms stoutly resisted by the latter. American policy in these negotiations was determined at an early stage. Knox informed the British that the United States would approve no loans to China unless they were accompanied by adequate provisions for the supervision of expenditures. Similarly, the British were of the opinion that effective control of expenditures was essential. Such supervision was necessary no matter what the size of the loan. The consortium also should secure from the Chinese a commitment not to negotiate any subsequent loan that might conflict with the legitimate interests of the bankers or impair the security for the loan. Members of the group should themselves agree with their respective governments not to participate in any loans except through the aegis of the consortium. Knox, however, temporarily refrained from endorsing the concept of a fiscal agency or itemizing the particulars of any proposed agreement.[20]

The consortium formulated its financial policy toward China very early in the negotiations. Specifically, the financiers wanted the customs tariff revised to bring in enough revenue to cover all previous loans and the Boxer indemnity. The emergency measures initiated after the revolution, requiring the deposit of customs revenues in foreign receiving banks, were to continue and the railroads and accounting departments of the Republic were to make extensive use of foreign personnel. If the railroad department could not generate sufficient revenue to cover the railway loans, the deficiency was to be made up through the salt tax and a foreigner was to be appointed chief financial adviser to the Chinese government. Finally, the financiers hoped to encourage the development of mining and industry through the attraction of foreign capital. Yuan, deprived of any revenue from the provinces by the revolution and desperate for funds to reconstitute the shattered authority of the central government, gave his general approval to these recommendations.[21]

Difficulties soon developed over the specific terms of the Reorganization Loan, a loan designed to reestablish a viable Chinese government under the control of the foreign powers. Generally, it was agreed that the loan would not exceed £60 million to be distributed over five years. There were to be adequate provisions for control and supervision of loan expenditures and a binding commitment from the provisional government not to negotiate future loans or advances except through the consortium. The bankers also sought the inclusion of an unlimited force majeure clause which would render their commitment illusory: "It is understood that in the event of the political or financial situation in China, Europe, or elsewhere, rendering in the opinion of the Four Groups the issue of further Treasury bills and/or the reorganization loan impossible on the terms named, the four groups have the right to withdraw from their engagements."[22] The financiers entered the negotiations with a one-sided, condescending attitude. The Chinese were to bind themselves exclusively to the consortium, which, in turn, was free to withdraw from the deal at its own discretion. This unilateral approach made an equitable agreement most difficult to achieve.

The Reorganization Loan hinged on the success of the negotiations. H. P. Davison detailed the financiers' conditions for this loan: The Chinese would not have the discretion to spend loan funds as they chose but would have to specify a purpose for the expenditure of funds satisfactory to the consortium prior to each advance required by the agreement. Moreover, the Maritime Customs Service, which was managed by foreigners, was to administer the salt tax and other revenue-raising devices pledged as security for the loan. Foreign financial agents were to supervise expenditures of the customs receipts and the Chinese government was to furnish, prior to the conclusion of each installment of the Reorganization Loan, a detailed statement of purpose for the expenditure of that money. The Chinese were to employ foreign financial experts who would control the requisition of all loan funds, as well as the disposition of other internal revenue sources. Finally, the Chinese were to pledge not to negotiate with any other group while the Reorganization Loan was outstanding. The consortium thus sought more than supervision of the expenditure of a particular loan; it sought absolute control of China's overall financial affairs.[23]

Despite the stringent terms offered by the consortium, the Chinese remained conciliatory. The Chinese minister of finance, Tang Shaoyi, accepted in principle the proposals for the supervision of advances which, in John Jordan's words, guaranteed a "stricter measure of supervision than has ever been exercised over the expenditure of foreign money in the past." An Audit Department would be created as an adjunct to the Chinese Board of Finance; it would be composed of one foreign auditor paid by the consortium and one other auditor, not necessarily Chinese, reimbursed by the Republic. The auditors would then countersign all requisitions on the basis of a detailed statement of purpose, pay sheets, and vouchers of actual expenses incurred. The Chinese also would hire a chief technical expert and the commissioner of customs would be given joint responsibility for disbanding and paying the troops. Calhoun was particularly sympathetic to the bankers' desire to supervise troop disbandment, since there was no adequate intelligence on the number of troops and the military governors, who otherwise would be responsible for this task, were either "irresponsible or unknown" and of questionable "integrity." [24]

There were, however, some points on which the Chinese would not compromise. While they would employ foreigners to supervise loans made for industrial purposes, they would not permit foreigners to supervise loans made for administrative purposes. Nor would foreigners be permitted to supervise the disbandment of troops. Regarding these items, the minister of finance would simply publish a list of expenditures. [25]

Tang Shaoyi stressed China's opposition to foreign supervision of troop disbandment and attacked the bankers for hardening their terms following the institution of republican rule in China. He now insisted that auditing and supervision of expenditures be carried out exclusively by Chinese. Tang's policy was especially popular in southern China, a region particularly sensitive to foreign intrusion. [26]

The southerners' nationalism also was laced with a strong dose of regionalism. They perceived correctly that extensive borrowing would strengthen the central government greatly and thus curtail provincial autonomy. In the opinion of American policymakers, these "young leaders" of the revolution did not appreciate the "responsibilities which come with self-government," preferring to address China's fiscal problems with "idle bombast." Regional Chinese rivalry was contributing to the stalemate in the negotiations. [27]

The Chinese press actively criticized the government for even considering loans that surrendered supervisory authority to foreigners, and the National Assembly, in an attempt to assert its maturity, demanded that any contract made with the foreign powers first be submitted to it for approval. In addition to these disputes, a growing political rivalry between two of China's leading figures, Yuan and Tang, was instrumental in stirring up controversy over the loan. Tang, who was closely identified with the antiforeign movement in the south, sought to use this rising nationalism to improve his political fortunes by steadfastly opposing any further compromise with the consortium. Huang Xing, a prominent revolutionary leader, urged Yuan to reject any loan that would give the bankers supervision over the army. "In spite of the long delay in issuing their pay and the danger of the situation, we are unwilling to accept this loan which means the destruction of our country and the extinction of our race; this would be drinking poison to quench a thirst." Huang also pointedly warned Yuan that "[t]hose who attempt to ruin our people and betray our country will be regarded as public enemies of the Republic." American consuls throughout the country reported that nationalistic sentiment had grown so strong that the merchant and gentry classes were organizing to raise sufficient funds to make a foreign loan unnecessary. Nationalism was threatening the success of the loan negotiations.[28]

The Chinese stance grew tougher. They informed Calhoun that even the commissioner of customs, a foreigner in their employ, would be unacceptable as supervisor of troop disbandment. This amounted to a de facto nullification of the precautions that the powers had attempted to insert into the proposed Reorganization Loan contract. Furthermore, in what the consortium claimed was a result of passive resistance by the Chinese government to its policies, foreign inspectors were finding it difficult to enforce regulations designed to allow supervision of preliminary loan advances made to cover the costs of troop demobilization. The minister of finance simply would not make available any actual troop figures, with the result that the inspectors could do no more than check his arithmetic. Verification of the actual existence of the soldiers for whom the money was disbursed was impossible and, as Jordan reported, "even at the ports supervision proved a mockery." Agitation against the loan terms also was becoming quite pronounced, especially in the provinces, making it difficult for the Chinese government to accede to the groups' demands.[29]

Calhoun attempted to break the impasse in the negotiations by suggesting that the consortium make a small loan without any provisions for foreign supervision, to boost the sagging prestige of the new republic. The consortium was unmoved. Sir John Jordan quickly informed his colleagues that the British government would not compromise on the issues of control or supervision. If money were advanced without the necessary safeguards, the consortium would lose its bargaining power and the Chinese would more stubbornly resist the bankers' demands. To Jordan, the Chinese demands were a patently outrageous attempt to hide from foreigners the fraudulent padding of the military payroll, enabling the government to bribe military satraps throughout the country.[30]

For all his vehemence on these matters, Jordan remained personally convinced that the central government did not have "the power to enforce obedience to the terms of the contract, or the courage to attempt it if they had the power" in light of the widespread popular opposition to the proposed measures of control and supervision. His views on the effectiveness of the salt tax as the financial security for the Reorganization Loan were similarly pessimistic. Unless radically reformed, the salt tax could not possibly generate sufficient revenue to secure the massive loan. Reform of this tax also would be difficult to achieve because the provinces opposed interference with this source of income.[31]

Under the circumstances, Chinese rejection of the consortium's terms was hardly surprising. The premier and the minister of finance informed the resident diplomatic corps that the National Council and public opinion simply would not tolerate acquiescence to the consortium's demands. Faced with stubborn Chinese resistance, the consortium, led by the United States, nonetheless continued to insist that any agreement would have to contain provisions for adequate security. That was the sine qua non for a loan.[32]

While the United States continued to advocate a hard line in the negotiations, the British began to move toward compromise. Foreign Minister Sir Edward Grey rejected John Jordan's criticism of the British bankers for having "little intention of placing salt under any foreign control" and for having "relaxed the provisions for superintending the expenditure of advances," stating that his government did not want to be placed in a position of insisting on terms so onerous that their acceptance by the Chinese government would precipitate civil war. Grey hoped that by imposing proper conditions and safeguards on independent loans to China, the new republic would be able to stabilize itself. Once this had been achieved, the general scheme for reorganization could be taken up. The British financiers were "delighted" with Grey's willingness to relax the loan conditions and suggested that advances should continue, to enable the Chinese to restore order and reestablish central rule. A policy of withholding all advances, except as part of a comprehensive loan, could destroy any hopes of profitably exploiting the Chinese financial market.[33]

The American group could not accept the British approach. It felt that preliminary advances would be insufficient to prop up the Chinese government, which was too weak to implement the terms of the loan, and would merely postpone the inevitable fragmentation of the country. To impress the Chinese with their earnestness, the Americans proposed withdrawing from the negotiations until the Chinese accepted their terms.[34]

Led by the Americans, the powers informed Yuan that no compromise was possible on the conditions of the loan. To preserve this adamant stance, Secretary Knox proscribed loans by American nationals that did not contain provisions essentially identical to those demanded by the consortium. Such a policy effectively denied the Chinese access to competing lenders and compelled them to choose between accepting the the consortium's terms or continuing the struggle to exist as a nation without adequate financing.[35]

Despite their predicament, the Chinese still found the proposed foreign control of the salt tax totally objectionable. The minister of finance insisted that the tax was too complicated for foreigners to administer and that their intrusion into the system would disrupt the lives of millions of Chinese workers. Also distasteful to the Chinese was the mandatory employment of foreign experts in government offices. The Chinese preferred to select their own personnel to govern the administration of loan expenditures and financial collateral. In addition to these economic concerns, the Chinese realized that a foreign foothold in the salt administration would further impinge upon the nation's sovereignty. A foreign chief inspector empowered to withhold salt revenues in excess of what was needed to service the foreign debt would possess a powerful political lever against the Chinese government. Although the Chinese had been unable to prevent the expansion of foreign control over the Customs Service and the Mixed Court immediately following the outbreak of the revolution, they were determined to resist this new attempt at encroachment.[36]

To temper the enthusiasm of the foreigners for control of the salt tax, the minister of finance candidly admitted that the central government was receiving absolutely no revenue from the tax. Imposition of the bankers' terms would not guarantee that there would be resources available to support such a huge loan. This argument, however, served only to reinforce the belief of the bankers that foreign control was absolutely necessary to provide security for the loan.[37]

America's adamant position deeply troubled Yuan's supporters and threatened to alienate completely a faction whose support was critical to the successful conclusion of a loan agreement. Accordingly,

Calhoun informed Yan Huiqing, Chinese vice-minister of foreign affairs, that America's hard line did not signify disfavor with Yuan but was an effort to wear down the resistance of the revolutionary "hot heads" within the Chinese government.[38]

Yuan's presence may have reassured the bankers somewhat, but Tang's candid reference to the sorry plight of the Chinese economy touched an acutely sore spot in the bankers' feelings about investing in China. Calhoun reflected their concern. He believed that the empire's attempt to secure control over the salt tax had strongly contributed to the outbreak of the revolution. He feared that, even if the Republic should succeed where the empire had failed, the proceeds from the salt tax probably would be inadequate to cover the pre-1900 indebtedness to which part of that tax was pledged. These 15 to 18 million taels annually were diverted from its proceeds to pay the Boxer indemnity and the requirements of the proposed Reorganization Loan. The maritime and inland customs funds provided no surplus and the land tax was used primarily by the provinces to finance local administrative costs. The fiscal plight of China was so desperate that any investment in its economy was subject to great risks.[39]

If Calhoun and the bankers needed additional reasons for tightly regulating the Chinese economy to preserve their potential investments, they found one in the behavior of such Chinese leaders as Vice-Minister of Foreign Affairs Yan, who was quite willing to use foreign funds to buy off military rivals. As Calhoun remarked, "It is a sad commentary on the patriotism that is supposed to have been inspired and led by the Revolution, to be told that some of the leaders had to be bought off, to secure their loyalty to the new government." Calhoun was not convinced by Yan's argument that such a tactic was representative of traditional Chinese politics and that, in any event, it was cheaper than fighting.[40]

In the hope of breaking the deadlock, the Chinese government, represented by Zhao Bingzhun, submitted a detailed counterproposal to the consortium. Zhao stipulated that the administrative power of the Chinese government must be preserved intact and that the feelings of the Chinese people must be considered. If the consortium agreed to these two principles, then the loan could be dealt with under two headings. First would be the liquidation of current expenses, such as the disbandment of troops and the repayment of past debts, which would require approximately £20 million. The second phase would cover the financing of economic enterprises. Loans would be arranged individually according to the particular needs of a project. Zhao was conciliatory on the matter of the salt tax. Foreign experts would be used not as supervisors but as technicians who would mechanize the production of salt. In the treaty ports, Chinese and foreign officials appointed by the minister of finance would collect revenues jointly. The Chinese government also would consent to the employment of a chief financial adviser who would cosign all drafts on loan funds. Depending on the nature of the economic enterprise to be financed, the Chinese would appoint foreign experts as the need arose. The latter provision was not to be part of the loan agreement, however, but part of an informal understanding. Finally, China agreed to deal with the consortium in all future loan transactions, if the terms compared favorably with competitive offers.[41]

Zhao's proposals would have eliminated many troublesome points of dispute, but the consortium still found several areas of disagreement. The financiers insisted that, because of extraordinary circumstances in China, stronger controls were more than ordinarily necessary. To ensure fiscal responsibility, the consortium insisted on either a clause to establish a financial agency or the right to name the financial adviser mentioned by Zhao. This adviser was to possess genuine authority to regulate China's finances. Foreign control of the salt tax was also a must. Under Chinese direction, the value of the salt tax would be considerably diminished, making more difficult the task of marketing the bonds needed to finance the loan. To exercise this control, the consortium favored the Maritime Customs Service or a similar, foreign-dominated organization; the receipts collected by this organization would be deposited in banks controlled by members of the consortium. Lacking faith in the judgment of the Chinese authorities, the financiers repeated their demand that the purposes of the loan be specified. Among the uses to be itemized were repayment of provisional advances, payment of the Boxer indemnity, and payment of provincial loans made by the consortium.

In addition to these external matters, the bankers desired financial details on the disbandment and payment of troops and police and government officials and on the allowance to be provided to the imperial family. Moreover, the financiers insisted on the right to name foreign experts to supervise and administer loans for industrial purposes, regardless of the availability of native Chinese talent. Finally, China was to give the consortium an absolute five-year option on all future loans. Equal preference was not sufficient "to protect the issues already made or to be made by the Groups, and to give the Groups an uninterrupted period in which to conduct the delicate operation of re-building China's credit."[42]

As could have been predicted, the Chinese responded unfavorably to this unyielding counterproposal. They argued that to specify the purposes of the loan would be to ignore unforeseen needs that surely would arise. The foreign administration of the salt tax was imprac-tical because the majority of the revenue was collected from deep in the interior of the country, where conditions were very arduous. In the spirit of compromise, however, the Chinese offered to appoint a for-eigner to assist in the collection of the salt tax wherever feasible. The supervisory powers desired by the consortium also conflicted with the constitutional prerogatives of the National Assembly, as well as being anathema to the Chinese people. Similarly, the financial agency plan violated China's sovereignty, as did the bankers' insistence on fore-closing China's freedom of action regarding future loans.[43]

The attitude of the consortium absolutely precluded acceptance of the Chinese counterproposals. Particularly galling to the Chinese were the financiers' attempts to make grossly exaggerated indemnity payments for damages incurred by foreigners during the revolution, a prerequisite to the loan. The minister of finance flatly rejected the in-clusion of foreign claims because liability had not yet been estab-lished. Nor would the Chinese government make a commitment to hire foreigners; it offered only to discuss the matter informally.[44]

The negotiations were far from over, however. The Chinese gov-ernment urgently needed funds but drew back from surrendering na-tional sovereignty. Yuan's proposal for an upward revision of the treaty tariff, which might have eased the need for such a large foreign loan, was flatly rejected.[45] The government's only viable option was to seek funds from other sources in the hope that the consortium would not be able to quash its efforts as it had with the Belgian loan. Mean-while, it would continue to negotiate with the consortium. The con-sortium members remained confident, however, that if they could maintain a united front against the Chinese, they would be able to drive the bargain they wanted. The rub was that they were beginning to worry that the consortium would not hold together. The financial Open Door, which was in truth a financial monopoly as far as the Chinese were concerned, had become grist for the rumor mills in fi-nancial circles during the late summer and early autumn of 1912.[46] Against a background of rumors that the British had betrayed the consortium by agreeing to compromise on the issues of control and

security, the Japanese government began to press hard for the maintenance of a united front against the Chinese. In a confidential memorandum to the British government, Japanese officials observed:

> Considering the circumstances which have brought about
> the present deadlock of negotiations for the Chinese Reorganiza-
> tion Loan, the Imperial Government are of the opinion that it
> will be unwise for the six groups to proffer at this juncture relax-
> ation of terms. Such a move on their part will be construed by
> China as a confession of their weakness and may encourage her
> to set one capitalist against another, simply in order to make a
> good bargain without due regard to the true interests of the con-
> solidation of her finances.[47]

Although Chinese nationalism was still in its incipient stages, it
had achieved a considerable victory by stalemating negotiations over
the Reorganization Loan. By insisting on fair and equitable treatment,
China's leaders demonstrated that they would not sit idly by and allow
the nation's independence to be subtly eroded. Chinese resistance to
the consortium's onerous terms also was beginning to stir dissension
among the powers themselves. This development soon would lead to
American dissatisfaction with the cooperative approach so favored by
the Taft administration and would secure terms for the Chinese that
were beyond their reach as long as the international monopoly remained intact.

5

The United States and the Breakup of the Foreign Financial Monopoly

W HEN John Hay promulgated the Open Door Notes, he sought to monopolize the China trade by combining China's main trading partners in a united front. Similarly, when William Howard Taft brought the United States into the international loan consortium, he was looking ahead to the industrialization of China and attempting to extend the principle of monopolization to China's embryonic industrial sector. Eventually, just as U.S. Steel had formed a trust in the American iron and steel industry and then gone on to buy out its main competition, the ultimate goal was an American takeover of the trade and finance of China. Until this occurred, the United States would exert every effort to maintain a united front among the potentially competitive members of the consortium.

Chinese resistance to the bankers' terms threatened to disrupt the consortium, and American strategy with it. Even more threatening was China's successful exploitation of international competition. This disruption, and Chinese success at exploiting it, eventually led the United States to abandon the consortium as a diplomatic tool. The Chinese, in effect, busted Taft's financial trust.

As early as September 1912, rumors began to develop that in London Lloyd's Bank had floated a £10 million loan to the Chinese, with the salt tax income earmarked for collateral. At first, there seemed little cause for alarm. The British government informed the United

States that in the spirit of international cooperation it would quash any disruptive or conflicting loan scheme contemplated by its nationals. In Beijing, Morgan, Greenfell & Company reported optimistically that the Chinese could be persuaded to cease their negotiations with Lloyd's. But as China's credit gradually improved following the revolution, the threat from potential lenders multiplied rather than receded. Indeed, it was apparent to much of the international financial community that even without a reorganization of the salt tax, China could carry a loan of as much as £20 to £30 million.[1]

The British government rapidly concluded that its earlier confidence that China would yield quickly to the consortium's demands had been misplaced. The government now sought to consummate the Reorganization Loan immediately, before further competition surfaced. The British even were willing to accept certain modifications in the terms and conditions of the loan, to facilitate a quick agreement with the Chinese. The American group, however, did not share Britain's sense of urgency and took the position that to compromise at this point would be an admission of weakness. The State Department supported the American bankers in their decision to remain firm but counseled against unwillingness to compromise should the Chinese present alternative proposals that included adequate and reasonable terms of supervision.[2]

These tactical differences between the American and British groups presaged a divergence in national interests that ultimately would lead to American withdrawal from the consortium. Britain had too much at stake in China to risk its entire position by following the Americans in an attempt to subject China to total domination.

Despite great pressure, China continued to negotiate with the independent British group led by Lloyd's. Employing tactics similar to those used during the Belgian loan crisis, the bankers asked the ministers of the six powers to warn the Chinese that unless the flirtations stopped, the consortium would demand the repayment of all advances. Assistant Secretary of State Huntington-Wilson instructed Minister Calhoun that, in handling such delicate matters, the first priority of the United States was to foster the principles of international cooperation and concerted action, as embodied in a loan with adequate measures of supervision and control. Calhoun was to avoid any action that would jeopardize the success of this policy.[3]

Led by the Americans, the consortium sought to reestablish its preeminence in Chinese financial affairs. The financiers reiterated their willingness to undertake the huge Reorganization Loan but stressed that, to ensure a sound investment, they would insist on strict supervisory powers as well as adequate security. The necessity for such measures grew out of unsettled conditions in China and that nation's record of default on previous loans and indemnity payments. Frank McKnight argued that the Chinese remained, even after the revolution, "ignorant of the value of money, extravagant and improvident," and not capable of handling a loan of such magnitude without tight foreign controls. In addition to accepting these general principles, all China had to do to conclude the Reorganization Loan was agree to cancel the London loan.[4]

As expected, the Chinese refused to comply with these demands and, to make matters worse for the bankers, British financier C. Birch Crisp's treasury bills for the Lloyd's loan remained on the market. Of some small solace to the consortium was the lack of investors interested in associating with Lloyd's.[5]

This new crisis prompted such men as Willard Straight and McKnight to call for drastic action. McKnight convinced the State Department that, to ensure the safety of previous investments, the United States should withhold payments due under the Huguang loan until conditions were more favorable. Straight, however, fared less well in urging the immediate repayment of all advances. Such a demand, in the opinion of Secretary Knox, would merely provide the Chinese with an additional pretext for securing further outside loans. Moreover, the powers simply did not possess the leverage to enforce such an ultimatum. But Knox expressed willingness to adopt harsh measures if the other powers joined in, so as to make their threats effective.[6]

The consortium kept the pressure on the Chinese. Sir John Jordan told Yuan that China's liabilities were becoming unmanageable. Among current debts were the Boxer indemnity arrears, the Belgian loan advance, advances by the consortium, various provincial loans, and miscellaneous obligations which alone amounted to £10 million. Jordan warned Yuan that the pledge to Lloyd's, for the London loan, of the only security available for the Reorganization Loan, i.e., the salt tax, plus the failure of the government to adopt a well-defined financial policy, was most reckless. In the eyes of the consortium members, this seriously jeopardized China's fiscal stability and solvency.

The warning did not bring the Chinese around to the consortium's way of thinking. The Chinese continued to advocate unacceptable counterproposals: reorganization of the salt tax under Chinese direction but with the aid of foreign experts; withdrawal of funds to be countersigned by a representative of the consortium, in accordance with an estimate sanctioned by the National Council; supervision of the loan account by the Chinese Audit Department, where foreigners would be employed; discussion by China of the employment of foreign experts in connection with industrial loans; and preference, on equal terms, to be given to the six groups for further advances prior to complete issuance of the Reorganization Loan, but not to the prejudice of loans already concluded.

It was apparent that the presence of alternative sources of foreign revenue had stiffened Chinese resistance to the groups' demands. Although the counterproposals were generally repugnant to the members of the consortium, the British representative, Charles Addis, reported that he had found nothing objectionable in the Chinese terms, with the exception of Article v, regarding existing loan contracts. The consortium's solidarity was beginning to crack.[7]

The London loan was proving to be a serious obstacle to the success of the Reorganization Loan negotiations. The British confessed that they had exhausted every diplomatic means to induce the Chinese to cancel the loan; they also admitted failure in their efforts to prevent the issuance of the loan from London. Unless the consortium relaxed its terms in order to secure an immediate agreement with the Chinese, outside sources would preempt the consortium in the China loan business. To justify their plea for compromise, the British pointed to improved conditions in China, as well as to steadfast Chinese resistance to any proposals that would subject the pledged security to foreign administration. Following the lead of their government, officials of Morgan, Greenfell & Company urged the other members of the consortium to accept China's reasonable counterproposals or be prepared to abandon the endeavor entirely.[8]

Unlike their British cousins, the Americans were not inclined to compromise with the Chinese regarding the terms of the loan. Huntington-Wilson felt that China's rejection of the consortium's proposal was to be expected, given the delicate and complex nature of the discussions. The United States, the assistant secretary said, "could hardly conceive for a moment of considering the question of abandoning so momentous and far-reaching a policy merely because confronted from time to time with some temporary embarrassment or untoward incident."[9]

Within State Department circles, the British view that conditions in China had significantly improved was regarded as mere sophistry. Nor did the State Department feel that China's ability to borrow small sums on its own terms placed it in a position to resist for long the consortium's demands. Furthermore, the mere size of a proposed loan did not affect the desirability of creating a precedent for conservative and safe lending procedures. Although the United States was willing to discuss the Chinese counterproposals, any final agreement would have to contain provisions that would absolutely secure the collateral for the loan. Besides, compromise on these issues had political as well as economic implications. Huntington-Wilson admonished the British minister to Washington, James Bryce, that if the British decided to depart from these principles, the United States would be most displeased: "In making this response, I trust that it is unnecessary to say the Government of the United States must rely upon your Excellency's Government to make sure that no temporary exigency of the British Group shall be allowed to jeopardize the negotiations in which many Powers are so greatly interested and for the success of which most surely the most patient efforts and much time would be well spent, while the lack of these could so easily make comparatively futile the work of so many years." [10] Huntington-Wilson conveyed his concern about British vacillation to President Taft. A proposal lacking adequate supervisory provisions was out of the question. To compromise on this principle would undermine the delicate balance of international power and cooperation which the United States was trying to maintain in China. If this policy were jeopardized, the United States would never be able to obtain equal stature with the more established powers in the Orient. However, Britain's inclination to follow an independent course, to protect its own considerable interests in China, had now developed into a serious conflict between the Anglo-Saxon powers. [11]

From Berlin came further evidence that British and American interests were rapidly diverging. The American minister there reported that China had informed Britain of the Lloyd's loan prior to its conclusion; Britain, however, had not seen fit to share this information with its partners in the consortium. Britain's lack of candor increased suspicions that selfish motives, rather than a spirit of international cooperation, were now dominating Britain's China policy. Suspicions also began to develop regarding the existence of a secret understanding that recognized the special interests of Russia, Japan, and Great Britain in Manchuria, Mongolia, and Tibet, respectively. [12]

The U.S. government feared that the consortium was in danger of collapse and, with it, the opportunity for the United States to attain Great Power status and to reap monopoly profits at China's expense. A

division of China into closely held and regulated foreign fiefdoms certainly would destroy the possibility of profiting from one huge market,
possibly would entail costly military efforts to establish an American
presence in one area of China, and probably would foreclose the possibility of reestablishing the foreign cartel. A cartel or monopoly was
clearly preferable to competition.

On September 19, 1912, the London *Times* publicly confirmed
that C. Birch Crisp had floated a loan of £10 million at 5 percent secured on the free surplus of the salt tax—which already was pledged
for the Boxer indemnity and, tentatively, for the Reorganization Loan.
Article xiv of the loan also gave Crisp a clear preference in future
loans, again allegedly in violation of the consortium's understanding
with China. Minister Calhoun reported from Beijing that news of the
loan had evoked from the Chinese a reaction of jubilance and de-
fiance. From the British Minister, John Jordan, it had elicited the excuse that improved conditions in China and the futility of attempting
to coerce the stubborn Chinese Government warranted an ameliora-
tion of the consortium's terms. To the United States, this explanation
amounted to the abandonment by the British of a policy that Britain
had been instrumental in creating. Acutely conscious of the lack
of British support for the American hard-line position, Calhoun
grudgingly recommended to Washington that the consortium not demand blanket acceptance of all its conditions but, rather, approach
the matter in piecemeal fashion. He hoped that an ad hoc approach
would mitigate China's resentment over those terms that would compromise its national integrity.[13]

Calhoun only belatedly recognized China's commitment to resist
further encroachments on its sovereignty. Yet, Great Britain was far
more sensitive than the United States to growing Chinese animosity
toward the financiers, which served only to aggravate anti-British feeling stirred up by Britain's aggressive behavior in Tibet. To prevent further growth of antiforeign and anti-British sentiment, the British government felt that the highly popular London loan should remain
undisturbed. This decision, coupled with British attempts to soften
the consortium's terms, somewhat diminished anti-British feeling in
China.

Domestically, Britain's new course made good political sense. In
forming the consortium, Britain had chosen the small Hong Kong–
Shanghai Bank to act as its sole representative in Chinese financial
affairs. This action generated considerable opposition from the large
British banking houses, which had been excluded from the consor-

tium, and led directly to widespread support for the Crisp loan. A successful move to quash the Crisp loan would have had severe political repercussions in British financial circles in The City. Under the circumstances, British efforts to avert the loan were not especially energetic. Loss of American support seemed, in those halcyon days before the outbreak of World War I, a small enough price to pay for tranquillity in domestic financial circles and along the fringes of the empire.[14]

Predictably, as a result of the London loan, China became even less compromising in its dealings with the consortium. China alone would reorganize the salt tax; the National Council would determine the purposes for which loan funds would be expended; and supervision of accounts would be the responsibility of the Chinese Accounting Department. The Chinese now held the initiative in the Reorganization Loan talks and only repudiation of the London loan would restore negotiating leverage to the consortium. The British, however, did not feel that the Chinese should be made to cancel the Crisp loan. The question of repudiation thus became a major point of contention between the United States and Great Britain.

Although the United States was somewhat wary of allowing the Chinese to set a precedent for repudiation, the lack of adequate alternative collateral necessitated such a move if the Reorganization Loan was to be secured. The Americans firmly laid out the points that they wanted to govern the ongoing discussions: China had to turn over administration of the salt tax to foreigners possessing sufficient authority to ensure the collection and deposit of funds; foreign technical experts would control the expenditure of all industrial loans; and, finally, the Chinese had to cancel the London loan before negotiations could be resumed. To the United States, these points were matters of principle on which there could be no compromise.[15]

Unlike the Americans, the British ardently desired to take the initiative in reopening the negotiations. Pressured by the large British banking firms, and anxious to preserve Britain's preeminent economic position in China, Sir Edward Grey did not want the United States to force Britain into a position of opposing reasonable independent loans simply because of a prior commitment made to unreasonable members of the consortium. Accordingly, he opposed the United States on virtually every point.[16]

The Hong Kong–Shanghai Bank, as well as the British government, became more and more dissatisfied with the situation. Each group, the bank proposed, should negotiate industrial and railway contracts in its own name. After the conclusion of a deal, participation could be offered to the other members of the consortium. Under such a procedure, widespread international agreement would no longer be necessary to begin a project. Behind this movement toward independent action was the British desire to complete the Reorganization Loan on whatever terms possible. As Calhoun reported to Knox, "The policies and interests of the different groups are so diverse that the effectiveness and continuance of the combination is doubtful."[17]

In an attempt to settle their differences, the members of the consortium, with the Americans conspicuously absent, met and agreed on certain issues. The conferees decided that it would be impractical to place the salt tax under an organization similar to the Customs Service. Regarding the control of expenditures, it would be necessary to insist on the appointment of an auditor approved by the bankers and possessing veto power. Finally, the groups present agreed to forgo the financial agency plan if they were granted an absolute preference in future loans. The agreement was not as conciliatory as the British had hoped, but still it offered some promise of success.

The absent Americans sought to disassociate themselves from the agreement. Alone, the American financiers continued to adhere to the discredited positions that had failed to bring about a resolution of the negotiations. Foreign supervision of the salt tax was absolutely necessary to ensure the integrity of this source of funds, and foreign technical experts were required to administer the expenditure of all industrial loans. The Chinese should be required to publish detailed financial reports and should give the consortium preference in all loans, in addition to the Reorganization Loan, as well as an absolute option on any loans needed to complete the latter.[18]

American obstinacy was especially alarming to the British who realized that the success of the Crisp loan was encouraging other financial competitors to attempt to fill the void created by the consortium's failure to complete the Reorganization Loan successfully. The United States blamed the British for the new competition. Had the consortium stood firm, the Americans believed, the Chinese would not now be able to play off one capitalist against another. McKnight, for one, believed that the British would rather dissolve the partnership than continue with a policy influenced by members of the consortium possessing such divergent points of view.[19]

To salvage the chosen instrument of its foreign policy, the State Department relented and attempted to persuade the American bankers to modify their demands. Perhaps the Chinese would allow a distinction between funds used for administrative purposes and money earmarked for industrial purposes. J. P. Morgan, master of the art of trust building and orchestrator of the great U.S. Steel monopoly, and a man who, from the beginning, doubted the economic prospects of the entire endeavor, would brook no tinkering with the American model for control of China's finances. In a dispatch to his British associates, the man who had demonstrated his mastery of the American economy by singlehandedly staving off an economic panic only a few years before insisted that the American way was the only way of dealing effectively and profitably with the Chinese:

> We believe that it is in the best interests of China and the Groups that the Reorganization Loan, to be effective should necessarily be of such a comprehensive character as to render impossible a single issue and in our interest as well as to protect quotations of the bonds of this loan first sold, we deemed it essential to secure option upon succeeding series. Upon this question involving matter of principle we did not find it possible to give way. . . . In any case we consider it unfair that because of the position which we adopted in an inter-group discussion we should be accused of blocking negotiations, the success of which depends entirely upon an agreement with the Chinese who objected not to an option of a future loan regarding which the Groups differed but to control of expenditures and security upon which the Groups and their Governments still insist.[20]

Morgan's protests notwithstanding, the British were reluctant to risk commercial and financial disaster simply so that the House of Morgan might increase its rate of profit. Calhoun warned Washington of British fears on this point. John Jordan confirmed the American minister's assessment of the situation during discussions regarding the American delay in completing the Huguang loan. Jordan pointed out that, although the United States had entered the loan negotiations because it was supposed to be so friendly toward China, the Americans were now "the most severe, the most technical in their objections, and the most obstructive in dealings with China." Britain's interests in China were too great to be impaired by America's obstructionist tactics. Chinese hostility following the British takeover of Tibet made conciliation a necessity if the British were to preserve their numerous economic enterprises in China without resorting to force. Calhoun realized that the British would make radical concessions rather than permit such an enterprise as the British and Chinese Corporation to lose its valuable railway rights. Either the consortium would follow Britain's lead or it would be dissolved so that the British would be free to make contracts and acquire concessions on their own terms.[21]

Britain's dissatisfaction presaged the rapid obsolescence of the consortium as an instrument of American foreign policy. No longer able to manipulate the other powers into taking a hard line against the Chinese, the United States would have to look for another approach to coordination of foreign interests in East Asia. Still, the bankers continued to seek a resolution of their differences in order to successfully conclude the potentially profitable Reorganization Loan.

A major obstacle to the financiers' success was the Crisp loan, Article XIV of which gave Crisp a clear preference in future loans. Moreover, a considerable portion of the salt tax had been pledged as security for that loan. The American group unsuccessfully attempted to persuade the British Foreign Office to pressure the Chinese into disregarding Crisp's preferential status. Failing in this endeavor, the consortium was forced to ignore Crisp and proceed with its own negotiations, in the hope that the matter could be settled later in a manner favorable to its interests.[22]

The issue of the salt tax could not be put off so easily, however. The loss of a lien on the entire salt tax seriously threatened the marketability of the consortium's bonds. Although Crisp asserted that the tax generated enough revenue to secure both loans, few bankers agreed. Without foreign supervision, the salt tax barely would be sufficient to cover the Reorganization Loan. Additional obligations virtually destroyed the likelihood of securing the consortium's investment through this source.

The negotiations seemed destined not to resume when suddenly the Chinese, in need of the larger funds that only the consortium could provide, canceled Crisp's preference clause and agreed to the need to reorganize the salt administration. Having lost his preference clause, Crisp decided to withdraw entirely from the China loan business and left the consortium a relatively clear field once again.[23]

Crisp was a victim of his own success. Consortium representative Frank McKnight learned from Dr. Robert Morrison, financial adviser to the Chinese government, that the Crisp loan had convinced the provincial governments that the central government could obtain foreign funds easily and that it had no need of provincial revenues. As a result of this misconception, the provinces stopped remitting funds to Beijing. Consequently, the financial woes of the central government increased to the point that the Chinese government was now very anxious to deal with the consortium, if only the groups could resolve their internal differences.[24]

The consortium remained divided. The American group continued to adhere to its strict attitude and refused to sanction the huge Reorganization Loan until some stability appeared in the political situation in China, characterized by increased friction between the central government and the provinces and by growing hostility to President Yuan's rule. Evidence also was available to the Americans that the Hong Kong–Shanghai Bank definitely was working to dissolve the consortium. Even the British associates of the House of Morgan were unhappy with the American group's unwillingness to enter into a large commitment to China. With such differences, a common front was difficult to maintain.[25]

When the members of the consortium convened another meeting to discuss their differences, controversy developed over whether to seek an option on future loans or merely a preference in them. Because of domestic pressure, the British and French opposed the monopolistic option plan. The Americans, however, remained adamant in their demands for a monopoly. They were reluctant to proceed without a firm option encompassing the Reorganization Loan as well as future industrial and railway loans. The Americans also insisted that Russia and Japan be included in all financial dealings with the Chinese, and that the Reorganization Loan carry an interest rate reflecting the consortium's monopoly position—5.5 percent, a full one-half percent above what the other members were willing to settle for. To round out their demands, the American bankers reiterated their earlier position that China pay any foreign claims resulting from the revolution. As far as the American financiers were concerned, if these proposals were not acceptable to the Chinese, the consortium should simply break off the negotiations and wait for China to come begging.[26]

Since the British bankers wanted a speedy agreement and strongly opposed inflexible loan conditions, the consortium would have broken down. However, the six ministers of the consortium governments met in Beijing, where they formulated a draft agreement calling for the Chinese to undertake to engage a foreign adviser in the Accounting and Auditing Departments, a foreign director of the National Loan Bureau, and a foreign chief inspector of the Salt Administration.[27]

Agreement came rapidly. The Chinese expressed approval of these terms, if they could make the appointments, in order to avoid conflict among the powers over the nationality of the appointees. Because the

Chinese had appointees of high quality in mind, even the U.S. government approved the compromise proposal. With the deadlock broken, the final shape of the loan agreement began to emerge. The aggregate amount of the loan was reduced from the initial figure of £60 million to £25 million, which was to be used solely for payment of liabilities of the Chinese government already due; redemption of provincial loans; provision for liabilities about to mature, including foreign claims for damages incurred during the revolution; disbandment of troops; redemption of military and provincial government notes; estimated current expenses of the central government; reorganization of the Salt Administration; and such other administrative purposes as might be agreed upon between the Chinese government and the banks. The loan was to be secured by the entire revenue of the salt tax, which would be reorganized with foreign assistance and controlled jointly by two chief inspectors, one Chinese and one foreign. Following American wishes, the bankers exacted a 5.5 percent interest rate and joint control of the Accounting and Auditing Departments was agreed upon, but the consortium settled for a preference rather than an option clause. Finally, the agreement contained a broad force majeure clause which would give the banks an easy way out if their commitment should become unprofitable or hazardous.[28]

Speedy conclusion of the loan negotiations was a matter of survival for the financially desperate president of China, Yuan Shikai. Unless he obtained large sums of money, he would be unable to organize the National Assembly under his own control; his domestic foes would then achieve dominance. But two issues—liability for damages suffered by foreigners during the revolution and the appointment of foreign advisers—continued to cause difficulties. On these matters, France and its Russian ally joined the United States in pressing for a hard line. When, for example, the negotiators reached a tentative agreement limiting liability for damages to areas within the zone of military operations, and allowing foreign advisers to be appointed at Chinese discretion, the French temporarily demanded the suspension of negotiations. The British and the Germans were so upset by these tactics that they threatened to do business independently of the other members of the consortium.[29]

The Americans refused to associate themselves with an independent British or German advance, but reserved the right to participate at a later date in any agreement arising out of such a transaction. The American financiers were attempting simultaneously to pressure the Chinese while preserving amicable relations with all the powers.[30]

American intransigence did not perpetuate the stalemate. The British were of the opinion that the appointment by the Chinese of three advisers, together with a statement of their duties and powers, would be sufficient. The French demanded the appointment of six advisers, one from each of the powers, in the various government departments, and two advisers from each power for the service of the loan. However, under British pressure, the French agreed to limit foreign advisers strictly to the service of the loan contract.[31]

With this obstacle removed, the consortium instructed its six representatives in Beijing to sign the Reorganization Loan, subject to "(1) Official communication from the Chinese Foreign Office to the Legations confirming the terms of provincial contributions; (2) Satisfactory evidence of cancellation of the Crisp loan; (3) Receipt by the legations of satisfactory assurance from the Chinese Foreign Office in respect to the payment of foreign claims from the Revolution and the employment of foreign advisers in the salt and audit departments."[32]

This consensus proved ephemeral, as the selection of the foreign advisers ruffled the sensitivities of the participating powers. The Chinese had notified the six ministers informally of the appointment of an Anglo-Irishman, Sir Richard Dane, as chief salt inspector, a German as director of the Foreign Loan Bureau, and an Italian as adviser to the Audit Department. The French balked because the Chinese had selected no French nationals. Britain and the United States, though opposed to the selection of neutral nationals because of the difficulty in controlling them, were willing to acquiesce in the Chinese appointments if the men were found to be qualified. But the French and Russians were relentless in their opposition to the Chinese appointees. The consortium seemed about to fly apart, to the detriment of the United States, which did not have the resources immediately at hand to compete independently in the Chinese financial market.[33]

Within days, more fissures appeared in the united front of the fragile consortium. Under pressure from their French and Russian allies, the British abandoned their previous position, which had been supported by the Germans. Sir John Jordan's attempt to replace the German designee for the salt inspectorate with a British national created an atmosphere of suspicion between the two nations. The German minister feared that France, Russia, and Britain were trying to rupture the consortium so as to exclude Germany and the United States, thereby extending the Triple Entente to China.

In an effort to salvage the situation, hectic discussions were held, which led to an unexpected compromise that somewhat alleviated the prevailing atmosphere of mistrust and suspicion among the powers. The director of the Foreign Loan Bureau was to be a German; the head of the salt administration, an Englishman; the supervisors of the Audit Department, a Frenchman and a Russian. The American financiers were willing to forgo national representation because the scheme maintained the principle of monopoly by eliminating potentially troublesome neutrals.[34]

This agreement reduced but did not eliminate the tension among consortium members. Britain ardently desired a politically weak yet economically viable China in order to provide a stable environment for trade. For the sake of a stronger position in Europe, however, Britain accepted Russian desires for a politically weak China that would be unable to resist encroachment and territorial loss in Manchuria and Mongolia. European attention to political ends frustrated the profit-minded Knox, who wrote disingenuously, "It is no longer a question of friendly international cooperation to help China but a combination of big Powers with common interests to accomplish their own selfish political aims." Jordan also concluded that the continuance of the consortium was impracticable, given the diverse political and economic interests of the participating powers.[35]

The Reorganization Loan agreement was finally signed April 26, 1913. With the knowledge and acquiescence of the powers, Yuan concluded this agreement without submitting it to the National Assembly for approval, as required by the Chinese constitution. The powers were willing to accept such an irregular validation of the loan because they deemed it essential that Yuan be given the financial wherewithal to consolidate his position. The great victory of his domestic rivals in the national elections of 1912–13 threatened Yuan's political survival. And Yuan did not disappoint his benefactors. To gain a financial advantage over his opponents, Yuan agreed to pay, over forty-seven years, £67,850,000 in principal and interest. Of this amount, Yuan would have only £8.5 million available for use at his own discretion. Yet this sum would prove to be sufficient to give Yuan a marked advantage over his rivals in his campaign to centralize all power in his own hands.[36]

Neither the Taft administration nor the American financiers were parties to the final Reorganization Loan agreement. The American group had become increasingly impatient over the delay in concluding the Reorganization Loan. The compromises in loan terms forced upon the Americans by the exigencies of international politics were particularly galling. As early as October 1912, the State Department began hearing rumors that the American group wanted out of the consortium. The deterioration of United States–Mexican relations was beginning to exert a chilling effect on the investment market, thereby dimming prospects for success in floating the Chinese bonds. If the situation in Mexico worsened, J. P. Morgan warned, the American financiers might have to withdraw from the consortium. The *Wall Street Journal* also reported that the Balkan crisis was lowering bond prices and that the European powers were reluctant to conclude the loan until the Balkan question was resolved. Davison informed Knox that, due to these factors, if the loan was not concluded by March 1, 1913, the American group would withdraw from the loan negotiations. Although Secretary Knox advised the bankers that such a move would seriously embarrass the administration, the group's commitment to the enterprise was clearly wavering. The bankers agreed to postpone any decision at least until the new administration took office in March 1913. They hoped, however, that negotiations would be concluded by that time.[37]

Under the leadership of the Taft administration, the monopoly-minded Americans had taken such a hard line in the negotiations, and stirred up so much Chinese resistance to the loan, that the negotiations dragged on into the new Wilson administration, which found Taft's cooperative approach odious. Aware of Wilson's antipathy toward the consortium and anxious to relieve themselves of the burden of being instruments of American foreign policy, the bankers quickly sought to discover the administration's position regarding their future participation in the Chinese loan negotiations. In a meeting with representatives of the American group held on March 10, Secretary of State William Jennings Bryan was told that the bankers would consider continuing their efforts to participate in the Reorganization Loan "only if expressly requested to do so by the Government." As expected, on March 18, 1913, Wilson announced that such a request would not be forthcoming from the government.

Although Wilson couched the reasons for his decision in terms of his solicitude for the Chinese and his dissatisfaction with the onerous terms sought by the consortium, in fact, he felt that working through the consortium deprived the United States of the right to take the independent action necessary to safeguard its interests in China. Wilson also hoped that the United States would reap tangible benefits from the Chinese by disassociating itself from the other powers, whose designs on that country were greatly resented by all nationalistic Chinese.[38] Indeed, simultaneously with his abandonment of Taft's cooperative policy, Wilson announced that he would seek the "legislative measures necessary to give American merchants, manufacturers, contractors, and engineers the banking and other financial facilities which they now lack and without which they are at a serious disadvantage as compared with their industrial and commercial rivals." [39] Having received the response from Wilson that they had both expected and hoped for, the American bankers decided to abandon the Reorganization Loan negotiations, and in June 1913, the American group formally withdrew from the original four-party agreement of November 10, 1910, which had established the consortium. [40]

The reaction to Wilson's decision was mixed. A few staunch proponents of Taft's cooperative policy, such as Huntington-Wilson, vigorously attacked the new administration. Others kept their peace, confident that the realities of international politics would prove the wisdom of past policies. As Straight remarked, while "competition at home is perhaps desirable . . . there must be cooperation abroad." Competition among American financiers would preclude "the undivided Government support which it is essential a Group should have to be successful in this essentially international . . . game." In large measure, the bankers were relieved to escape their expensive commitment to the Taft administration which had been "nothing but trouble and vexation." A few financiers were concerned, however, that alone the United States would not be able to compete successfully for its fair share of the China market. Bishop Bashford wrote Bryan that withdrawal from the consortium could spell "the destruction of American trade in the Far East." Although America's foreign partners resented Wilson's failure to consult with them before announcing his decision, they shed few tears at the departure of the obstructionist Americans. Last, the Chinese, responding to Wilson's expression of concern for their independence, declared that they welcomed the president's "just and magnanimous attitude." [41]

Such optimism was quite misplaced, however. Woodrow Wilson, his public statements notwithstanding, did not take the United States out of the loan consortium because of solicitude for the Chinese. International tensions, Chinese stubbornness, and an unfavorable investment market at home had stripped the consortium of its viability as an effective instrument of finance capital and foreign policy. Domestically, having campaigned on an anti–Wall Street platform, Wilson was not in a political position to support the bankers' China monopoly. Taft himself acknowledged that the prominent position of J. P. Morgan and other well-known New York financiers in the group made Wilson's decision a politically popular one. Wilson also felt that the cooperative approach enhanced the position of rival powers to the detriment of American interests. Through competition, rather than cooperation, the United States could achieve the dominance it sought in East Asia. Wilson, then, sought to achieve Taft's goal of maximizing American wealth, power, and influence in China by other means. While Straight despaired that a consistent foreign policy was not possible in a democracy, it would turn out that the means Wilson chose would prove to be as detrimental to China as those Taft had employed so unsuccessfully.[42]

6

America and the Recognition of the
Republic of China

A S LONG as the U.S. government felt that the opportunity existed to impose monopolistic financial terms upon the new Chinese republic, it was willing to stand with the other powers in denying diplomatic recognition to the recalcitrant regime. This policy of withholding recognition until the Chinese came to terms that were satisfactory to the international financiers was perceived as a departure from American custom and tradition.[1] It drew intense but initially futile criticism from various domestic interest groups. By the time of the 1911 Revolution in China, the United States had come to accept fully the self-interested aspects of recognition. In Latin America, for example, this diplomatic device had been used to foster or, alternatively, to undermine, regimes whose presence affected vital American interests. In the case of revolutionary China, American leaders would use recognition to gain protection for American citizens, property, and trade and to enhance America's position in the six-power consortium. American leaders, however, were not willing to reveal their whole agenda for China to the American people but preferred to mask some of their purposes in high-flown, prodemocratic, prorepublican rhetoric that did not correspond with actual U.S. policy.

Caution marked the initial response of American diplomats in China to revolutionary developments there and to the question of recognition of the new regime. Consul Roger Greene, who had the opportunity to witness the genesis of the revolution firsthand from his post in Hankou, exhibited this caution in a discussion with Wang Zhengding, vice-president of the Revolutionary Board of Foreign Affairs. In response to Wang's pleas for recognition in late November 1911, Greene pointed out that the United States could act only on facts; that while the revolutionary movement displayed a unity of purpose, it also totally lacked central organization; and that throughout the country, republican leaders were acting independently and without cooperation. Coupled with the realization that the Manchus controlled a considerable portion of Chinese territory, these factors made recognition both infeasible and impolitic. Moreover, Greene argued that any undue interference in Chinese affairs, particularly recognition of one of the competing factions, would likely trigger an anti-foreign outburst.[2]

Greene's rationale accurately reflected U.S. policy. The United States chose not to favor the cause of popular government but rather took the legally proper stance that in any civil disturbance alien powers should follow a course of strict neutrality. Accordingly, Secretary Knox ordered American diplomats in China to abstain from formal diplomatic contact with all but the imperial regime. Despite extreme pressure from the revolutionaries for recognition, Knox would not move from his position as long as the Manchus retained some semblance of power.[3]

In an effort to circumvent American policy, the rebels appealed to republican sympathies in the United States that the Taft administration had ignored. The rebels' minister of foreign affairs, Wu Tingfang, for example, pointed out in a letter to Secretary Knox that the Manchus had wrought great oppression upon the Chinese people and that their overthrow was nothing less than a manifestation of democracy and popular will. Wu reaffirmed the peaceful character of the Chinese people and attributed to the Manchus responsibility for such diverse evils as closing China to foreign intercourse, obstructing commerce, levying unfair taxes, retarding industrial growth, and denying China a proper system of justice. Wu stressed the insurgents' desire to foster foreign trade, to create favorable conditions for loans and concessions, and, most important, to respect all previous treaties and commitments as well as foreign lives and property.[4]

These promises, if realized, offered much hope to the foreign powers. The merits of the proposed reforms were not so much in doubt, however, as was the ability of the revolutionaries to carry them out. Moreover, a rebel government strong enough to enforce such changes might be too strong to be manipulated easily.

In February 1912, when the Manchu dynasty finally abdicated its claim to the throne, it designated Yuan Shikai as its legal successor with whom the United States would maintain formal relations. Yuan's regime held more advantages for the United States than did the rival regime maintained by Sun Yat-sen in the south with which the United States maintained no formal relations. However, given the possible dangers of alienating Sun's government altogether, the United States withheld actual recognition of Yuan's regime and initially sought to discourage loans to either of the contending factions.[5]

American leaders proceeded warily, conscious that the disintegration of China would destroy the commercial and financial potential of that huge market. President Taft, in his annual message to Congress, elaborated on the rationale behind American China policy:

> From the beginning of the upheaval last autumn it was felt by the United States in common with the other Powers having large interests in China, that independent action by the foreign governments in their own individual interest would add further confusion to the situation already complicated. A policy of international cooperation was accordingly adopted in an understanding reached early in the disturbances, to act together for the protection of lives, and property of foreigners if menaced, to maintain an attitude of strict impartiality as between the contending factions, and to abstain from any endeavor to influence the Chinese in their organization of a new form of government.[6]

The united foreign front of which Taft spoke was as much offensive as defensive, and for the United States, which had insisted that Japan and Russia be brought into the front, the goal was to achieve Chinese acquiescence to foreign privilege and encroachment. Thus, in response to a Japanese request for cooperative action to secure guarantees for all existing rights and privileges before recognizing the Republic, the United States replied that "it welcomes this fresh affirmation of the policy of concerted action and agrees in principle to its application to the Recognition of the Republic of China." This response cast doubt on Taft's lofty proclamation that U.S. recognition policy was guided by the "natural sympathy of the American people with the assumption of Republican principles by the Chinese people."[7]

Technically, the United States did not view its recognition policy as a resort to coercion and blackmail against the new Chinese government. Legally, all obligations of the previous government automatically passed to its successor regime. Yet, the obligations forced upon the Manchus and demanded of their successors could not be reconciled with a policy of friendly relations with China. Nor, for that matter, could the reluctance of the Taft administration to recognize the new Republic of China be seen as a ringing endorsement of republican principles.

The failure of the U.S. government to recognize the newly proclaimed Republic of China created a major controversy in America. Elements of the press, members of Congress, and concerned missionaries launched an informal campaign to dislodge the Taft administration from its cautious, calculating approach toward the Chinese Republic. The influential periodical *Independent* deplored American inaction in welcoming a sister republic into the family of nations and interpreted the prudent impartiality shown by the United States during the Chinese civil war as a betrayal of republicanism in favor of monarchical principles. The editors argued that the Chinese republicans had every right to expect positive encouragement from the United States because "America is responsible for the revolution. Its leaders are largely young men educated in the United States or in the American mission schools. They have imbibed from us the spirit of freedom. They have been inspired by our example to put their ideals into effect. They had a right to expect from us sympathy and encouragement, if not that more tangible aid which we have often extended to insurgents who had far less reason to revolt." [8]

Such chauvinistic pleading also appeared in political circles, much to the dismay of the Taft administration. Many leaders of American opinion and their political counterparts seemed to forget that the Revolution of 1911 was an indigenous Chinese phenomenon and should have been evaluated as such. Congressman A. W. Lafferty of Oregon, for example, a legislator who knew virtually nothing of Chinese affairs, personally submitted to the secretary of state an essay by fifteen-year-old Mildred Hudson entitled "Why the United States should be the first Nation to Recognize the New Republic of China." Lafferty contended that Miss Hudson's essay represented the sentiments of not only the people of Oregon but several members of Congress as well. The schoolgirl termed the Revolution of 1911 a sensational event that severed the bonds of slavery and despotism. "Is not the United States," she wrote, "the largest and greatest republic on earth? As such it should be the first to recognize a sister republic who has just been born into the great light of liberty." [9]

The Taft administration looked with disfavor upon such attempts as those of Congressman Lafferty to influence American China policy. Particularly troublesome to the administration were the efforts of the chairman of the House Foreign Affairs Committee, William Sulzer, who successfully sponsored a resolution congratulating the Chinese on their assumption of self-government. In a letter to President Taft, Assistant Secretary of State Huntington-Wilson pointed out the dangers of politicization of the recognition question. To forestall future congressional outbursts similar to the Sulzer resolution and to defuse the issue, Huntington-Wilson suggested that the United States issue a statement of sympathy. It would serve the purpose of securing Chinese goodwill without sacrificing the policy of withholding recognition from the new republic.

There is no doubt that the draft resolution that the Taft administration subsequently submitted to Congress was motivated by such political considerations rather than by a desire to assist the Republic of China. The innocuous resolution, passed on February 26, 1912, read:

> Whereas the Chinese nation has successfully asserted the fact that sovereignty is vested in the people, and has recognized the principle that government derives its authority from the consent of the governed, thereby terminating a condition of internal strife; and,
>
> Whereas the American people are inherently and by tradition sympathetic with all efforts to adopt the ideals and institutions of representative government therefore be it resolved by the Senate and the House of Representatives that the United States of America congratulate the people of China on their assumption of the powers, duties, and responsibilities of self-government and express the confident hope that in the adoption and maintenance of a republican form of government, the rights, liberties, and happiness of the Chinese people will be secure and progress of the people ensured. [10]

All the congratulatory messages in the world, however, could not obscure the hesitation and restraint that marked American handling of the recognition question. American policymakers continued to bide their time, weighing a variety of practical considerations.

To the advocates of immediate recognition, caution and restraint in recognizing the Republic of China were completely unacceptable. They were willing to disregard the debilities of the Chinese government, which by June 1912 were obvious even to the most optimistic observers. Tang Shaoyi, the new premier, as well as four members of the cabinet, had just resigned in protest over Yuan's arbitrary and dictatorial rule. Although the appointment of Sun Yat-sen as director of railways had temporarily prevented a split between Yuan and Sun's party, the Tongmenghui, the political situation was rapidly becoming chaotic. Nevertheless, the influential *Washington Post* remained sanguine about events in China and strenuously advocated a reversal of American recognition policy. "Can there any longer be doubt about the stability of the new Chinese Government? It is hardly possible that even the most skeptical person can believe that China is in danger of a sudden reversion to its original condition," the *Post* editorialized. "Why should the United States wait for the other nations to recognize China? Let the hand of brotherhood be extended from the pioneer republic of the United States and the cause of liberty will be advanced." [11]

The missionary community was even more fervently involved in Chinese affairs than the editorialists, schoolchildren, and congressmen, and it added the loudest voice of all to the chorus urging recognition of the Chinese Republic. J. W. Hammer, a prominent Protestant bishop, counseled the Taft administration to recognize China forthwith. He stressed that such action would be consistent with the tradition of cordial Sino-American relations and would serve as an acknowledgment of the extensive American missionary effort that had, in Hammer's view, laid the groundwork for the revolution. He argued that the courteous behavior of the revolutionaries toward foreigners and their property, and the similarity of the Chinese Republic to the republican form of government of the United States, merited recognition. Hammer's argument struck a sensitive chord when he noted that recognition also would disassociate the United States from such predatory powers as Japan and Russia and would strengthen already friendly ties with China. To clinch his argument for a change in American China policy, the bishop appealed to the commercial interests of the United States: "There is no single act upon our part which would so conduce to the uplift of the new nation as its prompt recognition. The full beneficial effect of this upon our country will be lost if action is postponed until others join. . . . The greatest republic ought to take the initiative and permit others to follow. . . . Gaining the favor of teeming millions of ultimate consumers will have a most salutary influence upon American trade." [12]

Thus, diverse factors motivated the campaign to secure de jure recognition for the Republic of China. Sympathy and altruism were involved, as was the mistaken impression that the Chinese Republic was modeled after the United States both in fact and in theory. But even missionaries, such as Bishop Hammer, who stressed the moral and philosophical aspects of the issue, were not oblivious to the question of American economic interest—the factor most important to the U.S. government.

Had the Taft administration been thinking only of the legal niceties involved in recognition, it could have justified its tardiness by explaining that, in international law, an untimely or precipitous recognition is considered an unlawful act and that while the Manchus retained some semblance of authority the United States should carefully respect that precept. The violent end of the Manchu dynasty also created an aura of uncertainty as to the permanence of the change and left open the question of the new regime's ability to govern. Until the new Chinese government exhibited not only domestic permanence and stability but also a willingness to fulfill China's international obligations, the United States could legally justify withholding recognition. The Taft administration, however, chose to follow the line initiated by Secretary of State William Seward making constitutional legitimacy the criterion for determining the effectiveness of a new government. Taft noted that recognition would not come "until a permanent constitution shall have been definitely adopted by a representative national assembly, a President duly elected in accordance with the provisions of such constitution and the present provisional government replaced by a permanent one with constitutional authority."[13]

The administration's legal scruples did not greatly affect de facto relations with the Chinese Republic, however. On February 14, 1912, the Chinese minister in Washington officially informed the American government that the emperor had abdicated and that the new regime had designated him "provisional diplomatic agent." The Department of State promptly admitted him to full relations with the department and ordered the American minister in Beijing to continue in the exercise of his office.[14]

The political realities of the situation in China were so open to conflicting interpretations about the efficacy of republican rule in China, and local American interests were so divergent from strategic American interests, that the Taft administration was in a position to justify either recognition or nonrecognition of the Chinese Republic. Nonrecognition would be a deliberate choice arrived at for strategic reasons in the face of strong domestic criticism.

The Taft administration certainly did not lack for pessimistic evaluations of the Chinese Republic. In January 1912, the American minister to China, William J. Calhoun, expressed his concern to Secretary Knox about the apparent weakness of the republic. Calhoun noted the prominence of unpopular Cantonese in the government and the leadership of a man whom he considered inexperienced in the affairs of state, Sun Yat-sen. Weak leadership, added to traditional provincial rivalries, did not augur well for the success of the Republic. The American consul in Qingdao subsequently commented on the "lack of any well defined policy on the part of the new government, the incapacity of those who are designated as leaders, and the antipathy of the peoples towards the Government as at present constituted." [15]

A State Department memorandum in February 1913 echoed these pessimistic evaluations of the Chinese scene. It noted that President Yuan had publicly admitted the shakiness of his regime and, although the Republic nominally controlled twenty provinces, military governors, all exercising varying degrees of autonomy, actually held the power. Had the central government been anything other than extremely passive, its incapacity to rule the country would have been exposed, together with discord between north and south, and the government's lack of financial support among the educated and wealthy. As it was, the Nanjing assembly, consisting of thirty-four members, none of whom were regularly elected by the people of their provinces, symbolized the Republic's weak support. [16]

Although American public opinion generally favored recognition, there was some support for the nonrecognition policy of the U.S. government. The *New York Times*, for example, urged that the United States retain greater diplomatic flexibility in dealing with China by withholding recognition and maintaining only unofficial relations until such time as the central government wielded effective authority. The *Times* editors proclaimed their sympathy with movements toward popular representative rule but, they warned, "in the matter of recognition our Government is bound to reflect that a Government called a republic is not necessarily one." [17]

There also were voices in the State Department that urged early recognition of the Republic, and though they never succeeded in changing American policy, they adduced more and more reasons for recognition as the months went by. George Anderson, consul general in Hong Kong, figured prominently in the movement to reverse American recognition policy. He argued that the new provisional government had been extremely successful in maintaining law and stability because the conservative business and property-holding classes controlled the revolutionary movement. He also argued that being the first power to recognize the new government would win both Chinese friendship and an advantageous position for American commercial and other interests: "This is our opportunity in China—an opportunity to establish for the future in a way never to be forgotten Chinese friendship for the United States, and not only to aid in a substantial way in the uplift and the peaceful development, and political advancement of one-fourth of the human race, but at the same time to secure such a position in Chinese affairs that American commercial and other interests may have a leading part in this great development." [18]

Gradually, other statesmen began to question nonrecognition. Withholding of recognition was essentially a negative policy that garnered meager results. It was not moving the Chinese to introduce the reforms and improvements that the United States felt were necessary. From Beijing, Minister Calhoun stressed this argument. The missionary community, in the persons of Bishops Bashford and Lewis, further developed this rationale by pointing out that recognition was needed to support the sagging fortunes of the Republic and its respected leader, Yuan Shikai. A strong Yuan was in American interests. [19]

The highly regarded American consul in Hankou, Roger Greene, eventually concluded that the United States should extend recognition for more practical reasons. The lack of de jure recognition created serious difficulties on the local level. Various American commercial and missionary organizations frequently sought Greene's aid in securing official sanction for land purchases. Because the United States had not recognized the new Chinese government, Greene was unable to ask officials of the new regime for approval of land transfers. The accumulation of many unsettled cases, involving such diverse groups as Standard Oil and the Seventh-Day Adventist Church, seriously aggravated relations between the foreign community and the Chinese. Greene and his colleagues throughout China thus were forced to cast aside their earlier caution and began to urge recognition of the Republic of China as a step which would promote local American interests in the area. [20]

Minister Calhoun echoed these calls for recognition. Calhoun feared that any further delay in recognizing the new Republic would jeopardize what he believed to be America's fine reputation in China. Delay would give the impression that the U.S. government was using recognition as a tool to extract a better deal for the international financiers. In a letter to Knox dated August 3, 1912, he urged the secretary to reverse American policy on recognition. He argued that the

Chinese government had supplied reasonable assurances that it would function for the indefinite future and thus had satisfied the requirement that a government have the appearance of stability and permanency in order to be recognized. He also pointed out that Yuan's strength was growing and that his government's authority now was quite generally accepted.[21]

Nonrecognition was not costing the United States its good reputation in China—its reputation there was anything but good—but it was stirring up anti-administration sentiment at home. Influential periodicals, such as *Outlook* and *Independent*, considered onerous the terms for the Reorganization Loan, which included giving the consortium a monopoly over foreign loans and foreign supervision of loan expenditures, and also included the requirement that the proceeds of the loan be spent abroad. They also claimed that the bankers had persuaded their governments to withhold recognition until the Chinese met their demands. In support of this contention, Congressman Sulzer flatly charged that the delay in recognition was due strictly to the requirements of the six-power loan. The thought that a financial operation could shape the contours of American foreign policy was very disquieting to many segments of the public, and a storm of criticism was the result.[22]

Former Secretary of State John Foster, a self-professed "friend of China," shared the popular suspicion of the financiers' good intentions. Although he dismissed the charges of impropriety on the part of the U.S. government, Foster realized that the six-power loan was indeed a political as well as a financial endeavor. Through it, nations such as Japan and Russia hoped to gain political control over the Chinese government.[23]

Without direct evidence, it is impossible to prove that primarily financial considerations motivated American recognition policy. Yet, it cannot be denied that the six-power loan was indirectly involved in the matter. Ample evidence exists that the business community, as represented by such organizations as the General Chamber of Commerce, sought to use recognition as a tool to further financial ends. In a report to Secretary of State Knox, Minister Calhoun indicated that the foreign business community considered a number of "reforms" absolute prerequisites for recognition. Among these reforms were the abolition of the inland customs tax, the establishment of a Mixed Court in Shanghai under absolute foreign control, a public registry of Chinese firms, a refund of 2 percent of the customs duties, as well as proper supervision of the expenditure of customs revenue, and an acknowledgment by the Chinese government of its duty to indemnify the foreign community for all losses suffered during the revolution.[24]

Although the U.S. government did not directly support these demands, its policy of cooperation with the other powers brought about the same result. The Japanese government, for example, made clear to the United States and to China that it connected recognition with acceptance of the international bankers' terms. "Such assistance which was designed to meet China's pressing financial need and to contribute to the restoration of order and the establishment of authority in that country has naturally a close connection with the question of recognition of the new Republic," the Japanese proclaimed. Similarly, the British made Chinese acknowledgment of their dominant position in Tibet a quid pro quo for recognition.[25]

To Taft and his administration, there was a larger issue involved than the stability of Yuan's government or even the profits of great financiers. Taft had invested a large part of his life in the great game of empire and had reaped handsome political rewards from his tenure as governor-general of the Philippines. He did not want to disown his past or deny to his compatriots the opportunity to play the great game in Asia. Thus, he would not break ranks with the other imperial powers. In matters ranging from the preservation of foreign lives and property to the possibility of foreign intervention, the Taft administration stressed the imperative nature of maintaining a cooperative policy with Japan and the other major powers.[26] Naturally, the powers considered the vital question of recognition an essential ingredient of this policy. In a message to Congress on December 3, 1912, Taft indicated his alternatives in formulating American China policy: "The choice would be between, on the one hand, acting in accordance with our precedents and getting for this administration any advantage that might be attached to the prompt recognition of the Republic, and, on the other hand, consistently adhering to our policy of cooperation which we believe has thus far been to the best interests of China."[27]

Cooperation with the other powers meant acceptance of their aims and methods in China. As long as the Japanese, Russians, and British withheld recognition from the Republic for political purposes, then the United States also would withhold recognition. In exchange for recognition, the Japanese wanted explicit guarantees that the new government would honor all the "rights, privileges, and immunities" that the foreign community had enjoyed under the Manchus, including formal acceptance of the Japanese position in Manchuria. The Russians wanted formal acknowledgment of their position in Manchuria and renunciation of Chinese sovereignty over Mongolia in favor of de facto Russian control. And the British wanted ultimate authority over Tibet.[28] Although the United States did not endorse explicitly the British, Japanese, and Russian use of nonrecognition to advance their territorial ambitions in China, Huntington-Wilson refused to oppose the other powers lest Taft's cooperative policy be jeopardized. The real reason for nonrecognition, Minister Calhoun realized, lay not within but outside of China.[29]

The Taft administration nevertheless was not completely satisfied with the collaborative approach to Chinese affairs. For one thing, all those uncertified land transfers were piling up, pending recognition of the Chinese Republic. Much more important, some of the powers were using the collaborative approach to secure special privileges that would work to their unique advantage and to the detriment of the United States. Recognition of the Republic would assist American property owners in China and remove some of the leverage that other powers were using to secure special privileges. The administration sought to remove this disadvantageous aspect of the cooperative policy and began prodding the other powers to recognize the Republic. In a circular note of July 20, 1912, to the major powers, the State Department claimed that the powers had agreed that a strong central government was "the first desideratum in China"; it claimed also that the provisional government was maintaining order and enjoying the acceptance of the people. "The situation accordingly seems to resolve itself to the question whether there are any substantial reasons why recognition should longer be withheld."[30]

The major powers were uniformly negative in responding to the rather disingenuous American ploy. They had no desire at all for a strong China and were not inclined to relinquish any advantage that recognition might offer the central government, unless the Chinese Republic guaranteed all of the rights and privileges exacted from the old regime. The French succinctly stated the powers' position: "Until the Provisional Government shall have been succeeded by a regularly constituted parliamentary regime according to the properly expressed desires of the people and until such new and well established government shall have given formal guaranty of treaty stipulations [regarding] rights of foreigners in China, the French Government does not consider the question of recognition of the Chinese Government can be advantageously advanced."[31]

The Taft administration passed into history without abandoning its emphasis on Asia, its collaboration with the other powers, or its

refusal to recognize the Chinese Republic. Although it opposed flagrant instances of monopoly at home, it sought vainly to perfect the
foreign monopoly of China's credit, much as the McKinley administration had sought to perfect a shared commercial market in China.
America's hard bargaining in the six-power loan negotiations reflected
the style of J. P. Morgan and, indeed, Morgan would have controlled
China's economy much as he controlled any business.

With the demise of the Taft administration, there passed an era in
which finance capital was clearly stronger than government. The
Wilson administration turned away from the monopolistic style of finance capital. Domestically, the administration of the former governor
of New Jersey and president of Princeton University stressed competition in the private sector and was less conciliatory toward the
demands of Wall Street. Simultaneously, it developed a centralized
banking system and an income tax system, which gave the federal
government ultimate control over the resources of the nation. Henceforth, while the government might still be responsive to big business,
at least it would not have to go begging to someone like J. P. Morgan,
as Grover Cleveland and Theodore Roosevelt had done, for lack of a
central bank.

In foreign affairs, the Wilson administration also eschewed combination in favor of competition with other powers. The tendency of
the Wilson administration in its early years to compete rather than
combine in foreign affairs quickly manifested itself in the matter of
recognition of the Chinese Republic. The American chargé in Beijing,
E. T. Williams, who had opposed Taft's nonrecognition policy, pointed
out to the new secretary of state, William Jennings Bryan, that "to
withhold recognition of the Republic until we are all agreed to recognize it . . . may ignore our own interests and merely promote the aggressive designs of others." And the Chinese foreign minister, Lu
Zhengxiang, lost no time in cabling the newly inaugurated president
that the United States would draw China closer to itself by being the
first nation to recognize the Chinese Republic. The opportunity to
gain an advantage over the other powers in China was irresistible, and
on April 2, 1913, the Wilson administration decided to extend de jure
recognition to the Republic of China. Although Wilson accompanied
this move with a request to the other powers that they also extend
recognition, Secretary Bryan ordered the embassy in Beijing to make
sure that no other nation preceded the United States in granting recognition. The days of Great Power cooperation in China were over.[32]

The exact date for recognizing the Republic was closely determined by legal criteria, however. Bryan declared that not until the National Assembly had convened with a quorum, and was organized for business, would the United States extend diplomatic recognition to the new regime.[33] At last, on May 6, 1913, the United States responded to the establishment of a permanent rather than a provisional government, by recognizing the Republic of China.

Despite American recognition, the Republic of China remained both unstable and undemocratic.[34] The only benefits that American recognition conferred were upon Yuan Shikai's political fortunes, not upon the cause of democracy in China. Indeed, John Jordan was particularly disappointed with the timing of U.S. recognition; it had the effect of placing the United States squarely on Yuan's side in his struggle with Sun Yat-sen and the Guomindang, which was soon to break out in open warfare. As Jordan pointed out, "Neither in this step nor in their withdrawal from the groups have the Government at Washington shown any knowledge or appreciation of events in China, and their almost indecent haste to reverse the policy of their predecessors has neutralized any impression which their recognition of the Republic might otherwise have produced."[35] In abandoning the cooperative policy in China, the United States lost what little leverage it had over the other powers. And, finally, to complete the catastrophe, by switching from an Asia-first to a Europe-first foreign policy, the United States under Wilson abandoned China to the rapacious Japanese and unwittingly positioned itself to become entangled in the war that soon embroiled the European powers.

7

America and the Growth of
Dictatorship in China

Aₗₜₕₒᵤ₉ₕ the Wilson administration reversed Taft's cooperative approach to the problems of recognition and finance, withdrawal from the consortium and prompt recognition of the Republic represented a change of means, not of ends. As subsequent events demonstrated, American policies and attitudes under the Wilson administration were consistent with those of the Taft administration.

The republican government formed by Yuan was a "mixed bag of incongruous elements."[1] Initially, both Yuan and the republicans believed that "the best way to meet the present situation . . . is . . . to make our people feel conscious of the external dangers around us and of the absolute necessity in presenting a united front."[2] Yuan, however, particularly distrusted representative government; he believed it to be inimical to his goal of concentrating power in the hands of the central government, in order to enact the "reforms" necessary for China to regain its national sovereignty. However, the republican faction, led by Song Zhiaoren, felt that national reconstruction required the establishment not of a strong executive but of genuine parliamentary government and of a national political party. Unlike Yuan, who wished to place all power in the hands of the president, Song, and the provisional Nanjing constitution which he authored, strongly endorsed the concept of legislative supremacy.

In August 1912, Song took a major step toward his goal of estab-

124

lishing party government in China by bringing together the Tongmen-ghui and various lesser parties to form the Guomindang. The Guomin-dang commanded a two-thirds majority of the national deliberative assembly, whose representation of provincial interests and adherence to the principle of legislative supremacy formed an obstacle to Yuan's desire to concentrate power in the central government. What national harmony did exist at this time was attributable to the continuing danger of foreign intervention and to the weakness of both major factions.

Yuan chose to bide his time before attempting to consolidate his authority. However, his patience was tested by party politics, partisan opposition to certain ministerial nominations, disregard for central authority on the part of provincial military governors, and local resistance to his efforts to collect national taxes. This led him to proclaim the need to revive "the official discipline of government ordinance" and to build "the prestige of the nation." [3] The financial situation was particularly desperate. The swollen military establishment left over from the revolution constituted a serious drain on finances, and provincial autonomy made impossible the remittance of money from the provinces to Beijing. Since the revolution, all customs revenue had been diverted directly to foreign banks, to pay off past debts and indemnities, and attempts at voluntary subscription to avoid the necessity of foreign loans for current expenses had failed miserably. An abundance of expensive reform programs further exacerbated China's fiscal woes. But the principal culprit was provincialism. As Kang Yuwei wrote in 1912, "Under the present threatening circumstances, China's greatest cause for concern lies particularly in the independence of the military governors." [4]

Yuan, who believed that centralization was necessary to keep China from succumbing further to foreign rule, began to plot ways of rectifying the ineffectual nature of the central government. In November 1912, he attempted to appoint all provincial officials himself and to segregate national from local taxes, in order to stimulate the flow of revenue to Beijing. Two months later, in January 1913, Yuan bypassed the national deliberative assembly and unilaterally promulgated regulations concerning government organization within the provinces. Attempts also were made to separate civil from military authority in order to project Bejing's presence into the provinces. These moves proved unsuccessful, however, and served only to alienate the opposition, which attacked Yuan "for having no great policy or plan to strengthen and stabilize the country, for leaving finances unorganized, order unrestored, and the economy unhealthy. [5]

In the national elections of 1912–13, the Guomindang won a convincing majority in both the upper and the lower houses. While the election was an indirect one, with only literate males over twenty-one years of age allowed to vote, and while instances of corruption were frequent, the results reflected the will of the social elite and bode ill for Yuan. The Guomindang not only endorsed provincial autonomy and legislative supremacy but was led to victory by Song Zhiaoren, who was determined to oust Yuan from power or, alternatively, to reduce him to figurehead status. Yuan, whose antipathy to party government was well known, became convinced that he could remain in power and accomplish his goal of centralizing authority only by moving forcefully against the Guomindang.[6]

Americans representing both the Taft and Wilson administrations feared the democratic and nationalistic bent of the Guomindang and longed for the pliability and stability that they associated with strong, centralized rule under a person like Yuan. When the Guomindang emerged as China's strongest party, Chargé d'Affaires E. T. Williams expressed despair over the development, which seemed calculated to lead to increased radicalism and antiforeign activity. Williams also perceived the Guomindang as a threat to Yuan's desire to centralize all power in his own hands.[7]

Other Americans in China shared the views of diplomats like Williams. After the National Assembly convened, the influential American journal *China Press* editorialized that the dire predictions concerning the parliament had been realized and that the record of the assembly declared it "incapable of functioning constructively in practical administration of government. . . . Certainly, the progress made so far is not only negligible; it is worse than that. . . . Yuan Shih-k'ai should just go on and carry on the affairs of government without waiting for the Assembly."[8]

Missionary confidence in Yuan's ability to make a success of the Republic was strong at first, but even the churchpeople soon began to worry about widespread apathy among the Chinese toward republican institutions. Gradually, pessimism began to reappear as the Republic failed to either stabilize the nation or change the rapacious nature of government. Some missionaries lost their belief that a strong man, such as Yuan, could rectify the situation. Almost all became discouraged with the general illiteracy and ill-preparedness of the Chinese people.[9]

Fear of change, turbulence, and loss of property gnawed at the missionaries. Those who originally had been anxious about the iconoclastic elements of the revolution now feared that the sharp break with the past was fostering an unhealthy disrespect for authority. Although they believed that the philosophy of Confucius had not provided an adequate moral foundation for the nation, the American churchpeople believed nevertheless that it was unwise for the young Chinese to abandon their sages altogether, because the dissolution of traditional mores and teachings was at least partially responsible for the turbulence.[10] As one missionary wrote: "Society is dissolving to pieces. . . . The conditions over a wide extent of the country are accurately described as anarchy. . . . The disposition to take advantage of unsettled conditions to appropriate things that do not belong to you is ever ready to assert itself. . . . Much is written of the democratic tendencies of the Chinese Government and social life. But a Chinese Government that does not have its roots in customs of a society fully four thousand years old will not be able to begin the slow process of establishing true republican and Christian principles."[11]

The missionaries' new disposition to view established mores as a means of fostering respect for authority during times of crisis led to increased support for Yuan and criticism of his democratic opponents. Henry Martin of ABCFM saw Yuan's strength as a barrier against chaos in China. The Americans sympathized with Yuan in his struggle with the young men and women who were leading the republican movement, and who comprised the bulk of the new Guomindang Party in the National Assembly during 1912 and early 1913. Despite the fact that many of these young leaders were steeped in Western learning and were sympathetic to the West, the missionaries held them in low esteem. Many missionaries felt that Sun and his young adherents were either socialists or anarchists, and hence constituted an incompetent and insidious force. One missionary typically commented about the foreign-educated rebels, "They have imbibed the knowledge that puffs up more than the love that edifies."[12]

While the American community in China was fostering a negative image of the parliament and promoting the notion of dictatorship, an American intellectual arrived on the scene who would contribute greatly to Yuan's budding one-man rule. The herald of dictatorship was Dr. Frank Goodnow, a close personal friend of Woodrow Wilson and of Paul Reinsch. A constitutional scholar of great renown, he was the first president of the American Political Science Association and was later president of Johns Hopkins University. Goodnow had journeyed to China at the behest of the Carnegie Endowment for International Peace to act as Yuan's legal adviser. Goodnow found that he

and the president of the Republic shared a similar philosophical outlook that was anything but democratic.

Upon his arrival in China, Goodnow discovered that conditions
were quite different from those that had been reported in the United
States. Rather than finding a people wholeheartedly behind the Republic, he saw a people who "do not even know what law is." He soon
concluded that China had been ruled for so long by the ethical principles of Confucianism that it would be almost impossible to install a
workable constitutional system. Advocating gradual change and representation based on existing social groupings and interests, "rather
than on the abstract idea of universal suffrage," Goodnow wrote that
he was inclined "to look to concentration of power and responsibility
in the hands of the President for more satisfactory results."[13]

Goodnow sought to use his position as legal adviser to the president to design a constitution which would provide for a strong executive largely independent of parliament. He justified his efforts by
claiming that parliament, which was dominated by Yuan's foes in the
Guomindang, interfered unduly with Yuan's administration of government, while at the same time showing itself to be a "singularly ineffec-
tive body." To strengthen the presidency, Goodnow recommended that
the president be elected for a long term, that he be eligible for reelection, that he be commander-in-chief of the armed forces, and that he
have the power to appoint all officers of the Republic. The professor
summed up his thinking on the matter for the readership of the *Peking Gazette*: "What China would seem to need, for the present at
any rate, is a strong Executive. Such an Executive should be permitted, subject to a general control to be exercised by the Legislature over
the policy to be followed, to pursue that policy unhampered by vex-
atious restrictions which would interfere with its efficiency and make
it difficult to plan for the future."[14]

Goodnow was not a rogue scholar out of step with American
academe. He had been recommended for his position in China by
Charles Eliot, president emeritus of Harvard University. When Goodnow left China, he arranged for Westel Woodbury Willoughby, another former president of the American Political Science Association,
to be his successor. While Goodnow worked on Yuan's behalf in
China, Professor Jeremiah Jenks of Cornell University, chairman of the
initial organizing committee of the association, established a public
relations service in New York for the Chinese government. Woodrow
Wilson and his minister to China, Paul Reinsch, also had served as

president and vice-president, respectively, of the American Political Science Association.[15]

Goodnow's academic colleagues strongly endorsed his work in Beijing on behalf of Yuan. At the Conference on Recent Developments in China, held at Clark University in November 1912, Charles Eliot supported the notion of dictatorship in China. Commenting on whether Yuan should act in a dictatorial manner, Eliot said that "it is necessary that it should be so."[16] Thus, when Goodnow expressed a desire to leave Beijing to return to Johns Hopkins, he was told that he should stay in China because "important international influence was at stake." The Executive Committee of the Carnegie Endowment for International Peace further pointed out that "some of the businessmen here feel that American prestige in the East is at stake in your carrying the work through to the end."[17]

Chinese political events early in 1913 went generally the way American diplomats and academics hoped that they would go, as Yuan steadily increased his power. On March 3, 1913, Song Zhiaoren, head of the Guomindang and the leading advocate of increased power for the legislature, was assassinated in Shanghai, shortly before the new assembly was to convene. There were some indications that Yuan himself had ordered Song's murder. Yuan's alleged involvement in the assassination triggered widespread denunciations of the president. Sun Yat-sen charged him with complicity in the murder of Song and appealed openly to the "civilized world" to withdraw its support from Yuan.[18] Yuan moved quickly to deal with the political furor that followed Song's murder. Military forces were deployed to critical points along the Chang Jiang, the National Assembly was suppressed, and Yuan moved to conclude the large foreign Reorganization Loan, to finance his program for centralization, without the approval of the National Assembly. Bribery of National Assembly members became widespread, with a large portion of the Reorganization Loan proceeds earmarked for this purpose.

Despite efforts by Sun Yat-sen and others to halt the Reorganization Loan which, they realized, would considerably strengthen Yuan's position, the five remaining powers within the consortium were determined to consummate the deal, regardless of, or perhaps on account of, its domestic political implications. Great Britain, in particular, was anxious to support Yuan even though the British were aware of his unconstitutional plan not to submit the Reorganization Loan to the National Assembly. On April 26, 1913, Yuan concluded the Reorganization Loan without parliamentary approval. In the words of the *North China Daily News*, "In concluding the loan contract, the Powers expressed their confidence in President Yuan's administration." Thereafter, armed with £8.5 million in discretionary funds, Yuan moved to assert the central government's power in the provinces.[19]

The missionaries found themselves easily able to excuse Yuan's flagrant blows against the parliament. When, for example, he disregarded the express wishes of parliament and signed the important Reorganization Loan, one missionary asserted that "[i]t was just the right boost of confidence which Yuan's government needs at this shaky time."[20] Not even Yuan's implication in the murder of Song Zhiaoren altered the missionaries' perception of Yuan. One cleric even saw the hand of God in Yuan's behavior.[21]

Neither the uproar over the assassination of Song nor Yuan's conclusion of the Reorganization Loan without parliamentary approval shook the U.S. government in its support for Yuan. Although the State Department was concerned that Song's murder might lead to disturbances, American officials insisted that Yuan had not been implicated and remained worthy of American backing. Chargé Williams, who felt Yuan was "too clever" to be involved in Song's assassination, had little sympathy for Yuan's political opponents. Writing of Song's murder, he claimed that the "resort to such a crime is not at all surprising when one reflects that the revolutionaries for years have preached and practiced assassination. They must expect to reap what they sow."[22]

The faith of State Department officials in Yuan was such that they remained oblivious to signs of growing opposition to his rule. In May 1913, Chargé Williams reported that "the common people take no interest in politics and the mercantile community is decidedly opposed to any further disturbance of the peace." Even in the fervently republican city of Guangzhou, Consul Cheshire reported that Yuan's position was strong and that "the better element of Canton are opposed to a faction composed of a limited number of political intriguers . . . whose main object is to cause trouble which must necessarily prove detrimental to commercial interests."[23]

Despite America's optimistic assessment of Yuan's prospects, several veteran leaders of the revolution, meeting in Shanghai, determined that Yuan's attempt to centralize power threatened the existence of the Republic and that he must be stopped. As a result, on July 11, 1913, a second revolution began. Unlike the 1911 Revolution, however, the 1913 Revolution failed to gain widespread support, either at home or overseas. An article in the *Journal of the American Asiatic Association* congratulated Yuan on his determination to suppress the revolt and charged that the "extreme Republicans" had "condemned themselves." This low opinion of the rebels also was quite prevalent in American diplomatic circles. Chargé Williams felt that the insurrection would soon collapse because the commercial classes of the south did not support it. Moreover, the revolution was not inspired by worthy goals. As he put it, "There does not appear to be any real principle at stake in the present quarrel; it seems to be chiefly a struggle for power and profit. . . . Yuan is the most talented man available and can harmonize these discordant elements." To those who thought that the rebels were pure idealists, Consul Amos Wilder pointed out that "[t]he rebels do not come to court with clean hands, that is, they do not command confidence because they have no achievements to show; their parliament has been bad business and disgusts the people. The Chinese have no confidence in this coterie who would turn Yuan out."[24]

Yuan successfully portrayed the 1913 Revolution as a politically motivated attack on national unity, and he exploited the overall lack of direction and programs of the revolutionaries. Williams reported to Bryan that there were no "real principles at stake" but rather that the dispute seemed to be "chiefly a struggle for power and profit." Claims by the rebel leaders that they had received a popular mandate in the 1912–13 elections were debunked. As one British observer noted regarding these elections, "The public took no part and exhibited no interest in the proceedings."[25] Given this attitude, the London *Times* was moved to call the 1913 uprising "the rebellion of jealous and rapacious politicians. . . . The revolt should decide whether China is to be subjected to strong centralized control or whether the provinces are to be a law unto themselves. . . . The Rebel leaders are certainly no patriots striking a manful blow against tyranny. . . . President Yuan may have been rough of late in handling of the provincial Governments . . . he may have treated the South with too much disdain, but to onlookers he still appears, for the present, the only man who can prevent the Chinese Republic from falling to pieces."[26] Similarly, on August 6, 1913, the *New York Times* noted that "The present so-called rebellion is not so much an uprising of the people against the Government at Peking as an effort by disaffected politicians and place hunters to force themselves into power. . . . The end of the civil war, which cannot be much longer deferred, will leave Yuan Shih-k'ai more strongly established than ever as ruler of China, an event in which the rest of the world cannot fail to find cause for congratulation."[27]

American policy during the short-lived 1913 Revolution did not differ greatly from that of 1911. As it had in 1911, the United States insisted that all treaty rights be respected, that its nationals remain aloof, and that not the slightest recognition be given to the revolutionary forces. But in 1913 the demand for law and order did not have to compete with a sentiment for republicanism. Apparently, America's republican sympathies had been spent in the effort to unseat the Manchus. Any further support for the radicals who sought to remove Yuan from power in 1913 would threaten to undermine China's order and stability. Whereas the moderate goals of the 1911 Revolution permitted at least rhetorical support, both the U.S. government and the press greeted the radical demands of the insurgents of 1913 with complete disfavor. For the United States, republicanism in China was a positive force only insofar as it did not interfere with law and order or with American aggrandizement in East Asia.

In theory, the United States, at the urging of Secretary of State William Jennings Bryan, adopted a policy of absolute neutrality. In practice, however, this policy clearly favored the established authorities. John Bassett Moore, legal counselor to the Department of State, warned American consular officials to abstain from any action that might be interpreted as recognition of the belligerent status of the rebels. This decision proved particularly beneficial to Yuan's government. For example, on July 23, a few days after the revolt began, the Chinese Foreign Office announced its intention to search both foreign residences and vessels for contraband. The Chinese government announced that it would arrest foreigners found to be aiding the revolutionaries. If carried out, these measures would have impaired seriously the privileges that the powers had secured by force of arms over the previous eighty years. And, in fact, the diplomatic corps vigorously protested directly to Yuan the contemplation of such measures. Although the United States formally joined in this protest, it allowed Yuan considerable leeway in practice, regarding treaty rights, in order to suppress the rebellion.[28]

When it came to the rebels, however, the United States adhered to a strict no-compromise policy. For example, when Yuan sent 1,300 troops to Shanghai to prevent the foreign arsenal from falling into rebel hands, Tang Shaoyi, the deposed premier-turned-revolutionary, urged Chargé Williams to have the troops removed pursuant to treaty rights. Williams refused to act, claiming that such interference would create the erroneous impression that the United States was sympathetic to the revolutionaries. Another instance of American partisanship occurred when the Shanghai consular body, in response to a request from Yuan and with U.S. approval, expelled the rebel leader, Huang Xing, from the foreign concession in that city. Similarly, the United States vigorously aided in suppressing illegal exportation of arms to the rebels and even provided military assistance to train Yuan's army. Although the United States claimed that all these actions were consistent with a policy of strict neutrality, they indicated rather clearly where American sympathies lay during the insurgency. The United States never allowed its neutrality to work to the rebels' advantage. When various Americans approached State Department officials with proposals that might have led to a peaceful settlement of the dispute, they were told that any such involvement would be a violation of American neutrality. Consul Alvin Gilbert, for example, turned down a Nanjing Chamber of Commerce request that he use his good offices to halt the fighting before a decisive struggle took place because he believed that Yuan's forces would soon crush the rebels. In similar fashion, the American legation simply ignored a plea from the Shanghai General Chamber of Commerce to use its influence to restrict hostilities to a distance of twenty-five miles from Shanghai.[29]

The rebels, with good reason, were unconvinced that the policy of the United States and the other Western powers was genuinely nonpartisan, so several of the provinces in revolt specifically requested the genuine neutrality of the powers. The United States left these requests unanswered. When rebel leader Huang Xing traveled to the United States, President Wilson refused to talk with him.[30]

Through its transparent policy of neutrality, U.S. support for Yuan showed clearly, to the dismay of Consul Amos Wilder in Shanghai. Wilder felt that the United States should be more cautious, for "the underdog today may be the fellow-on-top tomorrow." Wilder was simply trying to warn his superiors that they must protect American interests in case the insurgency was successful. At no time, however, did this caution translate into active opposition to Yuan Shikai. Nonetheless, Chargé Williams reprimanded Wilder for his less than wholehearted support of Yuan's government. His fate could have been worse, since Secretary Bryan felt that Wilder's attitude toward Yuan merited dismissal from office and brought the matter directly to President Wilson's attention.[31]

As far as the U.S. government was concerned, the only cause for alarm over the July revolution was apparent Japanese support of the rebel leaders. When the uprising began, there were reports that Japanese military personnel were assisting the insurgents. The American embassy in Tokyo confirmed that it was probable that Japan had helped the revolutionists by supplying arms and training troops. Chargé Williams believed that Japan was aiding the rebels because it did not want a strong China under Yuan as a neighbor. The evidence available to the Americans convinced them that Japanese denials of involvement in the uprising were false. Cynically, Williams hoped that Chinese resentment of Japanese interference would provide the United States with greater business opportunities in Manchuria.[32]

Japanese support would prove to be insufficient to overcome the revolution's lack of domestic support and the opposition of the other major powers. The merchant class supported Yuan because of its concern for law and order, while the general populace felt that little was to be gained by fighting another civil war. The army also refused to join with the revolutionaries against Yuan. Having secured ample funds as a result of concluding the Reorganization Loan, Yuan had sufficient resources to pay his troops and thereby retain their loyalty. Finally, the powers, especially Great Britain, having invested much capital in Yuan, lent him considerable assistance in putting down the revolt. With British help, navy vessels were kept out of rebel hands and loan funds were provided to the central government to assist in its time of need. By these actions, the British hoped to win new concessions, receive favorable settlements on cases pending in the provinces, and create an appropriate climate for trade. As the German chargé observed, American, British, and German cooperation enabled Yuan "to turn the tide in his favor." By September 1913, the revolt had collapsed.[33]

The missionaries also were not inclined to withdraw their support from Yuan when the southern provinces rose in revolt against the central government. Indeed, the members of the Methodist mission in China were especially vigorous in their support of the president. The Congregationalists were an exception, managing to maintain their neutrality after heated debate. Cooler heads won the day with the argument that if the insurgents won, "the Church will feel their wrath for foolishly being unneutral."[34]

When Yuan suppressed the 1913 uprising, the missionaries shed few tears. As one missionary exclaimed, "It was well that the revolting party was so poorly prepared for its rash attempt." These Americans felt that Yuan's opponents had forced him to act in a dictatorial fashion and that it was only fitting and just that Yuan forcibly crush them. As one contributor to the authoritative *Mission Year Book* wrote, the "rebellion of 1913 gave Yuan a legitimate excuse for dealing summarily with elements of political discord," and provided him with the opportunity to implement a "system of government that his sagacity and experience told him was the best adapted to the plane of political and intellectual development reached by the nation." Yuan's authoritarian methods were necessary, for "there comes a time when the needs of the situation . . . override the claims of a strict observance of law and statute." A mission chronicler revealed the self-interested nature of the missionaries' support for Yuan and their approval of his suppression of the uprising with the comment that "[i]f rebellions and troubles so injure the central government and allow too much freedom, the result may be injurious to the position of the foreigner in China." [35]

Because Yuan remained the one man in China who held out the promise of the order and stability required by American interests, support for him remained constant. His suppression of the insurgency only confirmed American faith in him, a faith unshaken by his sanguinary, dictatorial methods. As E. T. Williams observed to Secretary Bryan, "The United States does not disapprove of the methods employed by the President to preserve peace and good order." [36]

With his domestic foes in disarray and the threat of armed opposition removed, Yuan moved quickly to tighten his control over the provinces and to destroy the remaining vestiges of republicanism in China. Beijing now controlled all provincial appointments as Yuan consolidated his authority by instituting a campaign of terror and repression. Martial law, which had been declared on July 21, 1913, continued and members of parliament were arrested. On November 4, 1913, claiming that the Guomindang was a seditious organization and was responsible for the 1913 Revolution, Yuan dissolved the party and expelled its members from parliament. The representative assemblies, which had thwarted Yuan's previous efforts to centralize power, became particular targets of his wrath. Once the remaining members of the National Assembly were induced by money and threats to elect Yuan formally as president, on October 6, 1913, the assembly's days were numbered.

The United States looked on approvingly as Yuan took these steps to consolidate his power. Paul Reinsch, the U.S. minister to China and, like the American chief executive, a former professor with strong Christian leanings, accepted Yuan's justification of his suppression of his political opposition. Similarly, Dr. Frank Goodnow, Yuan's legal adviser, justified the expulsion of the Guomindang members of parliament as "necessary for the salvation of the State," and the *Journal of the American Asiatic Association* declared that Yuan's "service" in dissolving the Guomindang "will long be remembered by posterity with gratitude."[37]

The American missionary community also applauded Yuan's expulsion of the Guomindang from parliament, because the Guomindang, despite Sun's Christianity, was filled with "atheistic socialists," and was "undoubtedly a seditious organization."[38] Other missionaries were content to label the Guomindang leaders as politically immature persons who irresponsibly made dangerous demands for rapid and immediate change. Bashford went so far as to write an article warning Sun that he must stop his plotting and support Yuan for the good of the nation.[39]

Yuan's political supporters urged him to move even more forcefully against China's elective bodies. The military leader of Yunnan province, Cai O, claimed that "[a] purely parliamentary government will endanger the republican regime and the country itself; President Yuan Shih-k'ai must be invested with much enlarged powers. The political parties should disappear."[40] Liang Qichao resurrected the old argument that China was ill prepared for democracy. According to Vice-President Li Yuanhong, "The condition of the people is such . . . that an iron rule is necessary. The people are still in a preparatory state rendering the rule and control of the central government essential. China tried government by the people, for the people, and chaos resulted: government must be by the few for the many."[41]

Yuan, who called the current state of domestic and foreign affairs "unbelievably chaotic," blamed this confusion on the provisional constitution of 1912, which restricted the exercise of presidential authority. To deal with this unsatisfactory state of affairs, on November 26, 1913, Yuan convened a political conference consisting of his strongest supporters to discuss the future of republican rule in China. In early January 1914, the conference recommended that the remaining members of the National Assembly be sent home and, as a result, on January 14, Yuan dissolved the National Assembly, ostensibly for lack of a quorum. Liang Qichao applauded this move: "If by chance a sufficient number of members decide to attend a discussion, the result is invariably a free-for-all-like squabble among a group of fishwives or naughty children. They have dealt with none of the important matters of state, but each one of them is entitled to 6,000 yuan a year. . . .

Their dirty and evil deeds are well known."[42] Some six weeks later, the conference endorsed the abolition of the provincial assemblies, and in early February 1914, Yuan dissolved all self-governing associations, an act which John Jordan described as removing the last traces of popular government in China.[43]

Yuan's indiscriminate campaign of terror and his abolition of the local assemblies risked alienating the local gentry and social elite. According to John Jordan, this latter act would "cause a more widespread, if less vocal discontent than the expulsion of the National Party from Parliament, or the dissolution of the latter body. Whereas these moves only aroused opposition among the relatively small number of radicals, Yuan Shih-k'ai's latest measure will effect, pecuniarily and from the point of view of their local prestige, a vast number of petty gentry and bourgeois throughout the country and will range them on the side of his enemies."[44]

Yuan saw things differently, however, and proceeded with his campaign of centralization by reducing the power of both provincial administrators and the military. The rule of avoidance, which precluded officials from serving in their own provinces, was reintroduced, and civil governors were made directly subordinate to Beijing. Civil functions previously performed by military governors were transferred to civil authorities, the censorate was reestablished, and national taxes were imposed. These measures greatly enhanced the authority of the central government, and by 1914 the provinces were able to balance their budgets and remit surpluses to Beijing. While the remittances out of provincial funds and new national taxes alleviated Beijing's financial dependence on foreign loans, the proliferation of new taxes stimulated unrest among the gentry and the revival of the inland customs tariff outraged the merchant community.

Economic self-sufficiency enabled Yuan to establish a government that was openly dictatorial. In March 1914, Yuan sought to formalize his newly won power and ordered the formation of the Constitutional Compact Conference to amend the provisional constitution. The document was promulgated on May 1, 1914, and, as Paul Reinsch candidly admitted, "Its most important function is to give the color of popular assent to the actions of the President."[45] The ultimate details of the amended constitution displayed the extent to which Yuan's dictatorship had grown since the 1913 Revolution. The presidential term of office was set at ten years and could be extended indefinitely by the Council of State, an advisory body whose members were appointed by, and were responsible to, the president. If and when the president was required to run for reelection, the incumbent had the authority to nominate three candidates, one of whom was then selected by an electoral college consisting of members of the council and of the Lifa Yuan (the projected legislative body). At the president's discretion, however, the election could be suspended.[46]

The foreign interests applauded Yuan's efforts to centralize all power in his hands. The *North China Herald* editorialized that "the only real cause of complaint is surely that the resulting dictatorship is not, as yet, absolute enough, while the form of Parliamentary administration, admittedly impracticable in China, still retains sufficient vitality to clog the actions of those who know what ought to be done."[47]

Although the editor of the London *Times* declared that he did "not care a straw about any deviations from the strict 'constitutional' path which the President may have found necessary," and all the powers, with the possible exception of Japan, supported Yuan's growing dictatorship, there was some concern that Yuan's campaign to consolidate power had alienated much of China's social elite and that his authority rested "on too small a basis and is becoming more and more a one-man affair."[48] The United States, however, expressed little concern or anger as Yuan's dictatorship became more blatant. As Consul Amos Wilder wrote Secretary of State Bryan upon the inauguration of the new Wilson administration, "It matters little to the Powers who have the most at stake in China whether Yuan Shih-k'ai rules the country as Constitutional President, or as Dictator as long as he rules it." For all its rhetoric about democracy, the Wilson administration remained true to this advice.[49]

For the American press, whose hopes for the Revolution of 1911 were so much higher and so different from those of American policymakers, the failure of the democratic movement in China and the rise of Yuan's dictatorship were disillusioning developments. The *Washington Post*, which had been ecstatic over the promise of republicanism in China, sank into sarcasm and cynicism when it commented on Yuan's growing dictatorship: "Possibly Western methods will never be able to reduce republican government to so few working parts as the ingenious Chinese have devised. There is a finicky love of technicalities in the West, which causes men to interpose objections to having their heads cut off. We lack the fatalism of the Orient."[50]

But American public opinion, as registered in the editorials of the nation's newspapers, quickly followed the *New York Times* in echoing the principles upon which Taft and, later, Wilson based their China policies. Writing that China was a republic in name only and that Yuan was as arbitrary and despotic a ruler as any Manchu, the *Times* commented: "There will be a good deal of sincere and somewhat sentimental protest against the utter shallowness of the democracy professed by Yuan and his associates. But the progress of China depends upon the maintenance of order, and anything like real democracy would for a long time tend towards chaos."[51]

The view that China was a nation following a path of development similar to the American experience was gone. American public opinion makers now were forced to admit that the 1911 Revolution, which had haltingly begun an experiment in republican rule, had led to a dictatorship equal to that of any in Chinese history. The same opinion makers also exposed the shallowness of American protestations of support for republicanism by the speed and thoroughness with which they adopted the narrowly self-interested outlook of American government officials and financiers. Indeed, the republican sentiments espoused by American leaders were proving to be almost as shallow as Yuan's own political masquerade. Yet, as long as China remained a republic in name, the possibility existed that native dissidents would use democratic principles to rally support. Yuan therefore set about to eradicate republicanism and democracy in China, and in the process to undercut further the myth that republicanism had played a vital role in the formulation of American China policy.

To the missionaries, Yuan's triumph over his opponents and his subsequent consolidation of power seemed fortuitous, and they dismissed the suggestion that Yuan's assumption of dictatorial powers bode ill for the Republic. "This dictatorship," wrote one missionary, "may after all prove to be the guarantee of greater liberty for the people than the so-called Parliament which used the people's money but refused to make laws." The annual report of the Methodist Episcopal Mission for the year 1913 pointed out that conditions in China for the missionaries were more favorable than at any time in the past because of Yuan's consolidation of power. The 1911 Revolution had brought democracy to China too soon; now, this situation had been rectified. The missionaries were confident that, in the words of an ABCFM station report for 1913, "the best is yet to be in this great country."[52]

Having cast aside Protestant proclivities toward democracy in order to take up the cause of dictatorship, and having given up their faith in Christianity for Confucianism, the missionaries naturally were unreceptive to democratic voices heard in their own Chinese

flocks. The small number of Chinese Christians were not totally sub-
missive creatures, and they too were stirred by the sense of nationalism
that had contributed to the 1911 Revolution. Consequently, they began to demand a voice in controlling their own religious affairs. While
the missionaries felt that this was theoretically a good idea, they believed that "the bulk of the members are yet in the infancy of Christian life."[53] Though often expressed in terms of cultural and racial
superiority, such as the "white man's burden," or fear of the contami-
nation of the church by Chinese culture, the missionaries' reluctance to
turn over the church to the Chinese was fundamentally a matter of self-
interest, the preservation of their livelihood as missionaries.

The missionaries shared a common bond of self-interest that precluded a positive evaluation of the revolution. Although, at first, the
republican nature of the revolution had a positive effect on many missionaries, because they equated republicanism with Christianity and
expected the revolution to encourage a flood of conversions, they
soon came to fear the anti-authoritarianism and antiforeignism that
pervaded the revolution. Old China was docile; the new China might
be dangerous and would resist missionary efforts to change its culture.[54] Accordingly, it was easy for the missionaries to align themselves
with the law-and-order philosophy of the Taft administration and
Wall Street.[55] Authoritarian democrats and Christians at home, they
became monarchists and Confucianists in China. Self-interest prevailed once again.

As for American diplomats, they could not help but be impressed
by Yuan's generous employment of their former colleague in China,
William Rockhill, as his personal adviser. Given Wilder's near dismissal for lukewarm support of Yuan, and given Rockhill's bonanza,
national interest and personal fortune seemed more tightly bound up
with enthusiasm for Yuan's cause than ever before. Rockhill worked
assiduously to garner support among foreigners for the dictator's
policies. The former diplomat described Yuan's repression of the Guomindang as "the persistent determination of the President to build up
a workable, popular, and representative form of government." In London, he proclaimed that the Council of State was a far more suitable
and appropriate body than the ill-fated National Assembly, whose dissolution was "an indispensable condition precedent to any possible
reform of the state and whose continued existence could not have but
blocked all useful and necessary reforms, [and] retard[ed] the restoration of order, and the economic recovery of the country."[56]

If the U.S. government and its representatives needed further reasons to accept Yuan's growing dictatorship, Professor Frank Goodnow's

presence in Yuan's personal entourage provided them. Goodnow did not attempt to extenuate Yuan's dictatorial tendencies. Commenting on the necessity of reorganizing China's political and constitutional system, Goodnow asserted that "more stress will have to be laid in the immediate future upon power than upon liberty, upon the cultivation of respect for political authority than upon . . . private rights, upon government efficiency than upon popular representation." [57]

Goodnow was thoroughly committed to Yuan's dictatorship. He saw few possibilities for constitutional government in China. In his opinion, Yuan was the only official not steeped in graft and corruption, but the mass of people were so ignorant that true representative government was not a viable option for China. On occasions when he was ready to concede any prospects for representative government in China, he blamed the Guomindang's July 1913 insurgency for setting back those prospects at least twenty-five years, if not permanently. If, however, China had to have some representative institutions, they should "in large measure be consultative and advisory." [58] Although he professed to value the ideal of democracy, Goodnow realized full well that he was serving the cause of dictatorship. Commenting on Yuan's belief that China could be saved only through the establishment of autocratic government, Goodnow was "inclined to think he [Yuan] is right." [59] And, as he wrote to a stateside colleague, "Such influence as I may exert will probably be in the direction of aiding in the establishment of absolutism rather than in helping China get a constitutional government. This will not be because I am in favor of absolutism even for China, but because my advice will be asked with regard to some one point while the general problems will not be presented to me. I am thus in favor of a strong Executive which they know." [60]

Goodnow's presence in China and his efforts on Yuan's behalf confirmed American officials in their belief that China was not ready for democracy. Minister Reinsch, commenting on the proposed constitutional amendments, was pleased to report that they did not hamstring Yuan's executive powers. In a letter to President Wilson's private secretary, Secretary of State Bryan also expressed support for Yuan's rapid consolidation of power, claiming that Yuan had the support of both northern and southern Chinese and glossing over Yuan's dictatorial methods with the statement that Goodnow's assurances guaranteed the propriety of Yuan's tactics. To those who felt otherwise, Bryan responded that the United States could not criticize Yuan's admittedly authoritarian methods because it was not privy to all the facts. [61]

Following the events of 1913–14, Yuan seemed to hold power

commensurate with that of any of China's former imperial rulers. All opposition to him had gone underground. Yet, beneath the surface, Yuan's position was not as strong as it appeared. Domestically, Yuan's campaign of terror had not been a discriminating one. His dissolution of China's elective bodies deprived China's social elite of a recognized legal forum from which they could exert their power and alienated provincial interests at the expense of centralization. Of equal or even greater importance were his failures in foreign policy.

Yuan's willingness to compromise with the powers severely damaged his standing with Chinese nationalists. Yuan was fully aware that the Manchus' failure to resist foreign encroachment contributed greatly to their downfall in 1911. Following the 1913 Revolution, Yuan acknowledged this danger by declaring that "unless we set speedily to work, others may take the task in hand in our stead. When our finances are under alien supervision and our territories apportioned into spheres of influence, the fate of Vietnam and Korea will be upon us, and it will be too late for repentance."[62] In large measure, Yuan justified his break with republicanism by its failure to turn back the imperialist tide. Yet, Yuan's desperate need for money made him willing to yield to foreign demands with respect to the Reorganization Loan and to grant railway and resource concessions in exchange for short-term liquid assets. In return for British support during the 1913 Revolution, Yuan arranged for the settlement of many outstanding British grievances. He also refused to challenge Russia's recently won hegemony in Outer Mongolia despite the objections of the Guomindang-dominated National Assembly. These concessions to the powers further eroded Yuan's domestic support.[63]

The Japanese, who had demonstrated their economic aggressiveness in the Reorganization Loan negotiations, also desired to obtain political and territorial profit at China's expense. When war broke out in Europe in 1914, Japan was presented with a golden opportunity to expand its sphere of influence in China. Tied to Great Britain by the Anglo-Japanese Alliance of 1911, the Japanese moved to displace the Germans from their privileged position in Shandong province. The Japanese were not content simply to drive the Germans from their leasehold territories but exploited the situation to assert their dominance throughout the province. These moves greatly angered the Chinese government, which had hoped that the war would provide it with the opportunity to reduce foreign spheres of influence in China. As the other major powers were preoccupied with the struggle in Europe, China looked to the United States as the principal neutral power that was in a position to resist Japanese designs. This hope would not be realized, however. Acting Secretary of State Robert Lansing indicated that "it would be quixotic in the extreme to allow the question of China's territorial integrity to entangle the United States in international difficulties."[64] Minister Reinsch further declared that American policy was not anti-Japanese and that "Americans are in China for their own purposes . . . and that they expect to remain there and develop their interests, but that their presence is in no sense unfavorable to Japan."[65]

Shortly after the successful Japanese initiative in Shandong, the Japanese moved to expand their dominance throughout China with the presentation of the so-called 21 Demands. These demands sought to consolidate Japan's preeminent position in Shandong, southern Manchuria, and eastern Inner Mongolia; preclude the cession or lease to any other power of coastal facilities in Fujian province; give Japan control of the coal and iron complex of the Hanyeping Company in Hebei; and bestow upon the Japanese a variety of special privileges, posts, and concessions, including the requirement that China employ Japanese nationals as political, financial, and military advisers; and establish a joint Sino-Japanese police force in China. Although these demands were presented to Yuan in confidence, the United States soon learned their content. Minister Reinsch reported that acceptance of the demands would make China a de facto commercial and military protectorate of Japan. "The plan of Japan was not to make any annexations of territory, but with the maintenance of formal sovereignty of China, to place the Chinese state in a position of vassalage through exercising a control over important parts of its administration and over its industrial and natural resources."[66]

The direct threat to Chinese sovereignty posed by the 21 Demands began to arouse some concern in American diplomatic, business, and religious circles. Minister Reinsch reported that the American Association of North China feared that the demands constituted a "serious menace to the expansion of American trade with China," and that Chinese acquiescence would "lose for us forever the vast opportunities for legitimate American enterprise that now exist in China." American merchants were already angered by Japanese discrimination in setting freight rates for the southern Manchurian railways. Reinsch was particularly concerned that the Japanese demands regarding the Hanyeping Company would give them a monopoly in mineral production and manufacturing, to the detriment of their American competitors. Many missionaries worried that Japanese economic dominance would threaten their own large real estate holdings, many of which had not been recorded properly with the Chinese authorities, and that the Japanese demand regarding their right to propagate Buddhist religious teachings in China would adversely affect Christian missionary endeavors. As Bishop Bashford advised President Wilson, if Japan secured control of China, it would "hinder, cripple and if possible destroy the work of Christian missionaries in China." The demands therefore were seen as a direct threat to the development of American trade, commerce, and missionary activity in China and for this reason they should be opposed.[67] Bishop Bashford wrote Secretary Bryan that Japan, "a manufacturing rival of the United States," was threatening to preempt the United States from its fair share of the China market: "Any administration which fails to face the conditions now confronting us in the Pacific and fails to preserve the opportunities for commerce of the United States with China will be condemned to shame and contempt by the future historians of the United States. . . . The maintenance of our historic policy in favor of the integrity of China and of the Open Door is an absolutely essential condition for equal opportunity for our commerce in the Pacific basin."[68]

Although the U.S. government was under considerable pressure to resist the Japanese demands, in order to preserve its own political and economic interests in China, the Wilson administration preferred compromise to confrontation in dealing with Japan. Williams advised Bryan that it was "necessary to recognize that Japan has special interests in Manchuria. . . . Moreover, she needs the sparsely settled and fertile lands of that region for her surplus population." The demands would do no more than legitimize a situation that already existed; also, to attempt to dislodge Japan from its present position of dominance in these areas would not be feasible. As a result of such advice, in March 1915, Bryan informed the Japanese minister in Washington that the United States had no objection to those demands pertaining to the Japanese position in Manchuria, Inner Mongolia, and Shandong because it "frankly recognizes that territorial contiguity creates special relations between Japan and these districts." Bryan also raised no objection about the Japanese demand regarding the Hanyeping Company and endorsed joint-policing, but only in Manchuria and eastern Inner Mongolia. And he suggested that the Chinese should pledge not to discriminate in the employment of Japanese advisers.[69]

In exchange for these concessions, Williams recommended that the United States obtain a quid pro quo from Japan with respect to a reaffirmation of the Open Door principles and acceptance of anti-

Japanese land policies then in effect in the United States, especially in California. Robert Lansing found these suggestions worthy of careful consideration, stating that the United States could take the position that "while it has reason to complain of the Japanese 'demands' on China . . . it appreciates the internal pressure of the increasing population of the [Japanese] Empire and the necessity for overseas territory to relieve this pressure by emigration." In return, the Japanese government would "make no further complaints in regard to legislation affecting land tenures in the United States . . . reaffirm explicitly the principle of the 'Open Door' . . . and prevent any monopolization by Japanese subjects of the particular trades in these territories [affected by the Demands]."[70]

Although Wilson and Bryan rejected Williams's suggestion of linking U.S. policy on the 21 Demands to the California land problem, Bryan did warn the Japanese that the United States "could not regard with indifference the assumption of political, military or economic domination over China by a foreign power," and that Japan should refrain from pressing upon China proposals which would "exclude Americans from equal participation in the economic and industrial development of China."[71] However, general statements of principle could not obviate the disappointment of those who advocated a stronger U.S. response to the Japanese demands. Minister Reinsch feared that "unless our Government unmistakenly disassociates itself from the appearance of acquiescence in the unconscionable demands of Japan persistent misrepresentations of its motives . . . will embitter Chinese public opinion against it." Reinsch's call for a strong American stand was rejected as unnecessary, because Bryan had "the confident expectation that the rights and obligations of the United States will not be affected or its interests impaired."[72]

The Chinese were not as sanguine regarding the outcome of the negotiations as was Secretary Bryan. The demands were considered to be an "unparalleled outrage" that threatened China's very existence. Nationalists urged Yuan to take China into battle rather than to sit idly by while the nation was turned into a Japanese vassal.[73]

Despite the nationalistic uproar sparked by the demands, Yuan chose to negotiate rather than to fight. While the Japanese moderated many of their demands as a result of Yuan's skillful negotiating and his attempts to secure U.S. and British support through a series of carefully arranged leaks, the final agreement reached between Japan and China was, in Yuan's own words, a "national humiliation" and a "great disaster." The hoped-for support from the United States and

Great Britain was forthcoming only to the extent necessary to defend those nations' own interests in China against Japanese ambitions. Britain, whose policy was "to try and keep China intact as a commercial asset during the War," would not confront its Japanese allies over the demands once it became clear that they would not substantially jeopardize British interests in China. In fact, Britain explicitly informed Yuan that he would receive no assistance if he did not submit to the main thrust of the Japanese demands, particularly with respect to Manchuria, Inner Mongolia, and Shandong provinces.[74] Lack of foreign support, Japanese threats, the presence of 60,000 well-armed Japanese troops in China, and Japan's willingness to use them had made defeat inevitable. Nonetheless, Yuan's capitulation and his suppression of Japan's domestic opponents, including the prohibition of a proposed boycott of Japanese goods, gravely weakened him politically and united the nationalist opponents to his rule.

Realizing that his domestic repression and foreign policy compromises were jeopardizing his political survival, Yuan looked for ways to bolster his sagging appeal without repudiating his basic policies. The method he chose entailed a traditionalistic revival designed to broaden his base of support among the general populace, who allegedly had no affinity for republican principles but presumably would respond favorably to political symbols of the past. Thus, official sponsorship of the rites venerating Confucius was ordained, and the ancient ceremony of the Worship of Heaven, which previously had been performed only by the emperor, was reinstituted. Yuan hoped that the revival of such ancient ceremonies would work to his political benefit and repair the damage done by his failure to offer a coherent program that would serve the interests of the major Chinese social classes.

Paralleling the missionaries' support for Yuan's dictatorship was their support for his attempt to revive Confucianism. Many churchpeople felt that with the newly granted religious liberty, Christianity would have no trouble competing with and subduing Confucianism, but that in the short run Confucianism might serve as a useful moral tonic whose inevitable long-term failure would clear the way for the widespread acceptance of Christianity. They gave little thought to the fact that Confucianism was already in rapid decline. Some missionaries even went so far as to express the groundless belief that Confucianism was conducive to democratic development.[75]

Yuan's traditionalist revival was to be more than ceremonial. In 1915, Yuan initiated a movement designed to restore the monarchy to

China. As early as November 1911, the president's eldest son, Yuan Geding, had begun to explore the possibility of his father becoming emperor after a transitional republican period. While Yuan rejected the idea at the time, the possibility of a monarchical restoration remained a plausible option that caused the republicans considerable anxiety, especially at the time of the 1913 Revolution. By mid-1915, however, mounting domestic problems and foreign policy failures, such as the 21 Demands fiasco, convinced Yuan that he needed to do something "theatrical." As Yuan had never really believed in republicanism and felt that the "masses of the people . . . were intensely conservative and monarchical," it was easy for him to opt for a restoration of the monarchy as a means to resurrect his sagging political fortunes.[76]

Ostensibly, the movement to reestablish the monarchy was a spontaneous one which Yuan was reluctantly forced to accept. The key figures in this movement were Liang Shiyi, former chief secretary to the president and described by one observer as the "most unscrupulous political leader in modern China," and Yuan Geding, the president's highly ambitious son. In August 1915, Liang and his followers established the Society for the Preservation of the Peace—the Chou An Hui—which was to become the nucleus of the monarchical movement. This organization was hardly independent but was, rather, the tool of the president.[77]

Yuan's supporters argued that imperial rule would represent "a form of authority with which the people are more familiar." A return to the monarchy, according to the American-educated Wellington Koo, also reflected the need for a "government able to hold the country together, develop its wealth and strength, and help realize the intensely patriotic aspirations of its people."[78] Not only was a monarchy more suitable to China's needs but the low level of education among the people and loose talk about freedom and equality made China particularly ill-suited to a republican form of government. The Republic had brought disorder and dictatorship, and only through a monarchy could true constitutionalism be brought to China.

The campaign to restore the monarchy under Yuan also received a boost from his legal adviser, Frank Goodnow, who had prepared at Yuan's request an extensive memorandum discussing the respective merits of monarchical and republican government in the Chinese context. Eschewing parliamentary government in an underdeveloped country as a risky experiment, Goodnow advised Yuan that only a monarchy could give China a strong central government capable of coping with its social, economic, and political problems. The uneducated state of the people and their low political capacity also argued in favor of the monarchy. As Goodnow remarked, "It is of course not susceptible of doubt that a monarchy is better suited than a republic to China. China's history and traditions, her relations with foreign powers all make it probable that the country would develop that constitutional government which it must develop if it is to preserve its independence as a state, more easily as a monarchy than as a republic."[79] Goodnow conditioned his "endorsement" of a change to monarchical government, which he believed carried some serious risks: The change must not meet with opposition, either domestic or foreign, that would lead to a recurrence of disorders; the law of succession must be firmly fixed; and the monarchy must be constitutional. Nonetheless, the Chou An Hui trumpeted that Goodnow had flatly stated that monarchy was a better form of government than republicanism and was indispensable to China. Goodnow thereupon persuaded the *Peking Daily News* to carry a story clarifying his position and correcting the Chou An Hui's version of his memorandum. Willing or not, Goodnow generated interest in the proposed change.[80]

Having laid out the intellectual justification for restoration of the monarchy, Yuan accepted on December 11, 1915, his "election" as emperor. He claimed his election represented the will of the people and "How could I oppose their desire?" Although well aware of "the foolish belief amongst the Chinese that they will be in a better position to withstand Japanese aggression under a Monarchy than under a Republican form of Government," Yuan nevertheless viewed the monarchy as a valuable political weapon to fend off external threats and to build domestic strength:

> The frequent change of the head of state under a republic will be a source of great danger and disturbance, as witness recent events in other countries. Not only will life and property of Chinese be in jeopardy but the business and interests . . . of friendly Powers in China will likewise be insecure. The Republic has now been established for years; during this time men of wealth and capital have been unwilling to invest their money, the business and trade of people as well as the administration of the officials have lacked permanent policies and plans, a feeling of instability has prevailed, and government has been difficult. It is for these reasons that the people desire a change in the form of their government.[81]

The political fallout that ensued from Yuan's capitulation to the 21 Demands also contributed to his decision to reestablish the monarchy. Yuan believed that a strong monarchy would be better able to withstand Japanese ambitions than a weak republic. Rumors were rampant, however, that he had agreed to submit to the 21 Demands in exchange for Japan's support of his monarchical ambitions.[82] While the rumors regarding a deal have never been corroborated, it seems clear that Yuan assumed he would have Japanese support, or at least acquiescence, as he moved toward the throne. This assumption proved to be greatly mistaken.

Yuan's desire to change the Chinese form of government alarmed the foreign powers in China. Because the world war was demanding the overwhelming attention of the European powers, they feared that Yuan's unexpected ambition might lead to disturbances that they could not contain. Great Britain, the nation with the largest stake in China, was particularly anxious. Sir John Jordan, the British minister and a long-time personal friend of Yuan, cautioned the president against proceeding with the movement at that time. As Yuan had concentrated virtually dictatorial authority in the office of the president, there was no need to undertake the risks which such a radical change in government might entail.[83]

Yuan's attempt to disassociate himself from the monarchical movement did not fool Jordan. The presence of two of Yuan's closest associates in the Chou An Hui left "little doubt that the whole movement has the approval of the President, who is however bound to discourage it officially in view of the solemn declarations he made on assuming his present office." While Jordan did not dispute the contention that a "monarchy may be more suited to the genius of the Chinese people than a republic," he believed that "the present does not seem an opportune time for inaugurating a change which may meet with some opposition in the south and may have an unsettling effect generally."[84]

Despite British concerns, Yuan's attempt to enthrone himself did not worry the U.S. government. Since the 1911 Revolution, it had supported Yuan as the indispensable authority figure necessary to preserve law and order in China. The republican sentiments of the American press had been too superficial to offer more than a mild check upon the government's authoritarian preferences. By 1914, the press, disenchanted with events in China and distracted by the war in Europe and troubles in Mexico, adopted the government's position on China and on Yuan. Consequently, when Yuan embarked upon his attempt to reestablish the monarchy, only sympathetic bureaucrats of the State Department stood by to observe the event.

The United States did not share British fears that a change in governmental form would lead to disorder. American diplomatic officials throughout China discounted the likelihood of open resistance to the change. One American consul reported that the movement had not stirred the common people and that the upper classes looked upon the proposed change as conducive to both order and stability. Moreover, the new American chargé d'affaires, John MacMurray, claimed in a dispatch to Washington that any opposition that did exist stemmed not from democratic convictions but from the realization of men like Sun Yat-sen that Yuan's ascent to the throne would mean an end to their own political ambitions.[85]

With its diplomatic reporters in China convinced that the military and the merchants favored a monarchical form of government, and that only "hot-headed" students opposed it, the U.S. government had no reason to question a development that meshed so neatly with what it regarded as its own long-term best interests in China. It decided to adopt an aloof attitude and not to interfere unless it determined that foreign interests definitely were threatened. A plea from the Chinese Nationalistic League of America for the United States to join with the other powers in opposing Yuan's monarchical scheme was quickly brushed aside.[86]

The change to a monarchy could not be accomplished overnight. Yuan had pledged himself to the support of the Republic and a sudden turnabout would create embarrassing problems. Consequently, it was necessary to give the movement a populist tinge and to divorce it from official sponsorship. In the latter part of August 1915, the Chou An Hui began a massive public relations effort toward this end. Floods of petitions began to deluge the capital urging Yuan to support the change. The Council of State, the president's advisory body, also took an active role in the campaign. It issued instructions to the provincial capitals describing in detail the procedures and specifics to be included in this spontaneous expression of public sentiment.[87]

The widespread agitation for monarchical government that ensued caught the powers somewhat by surprise. The United States did not immediately detect Yuan's presence behind the monarchical movement. MacMurray reported, in late August 1915, that the movement was being sympathetically received by all segments of Chinese society, including the young men who previously had been closely identified with the republican cause. Despite prior diplomatic experience and native talent that would later help him to make his mark in China, MacMurray was new on the scene and did not yet comprehend the forces released by the 1911 Revolution. As a result, he naively discounted the possibility that the monarchical movement was officially inspired.[88]

Yuan soon made his true feelings known. On September 6, 1915, he took official cognizance of the movement. While he protested the proposed change, he also stated that it was obvious that the goal of the movement was to "strengthen and secure the foundation of the state and to increase the prestige of the country." Yuan's statement was a tacit endorsement of the movement and his supporters made the most of it. Word went out to the provincial governors to prepare for a popular election to decide the issue, but they were warned to see to it that, when the election took place, the electors would not cast their ballots "otherwise than directed."[89]

The monarchical movement now seemed to have the support of a majority of the cabinet, all the provincial governors, the military, and the leaders of the most prominent educational and commercial institutions in the country. These developments led MacMurray to conclude that Yuan was actually inspiring the movement and that the propaganda was merely a prelude to Yuan's actual assumption of the throne.[90]

To alleviate the growing anxiety of the British, Yuan sent his personal secretary, Liang Shiyi, to see Jordan and convince him that a monarchy would be beneficial not only to China but to the foreign powers. Liang could not sway Jordan. The minister told Liang that if Yuan proceeded with his plans, he would not be able to count on the support of any of the European powers, especially if the change provoked internal disorder. Jordan wondered why Yuan would seek the throne "when he has all the power that any occupant of it could wish for," and he pointed out that Yuan's reputation would suffer considerably if he repudiated his solemn oath to support the Republic.[91]

Because of British opposition, Yuan hesitated and began reconsidering his position. Chargé MacMurray reported that the government was beginning to disassociate itself from the movement, although the change would still be considered by the legislative assembly. Still, MacMurray believed that Yuan's hesitation might be only temporary and that China had not seen the end of his monarchical ambitions.[92]

MacMurray's suspicions were borne out over the next several weeks. By October 1915, Yuan had abandoned his short-lived policy of reticence and ordered the Council of State to enact a measure providing for machinery to decide the issue. Two days later, the president promulgated a law calling a convention of "citizens' representatives" to settle the matter. The central government went to great lengths to ensure that the convention would not exercise any independent judgment. The Chinese government carefully screened the candidates to the convention, and the minister of the interior prescribed the steps that the convention should follow when it convened. These measures created an aura of inevitability about the outcome.[93]

The Japanese were especially alarmed by the progress of Yuan's campaign and sought to rally the other powers against Yuan. Japan let its fears be known, that "the introduction of the new regime . . . might . . . lead to an outbreak of disturbances in the country with its deplorable consequences upon the peace and stability of East Asia . . . and to the interests . . . of the Powers." Because Japan was so fearful of internal disruption in China, it felt compelled to inform the other powers that "it would not sit idly by" and allow Yuan to embark on such an impetuous course. In addition to these fears, the Japanese leaders well remembered Yuan's troublesome activities in Korea before the Sino-Japanese War. The enthronement of an old antagonist was not appealing to the Japanese, who preferred to keep China weak and unstable.[94]

Japanese opposition to the monarchy was beginning to influence the attitude of the other powers, especially Great Britain. On October 15, Jordan counseled Foreign Minister Sir Edward Grey that Yuan enjoyed strong military support and that opposition from the powers, especially Japan, actually had given the movement considerable momentum. Under the circumstances, and given Yuan's determination, continued resistance probably would do more harm than good. But under prompting from Grey, who was fully aware of Japan's determined opposition to the change and of the opposition of several provincial governors and many high officials in Beijing to the monarchical movement, Jordan allowed that the change would stir up considerable disorder in the south. It would, therefore, be advantageous to Britain to join with its ally Japan in urging Yuan to suspend the proposed change. Jordan further advised Grey that the powers must speak unanimously on this point to Yuan and that, for this reason, it was particularly vital to secure the cooperation of the United States, especially since Dr. Goodnow, an American national, was so intimately associated with the monarchical movement. In response to this cue, the Japanese asked the United States to join in making a "friendly" suggestion to Yuan to refrain from drastic moves for the time being.[95]

Although republican rule in China was in dire jeopardy, the republican United States would not go along with the Japanese proposal to oppose the monarchy. The new secretary of state, Robert Lansing, proclaimed that the United States would not even consider interfering in the internal affairs of another nation. More important, the United States did not share Japan's belief that the proposed change would lead to disturbances or would present a threat to American interests in China. As Minister Reinsch pointed out, the Japanese were seeking to enhance their predominance in East Asia and it would be self-destructive for the United States to assist such a formidable rival. Should the change prove to be detrimental to American interests, however, Reinsch would not hesitate to support independent action to safeguard U.S. interests in China.[96]

On October 28, 1915, Great Britain, Japan, and Russia, with the United States conspicuously silent, presented a formal protest to the Chinese government against the proposed monarchy.[97] An additional warning was given to Yuan in December as the Japanese, fearful of the likelihood of domestic upheaval that would endanger their interests if Yuan should proceed with his plan, led the foreign opposition to the monarchy.

The Wilson administration's profession of the principle of non-interference seemed unconvincing in view of its maneuverings in Mexico, and positively Machiavellian in light of its private views of Yuan and his movement. Realizing that the monarchical movement might lead to disorder, the administration was pleased that the other powers were seeking to halt the movement. Secretary of State Lansing wrote President Wilson regarding the efforts of Japan and Britain to halt Yuan's progress toward the throne: "My own view is that it is not an action on their part to which we should object. In fact, I believe that if it accomplishes its purpose it will be beneficial. Our reports while varied tend to show that the proclamation of Yuan Shih-k'ai as Emperor would cause insurrections in various parts of China. He is to all intents Emperor at the present time and I see no reason other than ambition for the continuance of his family in power for the assumption of the title." Wilson agreed with Lansing that conditions were inopportune for such a radical reversal in China but that the United States should remain aloof since the other powers were conveying similar sentiments to Yuan. Furthermore, there was no necessity for the United States to take independent action as Yuan seemed to be holding any potential opposition in check.[98]

New intelligence reaching the British and the Japanese made them even more anxious to halt Yuan's movement. Sir John Jordan reported that Yuan's position was growing stronger as recalcitrant officials were brought into line. The Council of State had voted unanimously in favor of the change, and only a final determination by the national convention stood between Yuan and the throne.[99]

To American decision makers, the election reports from the provinces seemed to indicate the futility of opposing the monarchy. Reinsch was either oblivious to or unwilling to report the bribery, coercion, and manipulation that apparently had driven underground Chinese resentment of Yuan's blatant grab for power. The other powers, neither so naïve nor so devious about the matter, expressed their misgivings to the Chinese Ministry of Foreign Affairs. For their efforts, the powers were told that the matter was an exclusively domestic issue in which they had no concern. As the minister of foreign affairs, Sir Edward Grey, disingenuously described the monarchical movement, "The Government took no initiative in the matter of the proposed change of the form of government. The people had long since been demanding such a change, and the movement has recently gained in its strength to such an extent that forcible suppression was out of the question."[100]

By thwarting the Japanese efforts to create a united front, the United States had made it impossible for the powers to stop Yuan's accession to the throne. Realizing the inevitability of the situation, the British concluded that further opposition would serve only to endanger their interests in China. As a result, they adopted the American position that the matter was an exclusively Chinese concern. By late 1915, Minister Reinsch was able to report that the two Anglo-Saxon powers would recognize the monarchy as soon as it was established, and he expressed his pleasure that the movement was proceeding in an orderly fashion with no hint of serious opposition. Secretary of State Lansing was now convinced that the change would be permanent and beneficial. As for America's mythical sympathy for republican government, Lansing commented: "While the Government of the United States may feel a natural sympathy for republican forms of government which fulfill the hopes of the people of other countries, we recognize the right of every nation to determine the form of its government and that the People of China have our good wishes for undisturbed peace and prosperity."[101]

The United States anxiously awaited the advent of Yuan's new dynasty, which would be the protector and benefactor of American interests in China. Reinsch began to urge Yuan to consummate the change as quickly as possible and to establish himself on the throne, for the delay was having an unwholesome effect on commercial and industrial enterprises in the country. In Washington, the State Department argued that the Republic seemed incapable of providing the country with needed stability and competent leadership.[102]

On December 12, 1915, Yuan accepted but did not ascend the throne. Sir Edward Grey was pleased that the Chinese, in taking this step, also had taken strict measures to prevent internal disturbances. Yuan's hesitation had little to do with the exigencies of peacekeeping, however. The would-be emperor postponed his actual accession until a time more propitious for momentous undertakings—February 3, 1916, the Chinese New Year.[103]

The delay greatly distressed the United States and Britain, both of which had been prepared to recognize the new regime immediately, for they feared that Yuan's procrastination would encourage domestic opposition. The anxiety of the Anglo-Saxon powers was heightened by Japanese warnings that in the south and in the Chang Jiang valley, the more Yuan's government "attempts to hasten the realization of the monarchy, the stronger grows the opposition sentiment." Reinsch concluded from his observations that the situation was, in fact, becoming serious for the central government and that, while no systematic opposition had yet developed outside of Yunnan and Guizhou provinces, disaffection seemed to be growing in the hitherto tranquil Chang Jiang valley.[104]

Japan, unlike the United States, was correct in perceiving the existence of a high level of indigenous opposition to Yuan's monarchical plans. Most of Yuan's top political and military supporters opposed the monarchy, and popular backing for Yuan's plan was virtually nonexistent. The old monarchists viewed Yuan as a usurper; the republicans were opposed on ideological grounds; the reformers resented Yuan's cutbacks of their favorite programs; the nationalists were furious over Yuan's numerous capitulations to foreign pressure; and the gentry and merchant classes, which had been alienated by Yuan's centralization policies, continued to be enemies of the president. Japan realized that Yuan's domestic support had virtually evaporated, and that it would be in Japan's national interest to assist Yuan's foes in bringing him down rather than to engage in a futile effort to prop up the failing dictator.[105]

In December 1915, Cai O, the military leader of Yunnan province, led an armed revolt against Yuan. Military leaders in other provinces soon joined the uprising. Attempts by Yuan to secure foreign support in crushing the rebellion proved futile as the Japanese lent active support to the insurgents. As the *Peking Daily News* noted, "Beyond all question . . . the revolt in Yunnan is a direct result of Japan's intervention."[106] Nonetheless, it was becoming apparent that, as a result of both foreign and domestic opposition, the success of Yuan's plan to ascend to the throne was in jeopardy.

The United States began to reassess its attitude toward the proposed monarchy. Immediate recognition was out of the question until the central government fully reestablished its authority in the south. This conclusion presented a difficult problem for American policymakers. Both Great Britain and the United States had hoped to maintain the status quo in China, at least until the end of the world war. The growing opposition to Yuan was making this task quite difficult. Indeed, Reinsch reported that Yuan's power was waning and that opposition was spreading rapidly throughout the country. In an attempt to salvage the situation, the United States urged Yuan to establish a genuine constitutional government as the only means of preserving order.[107]

Faced with both formidable domestic and foreign opposition, in January 1916, Yuan postponed indefinitely his formal enthronement. In February, all formal preparations for the coronation were canceled. With defeat all but certain, Yuan ended once and for all on March 22, 1916, his dreams of restoring the monarchy.

Foreign opposition destroyed the myth that a monarchy would earn China the respect of the powers, while the Yunnan uprising overcame the presumption that a monarchy could ensure domestic tranquility. The myth of Yuan's invincibility had been destroyed as well. The numerous enemies he had made during his tenure as president had exacted their revenge. The monarchical movement was the last straw that brought Yuan down. China correspondent G. E. Morrison wrote of him that "he had restored a fair measure of order throughout the whole country, his word was law, he had at least as great control of China as had ever been obtained by any ruler, and yet he goes and sacrifices everything for the sake of an empty bauble."[108]

Shortly after he was forced to abandon the monarchical movement, Yuan died, a broken man. Reinsch observed that the monarchical movement was the "tragedy of the great man who dies as a consequence of his ambition."[109]

The monarchical movement in China shattered once and for all the illusion, held by so many in the early days of the 1911 Revolution, that China had established a genuine republic. American policy during Yuan's unsuccessful attempt to ascend the throne exhibited the shallow nature of America's republican sympathies and the guile of the Wilson administration. By this time, public opinion in America had lost interest in the struggle for democracy in China and was content to leave China policy exclusively in the hands of the State Department. True to their interest in stability, the policy-makers in Washington registered no objection when Yuan sought to destroy even the slightest vestige of republicanism in China. Only at the very end of his career, when his maneuvers seemed likely to stir unrest in China, did American policymakers try to check Yuan, and then not for purposes of preserving republicanism. The record of American activities in this affair is a compelling illustration of the leading role that one of the world's oldest republics played in discouraging republicanism in China.

8

China: Not a Special Case After All

THE DEATH of Yuan Shikai ended a unique chapter in Chinese history. Before 1911, the Qing dynasty had exercised absolute dominion over China, albeit with the cooperation of the local gentry. So secure had been their grip on China that the Manchus were able to withstand numerous internal challenges to their rule, including the White Lotus Rebellion of 1796–1804, the Taiping Rebellion of 1850–64 in south China, the Nian uprising of 1853–68 in north China, the Hui Rebellion of 1863–73, and a twenty-year war (1854–73) against the Miao aborigines. In addition to fending off these internal challenges to its reign, the Qing also found time to extend the authority of the empire to its farthest borders: Turkestan, Taiwan, Yunnan, Tibet, and Korea. The costs of these military campaigns were high, and to finance them the dynasty had to squeeze its subjects to an unprecedented degree. Yet, even though such financial exactions further contributed to domestic unrest, the hard-pressed Chinese people were unable to topple the Manchus.

It was not until the armed Western incursion into China began in the 1830s and 1840s, culminating in the Opium War, that the dynasty's fortunes began to slide, irretrievably as it turned out. Although England's war with China was fought ostensibly over the right of foreign nations to engage in the trade of a contraband product—opium—the impact of Chinese defeat extended far beyond the particular issue that had occasioned the conflict. Historically, China after the Song dynasty preferred to limit strictly its contacts with outside nations. The limited contacts that were permitted were so structured as to reinforce China's sense of cultural and political superiority. Equal intercourse among nations was not known to the Chinese. The Opium War changed this. China would have to deal with the West not as vassals but, at best, as equals or, at worst, as conquerors. The loss of political sovereignty over Hong Kong, the right of foreigners to reside and trade in certain Chinese ports, and the opening up of China to Christian missionaries, all won as a result of British victory in the Opium War, struck at the very foundation of China's cultural-political system. Thus, Western trade undermined the local economy while the influx of foreign missionaries destroyed the cultural underpinnings of imperial rule. These developments posed a grave threat to the very survival of the dynasty.

To meet the threat, the dynasty eventually embarked upon a series of expensive, far-reaching reforms that not only failed to halt Western encroachment but alienated both the populace who bore their cost and the local gentry whose institutional power base they undermined. The Chinese elite, already dissatisfied with the dynasty's domestic policies, found the Qing's foreign policy failures especially galling. Nationalistic sentiment in China was no longer directed against just the foreign powers. The dynasty, because it had failed to halt Western encroachment upon Chinese sovereignty, was singled out for responsibility in these untoward developments. The 1911 Revolution, which toppled the Manchus from power, represented the judgment of the Chinese people, especially the gentry, that the dynasty had failed the country.

The motives of those who led the fight to unseat the Manchus in 1911 were mixed. Political, economic, racial, nationalistic, regional, and democratic forces all contributed to the Manchus' downfall. Although the democratic factor was short lived, it temporarily proved to be the most powerful force of all. When the Manchus fell, they were replaced not by another dynasty but by a republic. Despite its past history and heritage, China appeared ready to embark on a new political course that was democratic in nature. As events later demonstrated, however, the Chinese experiment in republicanism was just that—an experiment. Within a relatively short time, it became apparent to all that China had become a republic in name only. Soon, an attempt even was made to restore the monarchy. It failed, and after a period of anarchy during which the warlords held sway, China was governed first by a military dictatorship under the Guomindang, and then by the equally authoritarian Communist Party.

How the United States reacted to China's brief, unsuccessful experiment in republicanism in 1911 had a significant but not decisive impact on political developments in China. When revolution broke out in October 1911, the rebels quickly gained the upper hand. It seemed likely that the dynasty would not survive the revolution. In a desperate attempt to salvage their position, the Manchus recalled Yuan Shikai to power. Even Yuan realized, however, that the Manchus' plight was desperate, so he sought a political accommodation with the rebels that would preserve his position while sacrificing that of the Manchus. The negotiations that ensued were delicate, and Yuan's eventual emergence as China's strong man was by no means foreordained. Had the powers openly sided with the revolutionaries, it is conceivable that the republican forces might have prevailed. But the European powers and Japan did not want to see democracy come to China, and the United States shared their antirepublican sentiments. At American urging, the powers, while ostensibly neutral, sought to tip the scales against the revolutionaries and in favor of Yuan, whom they viewed as indispensable to the preservation of order, stability, and continued foreign privilege in China.

Whether foreign and, in particular, American support for Yuan actually altered the outcome of the internal Chinese power struggle is not really important. What is important about American reaction to the 1911 Revolution is not its impact on China but what it tells us about the United States and its approach to the conduct of foreign policy. In this respect, the results are most revealing, especially in light of the myth of a special relationship between the United States and China, based on America's own revolutionary heritage.

Although nationalism clearly inspired the 1911 Revolution, the militant xenophobia that had characterized the Boxer Rebellion a decade before was conspicuously absent. Rather than preaching antiforeignism, the revolutionaries were extremely solicitous of the foreigners among them, pledging on numerous occasions to respect foreign lives, property, treaty rights, and financial obligations. The rebels demonstrated a reverence for order and stability in order to stave off foreign intervention as they strove to keep their own forces under control and to achieve a quick peace settlement with the would-be defender of the monarchy, Yuan Shikai. The rebels also made a blatant appeal to win the sympathy of the United States by proclaiming their allegiance to the American political model, drawing constant analogies between their revolution and America's own. Finally, the leader of the revolution, Sun Yat-sen, was a man who had spent years cultivating American public opinion, adopting not only Western political values but also Christianity. The presence of Sun Yat-sen should have been comforting to those who feared the emergence of an unfriendly regime in China.

On the surface, there appeared to be no reason for the United States not to support the revolution. Indeed, segments of the press and the missionary community were quickly swayed by the rebels' apparent good behavior and pro-American propaganda. However, the press and missionaries could offer rhetorical support at best. More concrete assistance would have to come from other quarters—the American government and financial community. Despite rebel hopes, such support failed to materialize. The Taft administration not only was skeptical of the rebels' ability to restore order and stability to China but was suspicious of their motives. Where the Manchus could be controlled, and therefore did not constitute a threat to foreign interests in China, the rebels might not be so amenable. These suspicions were reinforced by Taft's adherence to a cooperative approach with the other Great Powers in dealing with China. His cooperative policy was shaped by traditional balance-of-power considerations. Alone, competing against the other Great Powers, the United States would not be able to secure a position of preeminence in China, or so Taft believed. The possibility also existed that the Chinese would be able to exploit political differences among the powers to free themselves from foreign domination. By working with the powers, the United States could help to maintain the status quo and eventually share, on an equal or greater footing, the benefits of foreign privilege in China. The concern of the other powers for their tangible political and economic interests in China was not tempered by any emotional attachment to republicanism or to the Chinese. Nor was that of the United States. Pro-republican or pro-Chinese policies toward China would only jeopardize America's interests.

Unlike its government, the American financial community was never too enthusiastic about involvement in China. Funds available for investment were limited, and China, because of its primitive economy and unsettled political condition, did not represent the most attractive opportunity to invest scarce funds.[1] Yet, Taft and his advisers believed that they could achieve their political goals only if America actively became involved in China's economy. Taft therefore urged the financiers to join the international consortium that had been dealing with the Chinese government in matters of high finance. The American financiers, however, extracted a price for their participation in the consortium. The U.S. government would have to exert political pressure on the Chinese to create a secure and stable environment conducive to foreign investment. Also, just as the cooperative approach had removed mercantile competition among the powers as a factor in China, so the consortium would eliminate financial competition. Political control and economic monopoly were the prerequisites of American financial involvement in China.[2] China's internal disturbances promised uncertainty and domestic instability at best. At worst, a new regime might emerge that would halt foreign economic exploitation and control of China. The bankers, understandably, were not in the forefront pushing for democratic reforms in China. Thus, to preserve order, stability, and foreign control in China, the two most powerful elements of American society, the government and the business community, supported Yuan rather than his republican opponents.

While the rhetorical support initially given the revolutionaries by the press and missionaries had little tangible effect, the skepticism of the government and the business community manifested itself in more concrete terms. In 1911, despite the generally held perception that the United States was a second-rate power, it was able to deploy the largest of the naval forces assembled in Chinese waters. The threat of foreign military intervention induced the rebels to come to terms with Yuan despite their own apparent military advantage. Similarly, American membership in the international banking consortium enabled the United States to help prevent financial assistance being rendered to the Chinese except on terms that guaranteed continued foreign control of China. Thus, it was to Yuan's benefit that American political, military, and economic policies inhibited the forces of revolution.

Although the U.S. government had doubts about the rebels, it was realistic enough to realize that any effort to prop up the discredited Manchus would inevitably end in failure and alienate China's future leaders, whoever they might be. Yet, how could the United States preserve order and stability in China—and the foreign control of that nation, in which it hoped to share—without repudiating its democratic ideals? The solution to this dilemma lay in the person of Yuan Shikai. Yuan was an admitted authoritarian who would tolerate no internal dissent. Under his rule, China might not have democracy but it certainly would have order. Fortunately for the powers, Yuan also was a realist. If China directly challenged foreign privilege, Western political and economic interests would suffer, but in the end China would lose.

Yuan realized this and therefore chose to be conciliatory to the powers and, by doing so, to use them to solidify his own domestic control. When Yuan formally embraced democratic principles and was elected president of the Republic, the United States was presented with a way out of its dilemma. It could support Yuan, confident that its interests would not be threatened, while at the same time formally aligning itself with a form of republicanism that it knew to be a sham.

Domestically, Yuan was in an untenable position. He could not suppress his political foes and acquiesce in foreign privilege, while at the same time maintaining a truly democratic regime. Something had to go and Yuan, true to his authoritarian heritage, determined that republican institutions could be dispensed with. Consequently, in 1913, Yuan commenced a bloody and effective campaign of repression that resulted in the murder of his principal political opponent and the dissolution of China's nascent democratic institutions. When Yuan crushed the 1913 Revolution the U.S. government shed few tears. Taft's Democratic successor, Woodrow Wilson, viewed the insurgents of 1913 with even less favor than Taft had viewed the opponents to Manchu rule in 1911. Yuan's authoritarian measures were considered necessary to preserve order and, hence, foreign privilege, in China. Moreover, in 1913, America's democratic ideals and revolutionary heritage were unable to exert even the slightest ameliorating influence on the nation's China policy. The government, this time, was joined by the press and missionaries in supporting Yuan's cause, which had not been the case in 1911. For example, American Protestant missionaries not only scorned Yuan's opponents but endorsed Confucianism as an immediate antidote to the social turbulence surrounding the movement toward democracy, and opposed demands by Chinese Christians that they be permitted to manage their own religious affairs. As long as China promised to emulate the American political experience, these two groups did not feel threatened. However, when China appeared to be following a path of political development independent of the United States, these groups came down hard on the Chinese and joined Wilson in supporting the growth of dictatorship in China.

Wilson's allegiance to law and order was not the only similarity between his administration's China policies and those of his predecessor. When Wilson broke with the other powers, by pulling the United States out of the consortium and reversing Taft's nonrecognition policy toward the Chinese Republic, he was praised as a true friend of China. The decision to reverse the policy of cooperation with the powers was not, however, based upon friendship toward the Chinese. Wilson felt that the United States no longer needed to cooperate with the other powers to achieve preeminence in China, and these moves represented the opening salvos in a new round of international competition, from which Wilson was confident the United States would emerge triumphant.[3] Of course, this change in tactics did not accomplish its stated goals of promoting democracy and political and financial independence in China. Recognition strengthened Yuan's political position at the expense of his republican opponents, and it cost China a promise of special economic favors for the United States. Similarly, withdrawal from the consortium resulted only in removing the United States from a position in which it could assist, for good or ill, China's economic and political development. Any doubt that Wilson's decision to withdraw from the consortium was motivated by his desire to promote American economic interests in China, rather than to safeguard Chinese sovereignty, was resolved by his subsequent attempt to reconstitute a second China financial consortium. Despite Wilson's initial belief that the United States could successfully compete independently in China, events such as the 21 Demands episode, which revealed that Japan, not the United States, was most likely to emerge as the dominant power in China, forced Wilson to reconsider his China policy.[4]

Administration efforts to induce American banks to enter the China market independently bore little fruit. For example, in 1915, the United States attempted to finance the Huai River Conservancy project, to give the United States an interest on the southwestern border of Shandong, where it could challenge British and Japanese claims of "special interest." Other efforts to crack the spheres of influence included reconstruction of the Grand Canal and proposed loans to the Chinese by Chicago Continental and Commercial Trust and by Lee, Higginson and Company.[5] As one banker described an abortive effort to market Chinese treasury notes, there was "such an absolute lack of knowledge about, and interest in, China that it was evident that more time must be taken for a campaign of education before anything could be accomplished."[6] The sheer number of independent American initiatives was not totally without effect, however. British, French, Russian, and Japanese bankers decided that the United States should be persuaded to rejoin the consortium, to coopt further American initiatives.[7]

State Department efforts to arrange independent American loans to China did not bear fruit for three reasons. First, the original Ameri-

can members of the group would not compete with their former partners in making loans outside the aegis of the consortium. Second, the
bankers required government support to secure the loans, which was
something Wilson would not give. And, third, America's Japanese
competitors were able to offer better terms to the Chinese. Clearly, unless Wilson changed his approach the Japanese would use the opportunity created by the world war to preempt American financial interests in China.[8]

In addition to the growing realization that it was unable to compete in China, the United States had another reason for seeking closer
cooperation with Japan. The United States and Japan were now allies
against Germany and, in Secretary of State Lansing's view, a rapproche-
ment in China would cement the wartime coalition. A cooperative
financial arrangement could regulate Japanese economic and, hence,
political, expansion in China. Otherwise, with Russia, France, and
Britain distracted by the war in Europe, Japan would have a free hand
in loans to China.[9] Consequently, in November 1917, the Lansing-
Ishii Agreement acknowledged Japan's special interest in northern
China and Manchuria ("territorial propinquity creates special relations between countries and, consequently, the Government of the
United States recognizes that Japan has special interests in China, especially the part to which her possessions are contiguous"), in exchange for recognition of the Open Door in China itself.[10] Similarly, a
new consortium would internationalize all loans to China, and, with
the United States subsidizing British and French participation during
the war, it would give the United States the power to dominate Japan
in Chinese financial affairs.[11] As Lansing remarked, American membership in a new consortium was considered "from the standpoint of
expediency."[12]

On June 21, 1918, after a recommendation by Lansing "in no uncertain terms," Wilson approved in principle American participation
in a new consortium. Wilson pledged the American bankers full diplomatic support and, in turn, the bankers promised to open membership in the American group to any interested U.S. bank. This abrupt
reversal in policy had as its "ultimate objective to drive Japan out
of China."[13] However, the Japanese claims of "special interests" in
Manchuria and eastern Inner Mongolia had to be reconciled with this
new cooperative approach before an agreement could be completed.
As a result, the United States, while refusing to acknowledge directly
Japanese rights in these areas, agreed that the new consortium was
not intended to encroach upon "existing vested Japanese interests in

the region indicated." It would apply only to undertakings where there had been no substantial progress, and not at all to the South Manchurian Railway.[14] The United States explicitly accepted Japanese dominance in all existing, and in some projected, economic interests in Manchuria and Mongolia as the price required to resurrect the consortium and to preserve American economic opportunity in China.

In May 1919, American, British, French, and Japanese bankers organized a new consortium designed to eliminate the dangers to American interests that resulted from Wilson's competitive approach— except, of course, in Manchuria and eastern Inner Mongolia, which were implicitly exempted from the consortium's purview.[15] Assistant Secretary of State Breckenridge Long remarked, somewhat disingenuously, that the new consortium was not intended to deprive Japan "of the dominating position she naturally enjoys in regard to Far Eastern matters . . . due to her geographical location, to the stamina of her race and to the strong government that has been developed there"; rather it was to deprive her of political control over China, derived through financial means.[16]

Once the United States opted for cooperative development, via the new consortium, it chose to discourage American initiatives outside this framework lest they lead to the return of genuine competition, in which the United States was not likely to prevail.[17] Under the consortium arrangement, "the terms and conditions of each loan . . . [were to be] submitted to and approved by this Government, and the other cooperating Governments," thereby giving the government total control.[18]

Wilson was, as he often stated, genuinely concerned with preserving Chinese sovereignty. Yet, this stance was not derived solely from principle. A China dominated by Japan or the other powers would not be fertile ground for American economic expansion. In withdrawing from the first consortium, Wilson naively thought that the United States could independently secure a dominant position in China without the necessity of compromising its ambitions, as would be necessary in a cooperative arrangement. When this goal proved illusory, Wilson went full circle and revived the cooperative approach and, in the process, compromised China's sovereignty to the extent required. In other words, for all Wilson's idealistic rhetoric, his China policy, like Taft's, was neither moralistic nor benevolent. Indeed, conventional historical wisdom to the contrary notwithstanding, Wilson was more antidemocratic in his actions than his predecessor.

Yuan's dictatorial tendencies came to the fore in 1913, and a case could be made that they were precisely what China needed to reconstitute its national strength. Once order was restored and the central government firmly established, China could turn its attention to developing democratic institutions. Following his victory in 1913, Yuan no longer could use the disintegration of central authority as an excuse to postpone democratic reforms. Yet, he chose to move in precisely the opposite direction—he sought to reestablish monarchical rule in China with himself as emperor. The United States, which also now had no excuse for failing to support republican rule in China, chose to support Yuan's aspirations, which in large part were inspired by Yuan's American adviser, Dr. Frank Goodnow. With this decision, the United States betrayed its rhetorical allegiance to republicanism.

The American refusal to support democracy in China was not unusual or "special." It was, in fact, consonant with past and future American practice. The case of China in 1911 was no different from that of Haiti or Hungary or Mexico or Russia. Despite its own revolutionary heritage, the United States has not reflexively supported democratic revolutions occurring in other countries. If a revolution is pro-democratic, and does not threaten concrete U.S. interests, the United States has been willing to offer rhetorical encouragement, but little else. If, however, the political turmoil that inevitably accompanies revolution threatens U.S. interests, then not only has rhetorical support been withdrawn, but the United States frequently has lent actual assistance to antirevolutionary forces. The U.S. government's reactions to revolutions in Mexico and Russia during the Taft and Wilson administrations bear out this analysis.

When Taft assumed the presidency, it was apparent that social unrest, widespread poverty, and corruption were leading Mexico toward revolution. During the lengthy dictatorship of Porfirio Díaz, foreign investment in Mexico had flourished but prosperity had not filtered down to the masses. Indeed, in 1910 nearly half of Mexico belonged to just three thousand families, leaving more than ten million Mexicans with no land at all. Díaz's harsh treatment of his own people, when contrasted with his avid courtship of American business, was particularly resented. Many revolutionaries also wanted a redistribution of wealth to alleviate Mexico's social and economic problems, a policy which would adversely affect existing foreign property interests.

With almost $2 billion in direct American investment in Mexico, and over 70,000 Americans residing in that country, Taft viewed intervention in the event of revolution as "inevitable." Thus, in the hope of propping up the decaying Mexican dictatorship, in 1909 Taft visited

Díaz to "strengthen him with his own people, and to discourage revolutionists' efforts to establish a different government." However, Díaz's troubles continued to mount, and in early 1911 Taft mobilized 20,000 troops on the Mexican border in case the United States decided to intervene.

Contrary to Taft's desires, revolution erupted, and on May 24, 1911, Díaz resigned from office after heavy rioting in Mexico City. In June 1911, Francisco Madero replaced Díaz as president but was unable to bring order to the country.[19]

This domestic turbulence worsened economic conditions and Taft and Knox let it be known that if Madero could not bring things under control, the United States would act to protect its substantial interests in Mexico. The pressure from American oil and business interests for intervention was particularly acute and Taft's ambassador to Mexico, Henry Lane Wilson, became a staunch foe of the ineffectual Madero. Ambassador Wilson was particularly concerned that the success of Madero's revolution would lead to a "permanent disrespect for constituted authority." Insofar as the revolution itself was concerned, according to Wilson, "By far the greatest change about to be effected is the adoption of universal suffrage." In Wilson's opinion, the Mexican people were totally unprepared and unsuited for democracy and, without a strong man at the head of government, chaos would result. Although Taft refused to intervene militarily because he thought such a course would be counterproductive, the administration sent the navy to Mexican waters as a show of force to aid in the reestablishment of law and order.[20]

Circumstances remained unsettled in Mexico, however, and on February 18, 1913, a military coup d'état removed Madero from office. Although no direct evidence exists linking the United States to this coup, Ambassador Wilson applauded the demise of Madero in favor of a more authoritarian regime headed by Victoriano Huerta.[21] Huerta's most pressing priority was to secure international loans so he could consolidate his position. But to accomplish this he required diplomatic recognition from the United States and the other major powers. While the European regimes quickly extended recognition, Taft and Knox refused to do so until Mexico agreed to settle various outstanding issues, such as damage claims and the distribution of Colorado River water, on terms favorable to the United States. As Taft remarked, formal recognition would be withheld until Mexico displayed an "earnest disposition to comply with the rules of international law and comity."[22] These issues could not be resolved over-night, however, and, despite his general support of Huerta, Taft left office without recognizing the new Mexican regime.

The Taft administration's response to the Mexican Revolution thus followed the same pattern as its response to the Chinese Revolution. Initially, authoritarian rule, whether by the Manchus or by Díaz, was favored over more liberal alternatives because the former was considered more conducive than the latter to order, stability, and American business opportunity. Similarly, when the initial experiment in democracy in Mexico, under Madero, proved unsuccessful, Taft favored the ascendancy of a new strongman, Huerta—or, in the case of China, Yuan Shikai. Finally, the United States under Taft eagerly used the weapon of diplomatic recognition to exert pressure on the new regimes in both Mexico and China to gain advantage for itself. In neither case did the United States display empathy or concern for the underlying causes of revolution.

When Taft left office to be replaced by Woodrow Wilson, the United States had not yet recognized the governments of either China or Mexico. Wilson, as we have seen, quickly moved to recognize China in an attempt to secure advantage for the United States, despite increasing evidence of the authoritarian nature of that regime. In Mexico, however, Wilson chose a different tack by refusing to recognize the Huerta government, ostensibly because it had come to power through force and had usurped legitimate constitutional government. However, the difference in reactions to the situations in China and Mexico was more apparent than real.

From the very beginning of his administration, Wilson sought to drive Huerta from office. As he explained in November 1913, "I am going to teach the South American republics to elect good men." In addition to refusing to extend recognition, Wilson worked assiduously to cut off all sources of foreign support to Huerta. As a State Department circular addressed to several nations put it, the United States was determined "to isolate General Huerta entirely; to cut him off from foreign sympathy and aid and from domestic credit, whether moral or material, and so to force him out."[23] Wilson even went so far as to remove the arms embargo—previously established by Taft to aid Díaz against the revolutionaries—so that the Mexican constitutionalists who had risen up against Huerta could secure arms from the United States. Finally, on April 21, 1914, without congressional approval, Wilson ordered the navy to seize the Vera Cruz custom house in order to deprive Huerta of needed revenue. With the United States actively arrayed against him, Huerta's days were numbered, and on July 15, 1914, his government collapsed.

Wilson's opposition to Huerta was not based solely on Huerta's unwillingness to adopt democratic principles. Wilson was particularly concerned about the method by which Huerta had come to power. By forcing Huerta out of office, in favor of the constitutionalists, Wilson hoped, by example, to prevent the spread of violent social revolution throughout the hemisphere. He was concerned especially with the Caribbean and Central America, where the United States had to protect the Panama Canal, then under construction.[24] The United States also feared that Huerta would "invalidate contracts and concessions . . . for his own profit, and . . . impair . . . all the foundations of business, domestic and foreign." Wilson's policy, therefore, was designed "to secure Mexico a better government under which all contracts and business will be safer than they have ever been."[25]

Venustiano Carranza, Huerta's successor, was a constitutionalist, and, as such, Wilson expected that Carranza would welcome American intervention in Mexico. Before Huerta's overthrow, Wilson had informed the constitutionalists that his support against Huerta was contingent on their willingness to protect American interests in Mexico. This demand was repeated when Carranza came to power. The United States would not recognize the new regime unless it agreed to respect foreign lives and property and Mexico's international debt obligations. As Secretary of State Bryan put it, the United States insisted upon "the utmost care, fairness and liberality" in the treatment of its interests, particularly "the delicate matter of Huerta's legitimate financial obligations," or the "most dangerous complications may arise."[26] No loans would be extended to Mexico unless the former rebels agreed to these demands.

The United States had good cause to be concerned about the actions of the new Carranza regime, despite its constitutional predilection. The constitutionalists deeply resented Wilson's heavy-handed interference in Mexico's internal affairs, especially American military intervention, which obviously was not an effort to protect Mexican self-determination but to promote American hegemony.[27] The State Department was particularly concerned about Carranza's plans to prevent monopoly in the oil industry and to ensure Mexico a greater share of the profits derived from foreign investment.[28] Fortunately for the Mexicans, however, international events quickly limited Wilson's freedom of action in Mexico. The spectre of growing German influence in Mexico forced Wilson to moderate his stance and to extend de facto recognition to the new Mexican government and to accept, albeit unwillingly, Carranza's nationalist policies. De jure recognition would be contingent, however, upon Carranza's "good behavior," which meant no basic changes in Mexico's socioeconomic structure and protection of foreign economic rights.[29] As he observed in *The Road Away From Revolution*, Wilson believed that revolutionary assaults upon capitalism threatened civilization and democracy.[30]

While Wilson did offer highly qualified support to a liberal-capitalist revolution in Mexico, he clearly could not accept a revolution that was socialist or nationalist in character. In Mexico, social and economic reforms were more important than political reforms, yet Wilson either could not understand this fact or would not accept it because these forces ran directly against U.S. interests. Even Wilson's support for political revolution was tempered by his concern for concrete political, economic, and strategic interests. In this respect, Wilson's reaction to the Mexican Revolution was similar to his reaction to the Chinese Revolution. For example, recognition was offered to Carranza to promote American interests just as it was offered to Yuan. Concern for order and stability, and for the protection of American economic interests, also was paramount in both theaters, as was a superficial concern for democracy, which disappeared when it threatened to unleash forces harmful to more tangible American interests.

In addition to China and Mexico, Wilson also had to confront profound social, political, and economic upheaval occurring in Russia. By early 1917, Russia was a nation broken by the strain of conducting a war that was draining the human and physical resources of the country. Dissatisfaction centered upon the despotic Czar Nicholas II who, in March 1917, was forced to abdicate in favor of a liberal democratic government headed by Alexander Kerensky. While Kerensky was determined to institute republican rule in Russia, he did not share the opposition of the Russian people to the war, which had been the root cause of the czar's downfall. As with China and Mexico, Wilson failed to appreciate the social and economic aspects of the Russian Revolution and focused entirely on the political changes wrought by the czar's demise. By removing the stigma of czarist reaction, the March revolution had, in Wilson's view, purified the entente so that the war in Europe became truly a contest between autocracy and democracy.[31] Thus, on April 2, 1917, when Wilson asked Congress for a declaration of war against the Central Powers, he was able to say:

> Does not every American feel that assurance has been added to our hope for the future peace of the world by the wonderful and heartening things that have been happening within the last few weeks in Russia? Russia was known by those who knew it best to have been always in fact democratic at heart, in all the vital habits of her thoughts. . . . The autocracy that crowned the summit of her political structure, long as it had stood and terrible as was the reality of its power, was not in fact Russian in origin, character, or purpose; and now it has been shaken off and the great and generous Russian people have been added in all their native majesty and might to the forces that are fighting for freedom in the world, for justice, and for peace. Here is a fit partner for a League of Honor.[32]

Wilson's euphoria over the turn of events in Russia did not last long. Within the year, the Kerensky government was turned out of office, replaced by the radical Bolsheviks whose pledge of peace at any cost was irresistible to the hard-pressed Russian people. The United States was unprepared for the triumph of Bolshevism. Not only did the Bolsheviks' political, economic, and social ideology—emphasizing as it did a repudiation of property rights and representative government—present a serious ideological threat to liberal democracy, but the stated Bolshevik intention of taking Russia out of the war jeopardized the ultimate success of America's war effort. Regardless of whether such a course might have been in the best interest of the Russian people, Wilson felt that the United States could not stand idly by and allow the Bolsheviks to have their way.

Under the influence of his secretary of state, Robert Lansing, who from the outset favored an anticommunist stance, Wilson, in December 1917, decreed that recognition of the Bolshevik regime was out of the question. As one scholar has observed, this nonrecognition policy was grounded in the belief that "the existing regime in Russia was based upon the negation of every principle of honor and good faith and every usage and convention underlying the whole structure of international law—the negation, in short, of every principle upon which it is possible to base harmonious and trustful relations."[33] Wilson also decided, as a matter of policy, to provide secret financial aid to pro-Allied and anti-Bolshevik forces within Russia. Eventually, these decisions led the United States to actual military intervention in Siberia and northern Russia, in an unsuccessful effort to unseat the Bolsheviks, keep Russia in the war, and aid in the "establishment of law and order."[34]

Wilson's negative reactions to the Russian Revolution undoubtedly were motivated by his ideological antipathy to the Bolsheviks, as was amply demonstrated by the fierce antisocialist domestic repression of his administration. But there seems also to be little doubt that his reactions were inextricably intertwined with concrete political and economic concerns that remained prevalent even after the defeat of Germany in 1918. In Wilson's view, America's commercial expansion required an economically stable, nonrevolutionary, capitalist order at home and abroad. The triumph of the Bolsheviks seemed as antithetical to this goal as the success of the Haitian revolution had seemed to the world order desired by the slavery-based American elite more than a century before. That many of the Bolsheviks' opponents were not democrats did not deter the United States; Wilson was as ready to support them as he had been to support Yuan in 1913 against more liberal opponents. In this consistent effort to maintain an international order open to American products, and to crush viable alternatives to the political system over which he presided, Woodrow Wilson differed from Taft only in his greater propensity for direct military action. Nor was he different from other presidents, back to George Washington, or from leaders of the elites of other nations, who believed that the key to their power lay as much without as within their borders.

Pursuit of self-interest by the American leadership has made it impossible for the United States either to adhere to its revolutionary heritage or to give substance to the myth of a special relationship with China. When the thirteen colonies won their independence from Great Britain, the considerable problems facing the new nation's leadership had to be mastered, the leaders realized, or the new nation would fail. It was especially important that the leader control the diverse economic, political, and regional interests that faced them. Such a task was a formidable one, however, and several approaches were tried over the years to accomplish it, ranging from the use of religious institutions and military force to control the citizenry to foreign intervention designed to stabilize the slave system.

But the most successful tactic of all was expansion of the frontier. As long as the American people were presented with the challenge of taming the vast continental frontier, their energies and their attention would be diverted outward rather than toward the performance of the leadership itself in meeting the needs of the people.

Whether the United States actually needed to expand its domain across the continent in the nineteenth century to serve the needs of the people is irrelevant. What is relevant, however, is that the American leadership believed it to be so and the people followed suit. However, with the century coming to a close and the frontier tamed, the agricultural and industrial unrest that so concerned the American leadership had not been eliminated but was, rather, on the increase. The leadership now proclaimed that for both economic and political reasons, the country had to reach outward beyond its shores to a new frontier to survive and flourish. There was only one possible direction: across the Pacific to China.

China was a great prize. Although it was the world's largest nation, it had proven itself incapable of resisting foreign encroachment. Politically, it was China that offered the United States the opportunity to prove itself a world power equal to any of its European rivals. Economically, the masses of China appeared to comprise the huge market needed to absorb America's agricultural and industrial surplus. The China market had the added advantage that it could absorb large amounts of raw cotton, the staple crop of the American South, the region that spawned the threatening Populist movement of the 1890s. Furthermore, to political leaders, such as Taft, who were striving to tame the rambunctious public behavior of the economic titans, there were significant political advantages in embroiling the captains of industry and banking in distant markets. The Taft administration not only pushed the finance capitalists and the railroad magnates to become active overseas but insisted that they conduct business there in a monopolistic fashion no longer legal at home. The administration also launched a barrage of antitrust actions that shook American capitalists, particularly the mighty House of Morgan, whose economic power rivaled that of the federal government. If the leaders of industry and finance drew more of their resources from abroad, there would be that much more available domestically to share both with other members of the elite and with the citizenry in general.[35] Finally, several hundred million potential converts to Christianity offered an unprecedented opportunity to the zealous clergy, who would establish a favorable cultural environment for the achievement of these political and economic objectives while also absenting themselves from an already highly charged religious arena at home. Penetration of the

China market would thus make the United States a greater economic power and, significantly, it would quell the economic, political, and religious unrest at home which so concerned the American leadership.

Despite the leadership's desire to use China for both domestic and international political and economic objectives, America's international weakness during the nineteenth century precluded the successful completion of such initiatives. However, things began to change as the United States entered the twentieth century. While still not quite a first-rate military power, the time was not far off when the United States would emerge as the preeminent power in the world. It was unfortunate for the Chinese republicans that their struggle to establish democracy in their country occurred during this period. If the 1911 Revolution had occurred fifty years earlier, the United States would not have rushed to the aid of the revolutionaries but probably would have offered rhetorical support. But the revolution reflected the desire of the Chinese people for a government that could restore China's political and economic sovereignty. The U.S. government realized this early on and stood with the other powers in trying to gain control of the situation through the aegis of Yuan. When the press and missionaries also realized this fact, even they withdrew their rhetorical support for the revolution and sided with the forces of dictatorship. American-style democracy would not threaten American interests but Chinese-style democracy would and, therefore, would not be supported.[36]

The American response to the 1911 Chinese Revolution certainly does little to substantiate the conclusions of some historians that the 1911 Revolution was the critical event in establishing a special relationship between the United States and China. Yet, the myth of a special relationship continued to grow long after the 1911 Revolution and after the fall of Yuan Shikai. Following the Allied victory over the Central Powers in World War I, Wilson's rhetoric regarding self-determination reached new heights, encouraging the Chinese to believe that the United States would support the elimination of foreign privilege in China and the return of Japanese-occupied Shandong. China's hopes collapsed, however, at the Versailles Peace Conference, when Wilson backed down in the face of Japanese threats to quit the League of Nations if Shandong were returned to Chinese control. Still, what the proponents of the "special relationship" remember from this episode is not Wilson's retreat from principle, but his rhetoric in favor of self-determination. Thus, for example, Iriye has observed that by 1918 Chinese nationalism had emerged as a force to be reckoned with in international politics and "the United States had done much to make it so."[37]

In the decade that followed, the United States was no more responsive to the demands of Chinese nationalism than it had been during Wilson's presidency. Despite China's ardent wish for treaty revision, the United States refused to yield any of its special privileges in the early 1920s.[38] This situation changed dramatically with the onset of the Nationalist Revolution of 1925–28. Realizing that the powers would be able to keep their privileged position in China only if they were willing to fight for it, the American leadership, beset by popular noninterventionist and pacifist tendencies, opted expediently to lead the way in the restoration of Chinese sovereignty, in the hope that the Chinese Nationalists would reciprocate this act of apparent friendship.[39] "By helping China . . . he [Secretary of State Kellogg] felt the United States would encourage the impression that it was the friend of China, thus exempting it from much of the anti-foreign feeling."[40] While American policy happened to be congruent with Chinese interests, it was rooted not in genuine concern for China but in a realistic evaluation of American domestic political interests. Just as the American response to the 1911 Revolution had been distorted, so too was the U.S. response to the Nationalist Revolution, following which Americans "once again . . . view[ed] themselves as 'champions of the sovereign rights of China.'"[41]

The next two decades were, for China, even more turbulent than the preceding generation. Beginning with the Manchurian crisis of 1931, China became the target of Japanese military aggression which ultimately evolved into World War II in the Pacific. The initial American reaction was embodied in Secretary of State Henry Stimson's non-recognition doctrine, a doctrine that was not based on concern for China's independence and integrity but on a calculation of the threat to American interests represented by Japan's resort to arms. Indeed, American policy during this period has been characterized as appeasement of Japan.[42] The *Washington Star* editorialized, "For the United States to go to war with Japan to prevent the seizure of China or to compel its release if seizure were already effected, would be a monstrous injustice to the American people, a sacrifice of American lives and treasure, for which there would be no justification."[43] Despite its moralistic condemnation of Japanese aggression, the United States offered little concrete help to China and even supplied Japan with vital war supplies, until Japan allied itself with Nazi Germany and began to look toward the European colonies in Southeast Asia.[44] Indeed, the aid given to China and the supplies sold to Japan were given for the very brutal, calculated reasons of self-interest noted by Stanley K. Hornbeck, chief Asian affairs specialist in the State Department:

> So long as they are tied up in and with the Chinese hostilities and lack assurance of material assistance from any other power, the Japanese simply are not in a position to engage in new adventures which in their estimation would involve risk for them of war with the United States.
>
> The strategy of the United States should be to keep the China hostilities going, by sending the Chinese reasonable (which means more than in the past) amounts of supplies and we should keep the Japanese fearful of a possible armed clash with us. In order to be able to deliver supplies to China, and in order to keep Japan fearful of a clash with this country, we should be currently allocating items for China and we must keep a sizable naval and air force in the Pacific.[45]

The war with Japan owed nothing to American friendship for China, and the wartime pattern of operations clearly demonstrated that China was of secondary or even less concern to the United States. Roosevelt compensated Jiang Jieshi (Chiang Kai-chek) and the Chinese Nationalists with rhetoric, calling China a "Great Power" and playing up the special relationship as a means of pacifying the Chinese.[46] Unfortunately, just as the 1911 and 1925–28 revolutions became integral components of the myth of a special relationship, so too America's public moral condemnation of Japanese aggression against China in the 1930s and its own war against Japan during the 1940s were misconstrued as indications of a special American friendship for China, a special friendship that soon turned into a special sense of betrayal when the Communists seized power in China in 1949.

One might well ask why it matters that the United States has failed to live up to either of these traditions in the conduct of its foreign policy. If no one believed these myths in the first place, little harm would be done. After all, a nation cannot be condemned for pursuing its self-interest so long as the means by which it chooses to do so conform to certain principles of civility and humanity. But, unfortunately, people do believe these myths, and, as a result, the leadership charged with conducting foreign policy can do so without being held accountable for what they discern the national interest to be, and the means by which they choose to pursue it. America's reaction to the 1911

Revolution is an important case in point. Popular misconceptions of this and other more recent episodes in Sino-American relations, fostered by the elite, created a romantic illusion that contributed to more than twenty years of Sino-American hostility, toughened the domestic repression of the McCarthy era, and facilitated American involvement in Vietnam, which was designed, in part, to halt mistakenly perceived Chinese aggression. If such dire consequences are to be avoided in the future, the nation's foreign policy must be opened up to well-informed public debate that does not leave the formulation of foreign policy the exclusive prerogative of the ruling elite.

Notes

PREFACE

1. Michael Hunt, *The Making of a Special Relationship: The United States and China to 1914*, pp. 12–13, 57.

2. Ibid., pp. 299–300; Edward Friedman and Mark Selden, eds., *America's Asia: Dissenting Essays on Asian-American Relations*, p. 14; Warren Cohen, *America's Response to China*, p. 213.

3. John K. Fairbank, *The United States and China*, p. 402; Dorothy Borg, *American Policy and the Chinese Revolution, 1925–1928*; Paul Varg, *The Making of a Myth: The United States and China, 1897–1912*, pp. 121, 169.

4. Akira Iriye, *Across the Pacific: An Inner History of American–East Asian Relations*, p. 125; Benson Lee Grayson, *The American Image of China*, p. 17; Foster Rhea Dulles, *China and America: The Story of Their Relations Since 1784*, p. 135.

5. Charles Neu, in *American–East Asian Relations: A Survey*, ed. Ernest R. May and James C. Thomson, pp. 169–72. It is particularly surprising that American diplomatic historians have ignored the 1911 Chinese Revolution, for when it occurred it was viewed as an event of enormous significance. See *San Francisco Examiner*, January 3, 1912, p. 1. Indeed, as Henry May has written in his cultural history of that time, "no event of the period was subject to more incessant and moral interpretation" than the Chinese Revolution (*The End of American Innocence*, p. 15).

6. Iriye, pp. 121–33.

7. Fairbank, in Iriye, pp. xi–xii; Neu, in May and Thomson, pp. 157, 161.

8. Tien-yi Li, *Woodrow Wilson's China Policy*, pp. 5, 6, 14, 18, 46, 205–6, 212.

9. Arthur Link, *Wilson: The New Freedom*, p. 286; Roy Watson Curry, pp. 16, 17, 20–21, 31, 312.

10. Burton Beers, *Vain Endeavor, Robert Lansing's Attempts to End the American-Japanese Rivalry*, pp. 17, 178–79; Jerry Israel, *Progressivism and the Open Door*, pp. 102, 123; Charles Vevier, *The United States and China, 1906–1913: A Study in Finance and Diplomacy*, pp. 207, 209; Noel Pugach, *Paul S. Reinsch, Open Door Diplomat in Action*, p. 55.

11. Cohen, pp. 78, 83, 86–90, 98–99, 213.

12. Hunt, *The Making of a Special Relationship*, p. 299.

13. Ibid., pp. 217–25; Wilson's activism in foreign commerce is amply documented in Burton I. Kaufman's *Efficiency and Expansion: Foreign Trade Organization in the Wilson Administration, 1913–1921*.

14. May and Thomson, p. 175; William A. Williams, *The Tragedy of American Diplomacy*, p. 61. Williams's work stands with Thomas A. Bailey's *Diplomatic History of the American People* and George F. Kennan's *American Diplomacy, 1900–1950* as one of the three most popular American diplomatic history books of our era, and perhaps the most influential. See Warren F. Kimball, "Seduction without Satisfaction: Textbooks and the Teaching of the History of American Foreign Policy and Diplomacy."

15. Varg, *The Making of a Myth*, p. 173; Harold Isaacs, *Scratches on Our Minds: American Images of China and India*, p. 195.

16. George F. Kennan, "A Fresh Look at Our China Policy," *New York Times Magazine*, November 22, 1964, p. 27.

Domestic Control and Overseas Expansion

1. Shortly after the establishment of the new Republic, American merchants moved into the China market and brought back not only the prized leaf but all sorts of porcelain paraphernalia associated with the tea habit. Chinese influences permeated the nation. Chinese art objects, handicrafts, and designs multiplied and were enjoyed by rich and poor alike, providing a strong counterpoint to the classic Western style favored by the political leaders of the nation. To pay for their tea habit and their beloved chinoiserie, and for other products imported from the nation that was generally acknowledged to be superior in its agricultural, industrial, and artistic achievements, Americans carried a variety of goods to Canton. Ginseng, sealskins, sandalwood, and specie sold well in China, but by far the most profitable cargo was contraband opium. As they had defied the British attempt to regulate the importation of Chinese tea into their own country, so the Americans defied the efforts of the ruling Manchus to ban the importation of opium into China. See Jonathan Goldstein, *Philadelphia and the China Trade, 1682–1846: Commercial, Cultural and Attitudinal Effects*.

Ineffectual attempts by the Manchu dynasty, which had ruled China since the mid-seventeenth century, to choke off the opium trade led first to the demoralization of the Chinese civil service and then to the unsuccessful Opium War of the early 1840s. The war in which tea had been the symbolic issue cost the Hanoverian dynasty in England a major part of its empire—an immensely wealthy continental domain—but not its throne. While the war in which opium was the symbolic issue at first cost China only a few square miles of territory and a small bit of its political sovereignty, the forces unleashed upon China beginning with the Opium War eventually cost the Manchu dynasty its throne.

2. Timothy M. Matthewson, "George Washington's Policy toward the Haitian Revolution."

3. Henry Cabot Lodge, ed., "The Works of Alexander Hamilton," in Norman Graebner, *Ideas and Diplomacy*, p. 64.

4. H. Martineau, *Society in America*, cited in Martin Marty, *The Modern Schism*, p. 129.

5. Ibid., p. 122.

6. Ibid., p. 131.

7. Charles G. Finney, *Lectures on Revivals of Religion*, pp. 205–6 (emphasis in original).

8. Marty, p. 114.

9. Charles I. Foster, *An Errand of Mercy: The Evangelical United Front, 1790–1837*, pp. 57, 128.

10. R. Pierce Beaver, *All Loves Excelling: American Protestant Women in World Mission*, p. 25. The use of missionaries to control and ultimately "Americanize" an alien population became an explicit instrument of U.S. government policy in 1869 when President Ulysses S. Grant adopted his so-called Quaker Policy, which called for the use of missionaries as Indian agents who, by civilizing the Indians, would eliminate an internal threat to the nation. See William S. McFeely, *Grant: A Biography*, p. 308. While such a policy was never explicitly adopted with respect to foreign missions, American leaders were not unaware of the political value of a missionary presence in nations, such as China, that were the objects of their ambitions.

11. Adams to Hugh Nelson, U.S. minister to Madrid, March 20, 1823, cited in Lester D. Langley, *The Cuban Policy of the United States*, pp. 11–12.

12. Thomas McCormick, *China Market: America's Quest for Informal Empire, 1893–1901*, p. 26.

13. Walter LaFeber, *The New Empire: An Interpretation of American Expansion, 1860–1898*, p. 14.

14. U.S. Dept. of Commerce, *Historical Statistics of the United States, Colonial Times to 1970*, pt. 2, pp. 903–7.

15. U.S. imports from Cuba dropped from $78,706,506 in 1893 to $15,232,477 in 1898. During the same period, U.S. exports to Cuba dropped from $24,157,698 to $9,561,656. Langley, p. 84, citing *Commercial Relations of the United States with Foreign Countries During the Year 1901* (Washington, 1901), 1:33, 37.

16. Philip Foner, *The Spanish-Cuban-American War and the Birth of American Imperialism, 1895–1902*, p. 197.

17. Brooks Adams, *America's Economic Supremacy*, p. 98.

18. Ibid., p. 49.

CHAPTER 1

1. Marilyn Young, *The Rhetoric of Empire: American China Policy, 1895–1901*, p. 21.

2. Ibid., p. 22.

3. Conger to Hay, November 3, 1898, quoted in Michael H. Hunt, *Frontier Defense and the Open Door: Manchuria in Chinese-American Relations, 1895–1911*, p. 30.

4. Ibid., p. 33.

5. Albert J. Beveridge, *The Russian Advance*, pp. 206–7.

6. Hunt, *Frontier Defense*, p. 41.

7. LaFeber, p. 302.

8. Hunt, *Frontier Defense*, p. 44.

9. Marilyn Young, p. 108; Harold Z. Schiffrin, *Sun Yat-sen and the Origins of the Chinese Revolution*, p. 287.

10. *New York Tribune*, June 11, 1900; *Independent*, June 14, 1900.

11. Jerry Israel, *Progressivism and the Open Door*, pp. 22, 44; see also Mark Twain, "To the Person Sitting in Darkness," *North American Review* 172 (February 1901): 161–76, and "To My Missionary Critics," ibid. (April 1901): 520–34.

12. Paul A. Varg, *Missionaries, Chinese and Diplomats: The American Protestant Missionary Movement in China, 1890–1952*, pp. 123, 138–39. In the 1890s one missionary remarked, "If I were asked what would be the best form of advertising for the great American Steel Trust or Standard Oil or the Baldwin Locomotive Works . . . I should say, take up the support of one or two or a dozen mission stations. . . . Everyone thus helped would be, consciously or unconsciously, a drummer of your goods, and the great church they represent at home would be your advertising agents" (LaFeber, p. 307).

13. Andrew Sinclair, *Corsair: The Life of J. Pierpont Morgan*.

14. Jesse Miller, "China in American Policy and Opinion," p. 48.

15. Hunt, *Frontier Defense*, p. 45, quoting Charles Denby, *China and Her People* (Boston, 1906).

16. Mary Wright, "Introduction: The Rising Tide of Change," in Mary Wright, ed., *China in Revolution: The First Phase, 1900–1913*, p. 10.

17. Straight, untitled article on the Chinese boycott (undated), Straight Papers.

18. Miller, p. 77; Howard Beale, *Theodore Roosevelt and the Rise of America to World Power*, pp. 42–43, 206, 215; Hunt, *Frontier Defense*, p. 92, quoting Roosevelt to Rockhill, August 22, 1905.

19. Straight, untitled article on the Chinese boycott.

20. Israel, p. 8; Huntington-Wilson's comment in Rockhill to Root, August 5, 1907, State Department [hereafter SD] 59.2413/79.

21. See Ssu-yu Teng and John K. Fairbank, *China's Response to the West*, pp. 28, 52–53, 177.

22. Marilyn Young, p. 108.

23. Meribeth E. Cameron, *The Reform Movement in China, 1898–1912*, p. 103.

24. Ibid., pp. 13–14.

25. Michael Gasster, *Chinese Intellectuals and the Revolution of 1911: The Birth of Modern Chinese Radicalism*, p. 60.

26. Ibid., p. 18.

27. Ibid., p. 59.

28. Ernest P. Young, *The Presidency of Yuan Shih-k'ai: Liberalism and Dictatorship in Early Republican China*, pp. 5–28.

29. Miller, p. 13.

30. Mary Wright, p. 1.

31. Ibid., pp. 18–19.

32. Hunt, *Frontier Defense*, p. 96.

33. Miller, p. 13; *Washington Post*, September 1, 1908, p. 6. The *Post* offered this assessment of China's attempt to implement constitutional rule: "What will the Chinese nation as it is today do with a constitutional government? The very question is enough to make the student of history shudder. How can a great, unwieldy, conglomerate mass of 400,000,000 human beings, living in the centuries before Rome fell, be expected to govern themselves in the twentieth century?

"At least 300,000,000 of these people have never heard of a constitution, half as many more do not know that a country exists outside their own, and almost half that number have never had a thought in their lives. Their forefathers thought for them; they follow in the footsteps of their ancestors and praise the ugly stone idols that they have their ancestors to venerate. They have never changed their religion or invented a new god in three thousand years. A people which cannot do that is almost beyond the pale of modern progress. It is at least not fitted to perform the functions of modern, civilized government."

34. Hunt, *Frontier Defense*, p. 94, quoting Adee to Denby, August 30, 1906.

35. *Foreign Relations of the United States* [hereafter FRUS], 1908, p. 190; Helen Kahn, "The Great Game of Empire: Willard D. Straight and American Far Eastern Policy," p. 119; *Congressional Record*, 59th Cong., 1st sess., 1906, 40, pt. II: 1020–23.

36. Contemporary observers of American diplomacy felt that Knox's corporate legal background had not prepared him to deal with the subtleties of foreign affairs. As the distinguished British minister to the United States, James Bryce, noted, "He [Knox] is hopelessly ignorant of international politics and principles of policy and is either too old or too lazy to apply his mind to the subject and try to learn. Nobody in his miserably organized department is competent to instruct or guide him." Quoted in Hunt, *Frontier Defense*, p. 224.

37. William Howard Taft, speech in Shanghai, cited in Kahn, p. 150; Taft to Rollo Ogden, April 24, 1909, letterbooks, Taft Papers.

38. Israel, pp. 60–82; Philip H. Burch, Jr., *Elites In American History*, 2: 167–69. Taft's affinity for Wall Street may have been more than simply ideological. In the 1908 presidential campaign, the House of Morgan contributed $150,000 to Taft, allegedly with the understanding that Taft's administration would cooperate closely with Morgan in matters of mutual interest. See Gabriel Kolko, *The Triumph of Conservatism: A Reinterpretation of American History, 1900–1916*.

Regardless of Calhoun's Morgan connections, he was, unlike Knox, well respected by his diplomatic peers. The British minister to Beijing, John Jordan, reported that Calhoun "has fully maintained his reputation for honesty and straight dealing. He is absolutely devoid of tendency to exalt America at the expense of the other Powers which too often characterises his countrymen in the East, and although inclined to be genuinely sympathetic to the Chinese, he does not hesitate to expose their faults when occasion requires it." Jordan to Grey, March 27, 1912, Foreign Office [hereafter FO] 405/517.

39. See Hunt, *Frontier Defense*, pp. 185–86; "Summary of State Department Policy and Actions," Fall 1909, Knox Papers.

40. William Phillips memo, May 10, 1909, Knox Papers.

41. Israel, p. 99.

42. F. M. Huntington-Wilson, *The Perils of Hifalutin*, p. 175.

43. Israel, p. 79.

44. Knox's view cited in J. B. Osborne memo, September 15, 1909, Knox Papers; see also Hunt, *Frontier Defense*, p. 187. Knox subsequently explained his reasons for seeking U.S. participation in this venture: "The proposed hypothecation of China's internal revenues for a loan was . . . regarded as involving important political considerations. The fact that the loan was to carry an imperial guaranty and to be secured on the internal revenues made it of the greatest importance that the United States should participate therein in order that this Government might be in a position as an interested party to exercise an influence equal to that of any other three powers in any question arising through the pledging of China's national resources." Statement, January 6, 1910, FRUS, 1910, pp. 159–60.

45. Hunt, *Frontier Defense*, pp. 188–90; see also Knox to Peking legation, October 6, 1910, SD 893.51/138.

46. Vevier, p. 106.

47. Hunt, *Frontier Defense*, p. 219.

48. Ibid., p. 238; Straight to Huntington-Wilson, quoted in Kahn, p. 337.

49. Lewis Einstein, "The New American Policy in China," Knox Papers; Einstein to Knox, October 17, 1910, ibid.

50. Huntington-Wilson to Elbert F. Baldwin, January 19, 1910, quoted in Hunt, *Frontier Defense*, p. 220.

51. Like so many other aspects of American foreign policy at this time, the intellectual origins of the principle of tying economic assistance to political control can be traced to the writings of expansionist nineteenth-century intellectuals. As historian Frederick Jackson Turner wrote, "Political relations . . . are inextricably connected with economic relations. . . . The government of a foreign state whose subjects have lent money to another state, may interfere to protect the rights of the bondholders, if they are endangered by the borrowing state." See LaFeber, pp. 69–70.

52. Report of P. Heintzleman, vice-consul, Shanghai, August 14, 1909, cited in Hunt, *Frontier Defense*, p. 252.

53. Willard Straight to J. P. Morgan, November 16, 1910, Straight Papers; Straight to J. P. Morgan, November 13, 1910, ibid.; Straight to H. P. Davidson, November 22, 1910, ibid.

54. Hunt, *Frontier Defense*, pp. 238–57. The Currency Loan, which was finally concluded on April 11, 1911, further solidified America's position as a full-fledged partner in the international banking consortium. As Straight exclaimed, "By virtue of this Loan Agreement . . . the American Group is now placed upon a footing of equality with the French, German, and British interests, which have been entrenched here for the last 30 years." Straight to J. P. Morgan & Co., April 16, 1911, Straight Papers.

55. Calhoun to Knox, January 11, 1911, SD 893.00/497; Calhoun to Knox, November 23, 1910, SD 893.00/482; Henry Fletcher to Knox, January 15, 1910, SD 893.00/369.

56. Calhoun to Knox, May 25, 1910, SD 893.00/405; Kirton to Knox, November 1, 1910, SD 893.00/456.

CHAPTER 2

1. Leon Stover, *The Cultural Ecology of Chinese Civilization*.

2. Edward J. M. Rhoads, *China's Republican Revolution: The Case of Kwangtung, 1895–1913*, pp. 61, 175ff.

3. Ernest P. Young, p. 1.

4. Gasster, p. 8.

5. Mary Wright, "Introduction: The Rising Tide of Change," pp. 5–8.

6. Akira Iriye, "Public Opinion and Foreign Policy: The Case of Late Ch'ing China," in Albert Feuerwerker, Rhoads Murphy, and Mary C. Wright, eds., *Approaches to Modern Chinese History*, p. 229.

7. Mary Wright, p. 17.

8. Gasster, p. 4.

9. Edmund S. K. Fung, *The Military Dimension of the Chinese Revolution: The New Army and its Role in the Revolution of 1911*, pp. 111, 142–49, 195.

10. Gasster, pp. 128–29; Comments of Father Hugh Scallan, Sianfu,

November 25, 1911, enclosed in Calhoun to Knox, December 11, 1911, SD 893.00/892.

11. Hu Hanmin, "The Six Principles of the People's Report," in W. T. deBary, ed., *Sources of Chinese Tradition*, pp. 763–64.

12. Gasster, pp. 86–87.

13. Fung, passim.

14. Ibid., pp. 121, 142–44, 168–69.

15. Gasster, p. 17.

16. Calhoun to Knox, SD 893.00/492; P'eng yuan Chang, "The Constitutionalists," in Mary Wright, pp. 146–50.

17. Fung, pp. 199–201; Ernest Young, pp. 23–24; Marie-Claire Berger, "The Role of the Bourgeoisie," in Mary Wright, pp. 229–53.

18. Chang, in Mary Wright, p. 172.

19. K. S. Liew, *Struggle for Democracy: Sung Chiao-jen and the 1911 Chinese Revolution*, pp. 87–88.

20. Taft to the prince regent, September 29, 1910, letterbooks, Taft Papers.

21. Knox to secretary of the navy, September 15, 1910, SD 893.00/452.

22. Chargé Henry Fletcher to Secretary Knox, March 5, 1910, SD 893.00/396.

23. Calhoun to Knox, June 3, 1910, SD 893.00/396; Hubbard to secretary of state, September 2, 1910, SD 893.00/432.

24. Memorandum of the Chinese secretary, Charles Tenney, March 11, 1911, SD 893.00/509; Consul Bergholz (Canton) to secretary of state, May 4, 1911, SD 893.00/523.

25. Fung, p. 203.

26. Jordan to Grey, October 16, 1911, FO 371/1090.

27. Straight to H. P. Davison, October 16, 1911, Knox Papers.

28. Reports of Captain M. Otter-Barry, enclosed in Jordan to Grey, November 5, 20, 1911, FO 371/1096.

29. E. T. Williams to Knox, October 26, 1911, Knox Papers.

30. Report of the U.S.S. *Helena*, Hankow, to secretary of the navy, October 29, 1911, SD 893.00/738.

31. Sir John Jordan to Sir Edward Grey, December 14, 1911, correspondence respecting the affairs of China, FO 405, No. 499 (152).

32. Calhoun to secretary of state, November 21, 1911, SD 893.00/826.

33. Ibid.; circular from Calhoun to all American consular officers in China, November 17, 1911, ibid.; Knox to Taft, October 27, 1911, Knox Papers; Taft to Admiral Wainwright, October 27, 1911, Taft Papers.

34. Memorandum to secretary of the navy, November 15, 1911, Knox Papers, Correspondence relating to China, XIV, Vol. 2; *New York Times*, October 22, 1911, p. 2.

35. Secretary of the navy to Knox, September 9, 1911, SD 893.00/545; Memorandum to Division of Far Eastern Affairs from Knox, October 14, 1911, Knox Papers, Correspondence relating to China, XIV, Vol. 2.

36. Knox to Senate Foreign Relations Committee, November 16, 1911, Knox Papers.

37. Mary Wright, pp. 54–55.

38. *San Francisco Examiner*, October 14, 1911, p. 6.

39. Harold Z. Schiffrin, "The Enigma of Sun Yat-sen," in Mary Wright, p. 457.

40. Ibid., pp. 460–61.

41. Consul Roger Greene (Hankow) to Chargé Williams, October 14, 1911, SD 893.00/570; *Christian Science Monitor*, October 18, 1911, p. 4.

42. *Washington Post*, October 15, 1911, p. l; Emily Cheng, "United States Policy During the Chinese Revolution," p. 83.

43. *Washington Post*, October 17, 1911, p. 2.

44. *Atlanta Constitution*, October 14, 1911, p. 6.

45. *Washington Post*, October 15, 1911, p. 1.

46. *Washington Post*, October 16, 1911, p. 6.

47. *Boston Herald*, October 15, 1911, p. 5.

48. *Christian Science Monitor*, January 3, 1912, p. 7.

49. Main to Stuntz, October 21, 1911, Archives of the Methodist Episcopal Mission.

50. Charles Ewing, Report of the Tientsin Mission Station, May 1, 1911, to April 30, 1912, Papers of the American Board of Commissioners for Foreign Missions [hereafter ABCFM]; James and Jennie Curnow to John Goucher, April 30, 1913, Goucher Papers.

51. Bishop James Bashford, Diaries, Vol. 37, October 19, 1911, Vol. 38, January 21, 1912; Bashford to Stuntz, October 19, 1911, Archives, M. E. Mission; Lowry to Stuntz, December 8, 1911, ibid.; George Newell to headquarters, November 22, 1911, ABCFM.

52. A. B. DeHaan, Report of the General Work of Panchuang Station, Shantung, July 14, 1913, ABCFM; DeHaan (Panchuang) to Enoch Bell, January 23, 1912, ibid.; Porter to Barton, January 4, 1912, ibid.; William Steele to Barton, December 21, 1911, ibid.; Bashford to Stuntz, November 11, 1911, Archives, M. E. Mission; Eastman (Tianjing Mission) to Headquarters, December 31, 1911, ABCFM.

53. Frederick Brown (Tianjing) to Stuntz, December 14, 1911, Archives, M. E. Mission.

54. Bashford to Stuntz, December 22, 1911, Archives, M. E. Mission.

55. Bashford to Stuntz, November 11, 1911, Archives, M. E. Mission; "The Revolution in China—Looking Backward and Forward," *China Year Book*, 1913, pp. 86–87.

56. Report of Mrs. E. S. Hartwell, Women's Work, Fuzhou Mission, 1911, ABCFM; *Annual Report of the Foochow Mission, 1911*, ABCFM; Bashford to Lowry, January 8, 1912, Archives, M. E. Mission; C. A. Nelson, "Revolution in South China," November 9, 1911, ABCFM.

57. Calhoun to consular officers, November 17, 1911, Archives of the Presbyterian Foreign Missions.

58. Arthur Brown to headquarters, October 26, 1911, ibid.

59. Annual letter of the Foochow Mission, 1911, ABCFM.

60. Bashford to Stuntz, November 11, 23, 1911, Archives, M. E. Mission.

61. Mary Newell to Barton, November 13, 1911, Report of the Foochow Missionary Hospital, ABCFM; Henry Martin to Barton, November 19, 1911, ibid.

62. Consul Brown (Chongqing), October 31, 1911, FO 371/1098, quoted in Mary Wright, p. 19.

63. Calhoun to Knox, November 27, 1911, SD 893.00/699; Knox to Taft, October 17, 1911, Taft Papers.

64. Jordan to Grey, December 28, 1911, FO 405, No. 520 (2021); Grey to Bryce, January 23, 1912, FO 405, No. 101 (4497).

65. Fung, pp. 217–26.

66. Knox to Taft, October 13, 1911, Taft Papers; James Reeves to Office of Military Attaché, Peking, October 23, 1911, Knox Papers, Correspondence relating to China, XIV, vol. 2.

67. Herbert Croly, *Willard Straight*, p. 429.

68. Willard Straight to Charles Norton, October 26, 1911; Straight to H. P. Davison, October 28, November 12, 1911; Straight to Frank McKnight, December 22, 1911; Straight to Jacob Schiff, January 22, 1912, all in Straight Papers.

69. Straight to H. P. Davison, October 28, 1911, Straight Papers; Straight to Frank McKnight, December 22, 1911, ibid.

70. Morgan, Greenfell & Co. to J. P. Morgan & Co., January 3, 1912, Knox Papers, Correspondence relating to China; Straight to J. V. A. MacMurray, November 27, 1911, Straight Papers.

71. Willard Straight to J. V. A. MacMurray, November 27, 1911, Straight Papers.

72. Straight to H. P. Davison, December 18, 1911, ibid.

73. Addis to Langley (Hong Kong–Shanghai Bank), January 3, 1912, FO 405, No. 345 (642); C. MacDonald to Sir Edward Grey, December 8, 1911, FO 405, No. 1 (291); Viscount Uchida to MacDonald, enclosure #16, ibid.

74. Aide-mémoire of British government, November 20, 1911, Knox Papers, Correspondence relating to China; Jordan to Grey, December 21, 1911, FO 405, No. 508 (952).

75. Straight to George Bronson Rea, December 18, 1911, Straight Papers.

76. H. H. Harjes (Paris) to J. P. Morgan & Co., November 18, 1911, Knox Papers, Correspondence relating to China; Miller, Department of Far Eastern Affairs, to McKnight, November 6, 1911, ibid.; Huntington-Wilson to Bryce, December 11, 1911, ibid.

77. Straight to H. P. Davison, December 18, 1911, Straight Papers.

78. Personal letter from Chargé Williams to Knox, December 8, 1911, Knox Papers; Minister Bryan (Tokyo) to Knox, December 26, 1911, SD 893.00/943; Straight to George Bronson Rea, January 11, 1912, Straight Papers.

79. Calhoun to Knox, November 21, 1911, Knox Papers.

80. Williams to Knox, December 8, 1911, Knox Papers, Correspondence relating to China; Memorandum to secretary of the navy, November 15, 1911, ibid.; Acting Minister of Foreign Affairs Neratov to Straight, November 14, 1911, Straight Papers; Schuyler (Tokyo) to Knox, October 15, 1911, SD 893.00/566.

81. Leishman (Berlin) to Knox, January 25, 1912, SD 893.00/994; Secretary of the navy to Taft, January 28, 1912, Taft Papers.

82. Bishop Bashford to Woodrow Wilson, November 18, 1912, SD 893.00/634.

83. Greene to Calhoun, December 29, 1911, SD 893.00/1041; Murdock to secretary of the navy, November 27, 1911, SD 893.00/889; Consul-General A. P. Wilder (Shanghai) to Calhoun, December 2, 1911, SD 893.00/898.

84. James H. Reeves to Knox, October 23, 1911, Knox Papers, Correspondence relating to China; Calhoun to Knox, November 21, 1911, SD 893.00/825.

85. Calhoun to Knox, December 15, 1911, SD 893.00/773; Calhoun to Knox, December 11, 1911, SD 893.00/759.

86. Calhoun to Knox, December 6, 1911, SD 893.00/745; Wu Tingfang to Calhoun, December 12, 1911, SD 893.00/737.

87. John Stuart Thompson, "The Genesis of the Republican Revolution in China from a South China Standpoint," in George H. Blakeslee, ed., *Recent Developments in China*, p. 88.

88. Jordan to Grey, December 12, 1911, FO 405, No. 495 (148); Percy Horace Kent, *The Passing of the Manchus*, pp. 256–57.

89. Knox to Calhoun, December 16, 1911, SD 893.00/776; Anatol Kotenev, *New Lamps for Old: An Interpretation of Events in Modern China and Whither They Lead*, p. 59.

90. Ernest Young, "Yuan Shih-k'ai's Rise to the Presidency," in Mary Wright, p. 433.

91. Jerome Ch'en, *Yuan Shih-k'ai*, pp. 92–93.

92. Ernest Young, p. 85.

93. Knox to Calhoun, December 21, 1911, SD 893.00/812; Secretary of the navy to secretary of state, December 31, 1911, ibid.

94. *China Year Book*, 1913, pp. 471–72.

95. Ch'en, pp. 104–5.

96. *Washington Post*, February 12, 1912, p. 6.

97. Ernest Young, p. 81.

98. Ch'en, pp. 105–6, 123; Ernest Young, in Mary Wright, pp. 436–39.

99. *Washington Post*, February 13, 1912, p. 6; *Boston Globe*, February 13, 1912, p. 8; *Washington Post*, January 24, 1912, p. 6; *Boston Herald*, February 13, 1912, p. 7; *Washington Post*, February 12, 1912, p. 6.

100. Jordan to Grey, May 3, 1912, FO 371/1318; Calhoun to Knox, November 12, 1912, SD 893.00/1515; E. T. Williams to Knox, March 3, 1913, SD 893.00/1595.

101. Frederick Brown to Stuntz, November 14, 1911, Archives, M. E. Mission; Henry Martin to headquarters, March 7, 1912, ABCFM.

102. Lewis Hodous to James Barton, February 15, 1912, ABCFM.

103. James and Jennie Curnow to John Goucher, April 30, 1913, Goucher Papers.

104. Lewis to Stuntz, November 18, 1911, Archives, M. E. Mission; Report letter no. 13, Ing Hok Station, March 20, 1912, ABCFM; *Missionary Review of the World* (May 1915): 338; *Missionary Intelligencer* (1912): 34; Arthur J. Brown to North China Mission, November 9, 1911, Archives, Presbyterian Foreign Missions; Bashford to Stuntz, December 22, 1911, Archives of the M. E. Mission.

105. Report letter no. 13, Ing Hok Station, March 20, 1912, ABCFM.

106. James and Jennie Curnow to John Goucher, April 30, 1912, Goucher Papers; Fred Pyke (Tianjing) to Fowles, January 17, 1912, Archives, M. E. Mission; C. R. Hager, comments on Sun Yat-sen, [undated], ABCFM.

107. Lewis Hodous to Barton, May 8, 1912, ABCFM.

108. Bashford to Stuntz, November 11, 1911, Archives of the M. E. Mission.

109. Annual Report of the Fuzhou Mission, 1911–1912, ABCFM.

110. Irene Dornblasser (Women's Board, Fuzhou Mission) to headquarters, January 20, 1912, ABCFM; "The Dawning of Religious Liberty in the Chinese Republic," Lowry to Stuntz, February 26, 1912, Archives, M. E. Mission; Edward Smith, Report letter no. 12, Ing Hok Station, February 8, 1912, ABCFM.

111. H. H. Lowry to Stuntz, February 28, 1912, Archives, M. E. Mission; Henry Martin to headquarters, February 10, 1912, ibid.; Report of Evangelistic Work, Fenzhou Station, 1911–12, ibid.; Annual report letter, Fuzhou Mission,

for year ending December 31, 1912, ibid.; *Annual Report of the Board of Foreign Missions of the Methodist Episcopal Church for the Year 1912*, Archives of the M. E. Mission; Brewer Eddy to Barton, June 14, 1912, ABCFM.

112. Bashford to Stuntz, December 22, 1911, Archives, M. E. Mission.

113. Headquarters to Bashford, January 6, 1912, ibid.

114. Brewer Eddy to Barton, June 14, 1912, ABCFM.

CHAPTER 3

1. Willard Straight, "China's Loan Negotiations," November 14, 1912, p. 16, Straight Papers; Paul Varg, *The Making of a Myth*, p. 94; Calhoun to Knox, February 23, 1911, SD 793.00/3; Huntington-Wilson to Elbert F. Baldwin, January 19, 1910, Reid Papers. The Tianjing-Pukou Loan Agreement, according to Straight, "marked the first recognition by the banks of the increasing efficiency of the 'Young China' party . . . [which] demanded the radical modification of the old loan terms. They considered 'control' subversive of China's sovereign rights. . . . The avowed purpose of these officials to weaken the hold of the foreigners on China was heartily applauded throughout the provinces. It served as a patriotic issue on which an appeal could be made to the masses and a cloak under which the provincial gentry could cover their real purpose, which was to restrict the extension of the Peking government's authority by railways built with foreign loans." See also Blakeslee, *Recent Developments in China*, p. 132.

2. Wu Tingfang to U.S. government, December 9, 1911, SD 893.51/737.

3. Aide-mémoire of British government to Secretary Knox, October 24, 1911, SD 893.51/632; J. P. Morgan & Co. to Willard Straight, November 1, 1911, SD 893.51/644.

4. Knox to J. P. Morgan & Co., November 18, 1911, SD 893.51/659.

5. Minutes of meeting of French, British, American, and German groups at office of Banque de l'Indo Chine, Paris, November 11, 1911, SD 893.51/670. Both the Currency and Huguang Loan agreements contained strict provisions for foreign control. Among the control provisions of the Huguang Loan were (1) specification of the purposes of the loan; (2) administration of provincial taxes by the Imperial Maritime Customs Service, if necessary; (3) placement of proceeds of the loan in foreign banks; (4) transfer of funds from foreign banks to Chinese banks in regular installments not to exceed £200,000 pounds in any one week; (5) submission of quarterly statements to the group regarding funds on deposit in Chinese banks; (6) statement of purpose of requisitions for funds to be submitted two days in advance, to permit corroboration; (7) opening of all accounts and vouchers to inspection at any time by two auditors appointed and paid by the foreign banks "whose duties it will be to satisfy the bankers as to the due expenditures of loan funds and to certify the monthly statements of the materials purchased"; and (8) appointment of a foreign engineer-in-chief.

With respect to the Currency Loan agreement, the following control conditions applied: (1) statement of purpose of loan and of revenue pledged as security; (2) detailed statement setting forth a program of currency reform, amounts to be applied to the operation of the program and nature of the proposed enterprises in Manchuria and amounts allotted thereto; (3) deposit of proceeds of the loan in foreign banks and transfer to specified foreign banks in amounts not to exceed £300,000 in any one week; (4) segregation of loan funds into special accounts; (5) signing of requisitions by the Board of Finance and handing to the foreign banks three days in advance; and (6) submission of quarterly statements to the banks showing disbursements on account of currency reform and Manchurian industry.

In addition to these requirements, the U.S. government insisted that the Chinese government employ an American financial adviser or monetary expert "empowered to countersign and certify to the accuracy of the quarterly and annual reports . . . and likewise to sign the requisitions for money for specific purposes." Although America's British, French, and German partners refused to go along with the U.S. desire to make the appointment of a foreign financial adviser a condition of the loan, in the face of strong Chinese opposition to the requirement, the attitude of the U.S. government displayed in this episode foreshadowed the approach it would take with respect to supervision of loan expenditures in the Reorganization Loan negotiations conducted with the new Chinese Republic. See "Provisions of Control for Chinese Loans and Note of the United States Government to the Governments of Great Britain, France, and Germany," February 9, 1911, SD 893.51/845 1/2.

6. Calhoun to Knox, November 25, 1911, SD 893.51/666; Calhoun to Knox, January 20, 1912, SD 893.51/766; Chinese Foreign Office to Knox, November 16, 1911, ibid.

7. Memorandum by dean of diplomatic corps, November 21, 1911, SD 893.51/766; Memorandum by inspector general of customs, November 22, 1911, ibid.; Meeting of managers of certain foreign banks, November 27, 1911, SD 893.51/767; Jordan to Langley, July 13, 1912, Jordan Papers, FO 350/8; Stanley F. Wright, *The Collection and Disposal of the Maritime and Native Customs Revenue since the Revolution of 1911*, pp. 1–9; Anatol Kotenev, *Shanghai: Its Mixed Court and Council*, pp. 169–78; Westel W. Willoughby, *Foreign Rights and Interests in China*, pp. 526–36; Mark Elvin, "The Mixed Court of the International Settlement at Shanghai," *Papers on China*, 17: 139–48; Ernest Young, pp. 43–47.

8. Calhoun to Knox, November 29, 1911, SD 893.51/730.

9. Straight to H. P. Davison, October 28, 1911, Straight Papers; Straight to J. P. Morgan & Co., November 18, 1911, ibid.

10. Straight to J. P. Morgan & Co., December 4, 1911, SD 893.51/729; Calhoun to Knox, December 16, 1911, SD 893.51/703a; J. P. Morgan & Co. to Morgan, Greenfell & Co., December 6, 1911, SD 893.51/678.

11. Minutes of meeting of four groups, Paris, November 11, 1911, SD 893.51/670; J. P. Morgan & Co. to Morgan, Greenfell & Co., December 6, 1911, SD 893.51/678; Knox to J. P. Morgan & Co., December 6, 1911, SD 893.51/686; Grey to Knox, December 8, 1911, SD 893.51/698; C. S. Addis (Hong Kong–Shanghai Banking Corp.) to E. C. Greenfell, December 7, 1911, ibid.

12. Knox to Calhoun, December 12, 1911, SD 893.51/692a; Consulate (Hong Kong) to Knox, December 11, 1911, SD 893.51/703.

13. Straight to J. P. Morgan & Co., December 6, 1911, SD 893.51/681; J. P. Morgan & Co. to Straight, ibid.

14. E. C. Greenfell to J. P. Morgan & Co., February 16, 1912, SD 893.51/767; Huntington-Wilson to J. P. Morgan & Co., February 19, 1912, ibid.

15. Morgan, Greenfell & Co. to J. P. Morgan & Co., February 23, 1912, SD 893.51/763; Straight to J. P. Morgan & Co., January 18, 1912, ibid.

16. J. P. Morgan & Co. to Morgan, Greenfell & Co., March 4, 5, 1912, SD 893.51/791.

17. J. P. Morgan & Co. to Morgan, Greenfell & Co., February 23, 1912, SD 893.51/777; Straight to J. P. Morgan & Co., January 18, 1912, SD 893.51/763;

Straight to J. P. Morgan & Co., January 9, 1912, Straight Papers. According to one contemporary observer, Lord ffrench, Great Britain would never offend either Russia or Japan: "As far as Great Britain is concerned, her attitude in the Far East is completely subordinated to European politics. . . . It is an essential factor of both French and British policy to keep Russia in sympathy with them. . . . Russia is really the dominating factor at present in European politics. . . . The result of all this is that there is not the slightest chance of any united action in the Far East having as its object the curtailment of Russian aspirations. I cannot see that any combinations in finance in the Far East are for a very long time going to carry their governments with them to the extent of defying either Russia or Japan, or both." ffrench to Straight, February 17, 1911, SD 893.77/1116.

18. Minister Reid (London) to Knox, October 23, 1911, SD 893.51/641.

19. Ibid.; Calhoun to Knox, December 5, 1911, SD 893.51/679.

20. Straight to J. P. Morgan & Co., January 9, 1912, SD 893.51/756.

21. Calhoun to Knox, February 23, 1912, SD 893.51/772; Langley to Jordan, February 29, 1912, Jordan Papers, FO 350/1.

22. Michael Hunt, *Frontier Defense*; Huntington-Wilson to Calhoun, February 24, 1912, SD 893.51/772; Leishman (Berlin) to Knox, February 25, 1912, SD 893.51/773; Bryce to Grey, March 25, 1912, FO 405/489. The State Department claimed that "[t]he utility of the principle of cooperation has been considerably enhanced by the admission of Russia and Japan into the concert of banks. The danger in the past has always been that the two countries realizing their financial inferiority to the Western nations should seek expression instead of military superiority." Now, the State Department declared, whether it came to military intervention or administrative supervision, the United States would have an equal voice with the other powers. Lewis Einstein, "The Chinese Revolution and American Policy" [undated], Knox Papers.

23. J. P. Morgan & Co. to Morgan, Greenfell & Co., February 26, 1912, SD 893.51/777; J. P. Morgan & Co. to Morgan, Greenfell & Co. February 20, 1912, SD 893.51/778; Morgan, Greenfell & Co. to J. P. Morgan & Co., February 26, 1912, ibid.

24. W. G. M. Mueller memorandum, February 26, 1912, FO 371/313; Grey to Jordan, September 19, 1912, FO 371/322; Jordan to Langley, May 21, 1912, Jordan Papers, FO 350/8.

25. Bryce to Huntington-Wilson, February 26, 1912, SD 893.51/774.

26. Huntington-Wilson to Calhoun, February 24, 1912, SD 893.51/772; Straight to J. P. Morgan & Co., March 8, 1912, SD 893.51/828; Straight to J. P. Morgan & Co., February 29, 1912, SD 893.51/784.

27. Huntington-Wilson to Calhoun, February 29, 1912, SD 893.51/790.

28. British memorandum on purpose of Reorganization Loan, SD 893.51/928.

29. Knox to German ambassador, February 3, 1912, SD 893.51/845; Huntington-Wilson to Bryce, March 16, 1912, SD 893.51/799.

30. Huntington-Wilson to J. P. Morgan & Co., April 1, 1912, SD 893.51/822.

31. Ibid.; J. P. Morgan & Co. to Morgan, Greenfell & Co., April 23, 1912, SD 893.51/834; Morgan, Greenfell & Co. to J. P. Morgan & Co., April 11, 1912, SD 893.51/840; F. M. McKnight to J. P. Morgan & Co., April 28, 1912, SD 893.51/865; Jordan to Mueller, June 17, 1912, Jordan Papers, FO 350/8. McKnight's rather belligerent recommendations for dealing with the Chinese typified his approach to the loan negotiations. As Jordan observed some time

later, "McKnight . . . is simply an impossible personality. He opposes everything and everybody. It is a refreshing spectacle to those of us who, two or three years ago, were roundly abused by the Americans for 'crabbing' the Chinese and were told that the American object in forcing entrance into the groups was to see that China got fair play. McKnight now whips them with scorpions." Jordon to Langley, October 3, 1912, Jordan Papers, FO 350/8.

32. Yuan Shikai to E. C. Hillier (Hong Kong–Shanghai Bank), March 9, 1912, SD 893.51/839. Whether Yuan gave the group an absolute option for the Reorganization Loan, regardless of how its terms compared with competing offers, is unclear. However, the consortium clearly felt that it had received such an absolute option. Group to Yuan Shikai, March 7, 1912, FO 405/470.

33. Morgan, Greenfell & Co. to J. P. Morgan & Co., March 10, 1912, SD 893.51/804.

34. W. G. M. Mueller, minutes included in Jordan to Grey, March 25, 1912, FO 371/1316.

35. Huntington-Wilson to Calhoun, March 18, 1912, SD 893.51/807a. American and British protests against the Belgian loan were delivered to Yuan in the form of a joint communiqué endorsed by the governments of the quadruple group. Although Calhoun was charged by his fellow ministers with the task of drafting the communiqué, according to Jordan, Calhoun's version was "so strong that we have been obliged to tone it down considerably." Jordan to Langley, March 25, 1912, Jordan Papers, FO 350/8.

36. Consul Gracey to Calhoun, March 26, 1912, SD 893.51/866.

37. Calhoun to Knox, March 29, 1912, SD 893.51/850; Gracey to Calhoun, March 26, 1912, SD 893.51/867; Calhoun to Knox, April 19, 1912, SD 893.51/881.

38. Straight to J. P. Morgan & Co., April 17, 1912, SD 893.51/871; Calhoun to Knox, April 19, 1912, SD 893.51/881; Morgan, Greenfell & Co. to J. P. Morgan & Co., March 13, 1912, SD 893.51/809; Calhoun to Knox, March 29, 1912, SD 893.51/843.

39. Knox to J. P. Morgan & Co., May 20, 1912, Knox Papers, Correspondence Relating to China.

40. Proposed loan contract for Reorganization Loan, SD 893.51/910.

41. Calhoun to Knox, June 12, 1912, SD 893.51/981; Herrick to Knox, June 21, 1912, SD 893.51/960.

42. Reid to Knox, June 13, 1912, SD 893.51/966; Knox to Herrick, June 19, 1912, SD 893.51/956.

CHAPTER 4

1. Calhoun to Knox, March 29, 1912, SD 893.51/850; E. T. Williams, Memorandum regarding Tang Shaoyi's address to the National Assembly on financial matters, SD 893.51/878.

2. Williams memo.

3. Tenney to Calhoun, February 8, 1912, SD 893.00/1187.

4. Calhoun to Knox, March 1, 1912, SD 893.00/1120.

5. Murdock to secretary of the navy, April 9, 1912, SD 893.00/1237; Consul Knabenshue to Calhoun, March 5, 1912, SD 893.00/1240; Calhoun to Yuan Shikai, March 4, 1912, SD 893.00/1226; Calhoun to Knox, March 6, 1912, SD 893.00/1146.

6. McNally to Knox, March 1, 1912, SD 893.00/1230.

7. McNally to Knox, June 17, 1912, SD 893.00/1377.

8. Calhoun to Knox, June 4, 1912, SD 893.00/1352; Calhoun to Knox, May 7, 1912, SD 893.00/1304.

9. McNally to Knox, March 28, 1912, SD 893.00/1286.

10. McNally to Knox, June 29, 1912, SD 893.00/1392.

11. Murdock to secretary of the navy, June 22, 1912, SD 893.00/1383.

12. Calhoun to Knox, June 25, 1912, SD 893.00/1376.

13. Calhoun memorandum contained in Herrick to Knox, July 31, 1912, SD 893.00/1403.

14. Calhoun to Knox, January 16, 1912, SD 893.00/1338.

15. Calhoun to Knox, June 2, 1912, ibid.

16. Ernest Young, *The Presidency of Yuan Shih-K'ai*, pp. 47–48, quoting Charles W. Eliot to Tang Shaoyi, May 1, 1912.

17. F. M. McKnight to J. P. Morgan & Co., April 28, 1912, SD 893.51/865; Calhoun to Knox, March 29, 1912, SD 893.51/850; Group representatives to groups, April 25, 1912, FO 405/553. The *Peking and Tientsin Times*, on May 6, 1912, summed up the reasons for control and supervision of China's finances: "The Chinese Republic has yet to convince foreign governments and financiers that it is capable of building up a stable, strong, and efficient administration. It is still in the experimental stage, and many months, if not years, must elapse before it can expect Western nations to believe that a Republic is suited to China, and that it will prove more efficient and stable than the Manchu regime. So long as there is uncertainty as to the outcome of the experiment it will be impossible to float foreign loans sufficient for China's needs, without adequate supervision over their expenditure, and the securities that are given for them."

18. Morgan, Greenfell & Co. to J. P. Morgan & Co., April 25, 1912, SD 893.51/860.5; Lewis Einstein, "The Chinese Revolution and American Policy" [undated], Knox Papers.

19. Calhoun to Knox, March 30, 1912, SD 893.51/825.

20. Knox to British Chargé Mitchell Innes, July 2, 1912, SD 893.51/977; Knox memorandum, May 18, 1912, SD 893.51/898D; Grey to Jordan, September 19, 1912, FO 371/1322.

21. Morgan, Greenfell & Co. to J. P. Morgan & Co., March 12, 1912, SD 893.51/797.

22. E. C. Greenfell to J. P. Morgan & Co., March 12, 1912, ibid. It is a well-established principle of law that to establish a binding contractual commitment, both parties to the agreement must be bound to its terms. The insertion of such an unlimited force majeure clause by the bankers violated this basic principle. Thus, despite subsequent claims by the bankers that the Chinese were contractually bound to refrain from negotiating loans from groups other than the consortium, it is clear that under elementary principles of contract law, no legally binding commitment was established at the time the first installment of the Reorganization Loan was negotiated. Hence, the protests of the bankers over Yuan's negotiations with the Belgian syndicate, for example, should be dismissed as mere posturing and not accepted as the expression of legitimate legal grievances.

23. H. P. Davison to J. P. Morgan & Co., May 15, 1912, SD 893.51/889.

24. Morgan, Greenfell & Co. to J. P. Morgan & Co., May 16, 1912, ibid.; Jordan to Grey, May 18, 1912, FO 371/1319; Calhoun to Knox, May 7, 1912, SD 893.51/918.

25. Calhoun to Knox, May 10, 1912, SD 893.51/877.

26. Minutes, meeting of Tang Shaoyi, Alfred Sze[Shi Zhaoji] and consortium representatives, May 2, 1912, SD 893.51/916; *Peking and Tientsin Times*, May 6, 1912.

27. Calhoun to Knox, June 10, 1912, SD 893.51/930; McKnight to J. P. Morgan & Co., May 29, 1912, SD 893.51/979.

28. McKnight to Morgan, ibid.; Calhoun to Knox, June 12, 1912, SD 893.51/981; Huang Xing to Yuan Shikai, ibid.; Kent to Calhoun, June 5, 1912, SD 893.51/985.

29. Consortium to Xiong Xiling, June 28, 1912, SD 893.51/1020; Jordan to Langley, September 21, 1912, Jordan Papers, FO 350/8.

30. Calhoun to Knox, July 2, 1912, SD 891.53/989; Jordan to Calhoun, July 2, 1912, SD 893.51/1015.

31. Calhoun to Knox and Jordan to Calhoun, ibid.; Calhoun to secretary of state, July 2, 1912, SD 893.51/1015.

32. Calhoun to Knox, July 9, 1912, SD 893.51/989; Calhoun to Knox, July 10, 1912, SD 893.51/997.

33. Reid to Knox, July 12, 1912, SD 893.51/999; Morgan, Greenfell & Co. to J. P. Morgan & Co., June 29, 1912, SD 893.51/982; Jordan to W. G. M. Mueller, June 17, 1912, Jordan Papers, FO 350/8.

34. McKnight to J. P. Morgan & Co., June 29, 1912, SD 893.51/982; McKnight to J. P. Morgan & Co., July 5, 1912, SD 893.51/1022.

35. Calhoun to Knox, July 15, 1912, SD 893.51/1028; Calhoun to Knox, August 10, 1912, SD 893.51/1032.

36. S. A. M. Adshead, *The Modernization of the Chinese Salt Administration, 1900–1920*, p. 204.

37. Calhoun to Knox, July 15, 1912, SD 893.51/1028.

38. Unlike Sun and his followers, Yuan was thought to have "more native ability, more experience in public affairs, more personality, and consequently more influence, than any other man who has so far appeared on the stage." As Yuan alone offered any hope of preventing anarchy, the United States felt that he should be supported at all costs, even if it meant the establishment of a military dictatorship at the expense of democracy in China. Yuan also stood between the nationalists, who wished to put China in "a position to resist the foreigners," and their achievement of political power through the National Assembly. Thus, when Yuan executed two prominent political opponents, Calhoun commented that "[w]hile the execution is regretted and on legal grounds cannot be justified . . . the situation requires some such summary measures in the interest of public peace and order." Calhoun to Knox, November 12, 1912, SD 893.00/1505; Murdock to secretary of the navy, July 19, 1912, SD 893.00/1428; J. P. Morgan & Co. to McKnight, August 13, 1912, SD 893.00/1440; Calhoun to Knox, August 31, 1912, SD 893.00/1455; Tenney (Nanjing) to Calhoun, February 10, 1912, SD 893.00/1555.

39. Calhoun to Knox, July 23, 1912, SD 893.51/1034.

40. Ibid.

41. Personal note from Zhao Bingzhun to Ogadiri, September 20, 1912, SD 893.51/1111.

42. Memorandum of the consortium, September 25, 1912, ibid.

43. Memorandum from minister of finance to the six groups, September 26, 1912, ibid.

44. Morgan, Greenfell & Co. to J. P. Morgan & Co., December 19, 1912, SD 893.51/1199.

45. *National Review* (Shanghai), August 24 and September 14, 1912; Stanley F. Wright, *China's Struggle for Tariff Autonomy: 1843–1938*, pp. 424–25.

46. Assistant Secretary Frederick Field, American Council, Institute of Pacific Relations, viewed the consortium as a last-ditch effort to salvage the Open Door and "the indispensable means of furthering the objectives of foreign interests with[in] China." Field endorsed the opinion of Stanley K. Hornbeck, State Department China expert, that "undoubtedly, the six banking groups contemplated as a unit monopolizing the business of furnishing money to China. With their Governments behind them they expected to exclude loans from independent sources." Such a financial monopoly was, in Field's opinion, absolutely necessary to stop "unbridled borrowing" that threatened China's sovereignty. Frederick Field, *American Participation in the China Consortium*, pp. 1, 42 (quoting Stanley K. Hornbeck, *Contemporary Politics in the Far East*, p. 393), and p. 189.

47. Confidential memorandum of Japanese government to Great Britain, October 16, 1912, SD 893.51/1155.

CHAPTER 5

1. Calhoun to Knox, September 11, 1912, SD 893.51/1051; Reid to Knox, September 14, 1912, SD 893.51/1053; Morgan, Greenfell & Co. to J. P. Morgan & Co., September 12, 1912, SD 893.51/1055; Ernest Young, pp. 125–26.

2. Morgan, Greenfell & Co. to J. P. Morgan & Co., September 12, 1912, SD 893.51/1055; State Department to J. P. Morgan & Co., September 12, 1912, ibid.

3. Calhoun to Knox, September 25, 1912, SD 893.51/1070; Huntington-Wilson to Calhoun, September 25, 1912, ibid.

4. J. P. Morgan & Co. to Morgan, Greenfell & Co., September 23, 1912, SD 893.51/1073; McKnight to J. P. Morgan & Co., September 5, 1912, SD 893.51/1086.

5. Morgan, Greenfell & Co. to J. P. Morgan & Co., September 24, 1912, SD 893.51/1073.

6. McKnight to J. P. Morgan & Co., September 5, 1912, SD 893.51/1085; Knox to Straight, September 26, 1912, SD 893.51/1075.

7. Morgan, Greenfell & Co. to J. P. Morgan & Co., September 26, 1912, SD 893.51/1078.

8. British Embassy to Huntington-Wilson, October 1, 1912, SD 893.51/1083.

9. Huntington-Wilson to British Ambassador James Bryce, October 4, 1912, ibid.

10. Ibid.

11. Huntington-Wilson to Taft, October 5, 1912, Taft Papers.

12. U.S. ambassador (Berlin) to Knox, September 21, 1912, SD 893.51/1087; U.S. ambassador (Berlin) to Knox, September 30, 1912, SD 893.51/1099.

13. London *Times*, September 19, 1912, p. 5; Consortium to Minister of Finance Zhou Xueshi, October 3, 1912, SD 893.51/1163; Calhoun to Knox, October 1, 1912, SD 893.51/1115.

14. Calhoun to Knox, October 1, 1912, SD 893.51/1115.

15. Ibid.

16. Phillips to Knox, October 8, 1912, SD 893.51/1095.

17. Calhoun to Knox, October 24, 1912, SD 893.51/1118.

18. Morgan, Greenfell & Co. to J. P. Morgan & Co., October 8, 1912, SD 893.51/1119.

19. McKnight to J. P. Morgan & Co., October 24, 1912, SD 893.51/1120.

20. State Department to American group, October 28, 1912, SD 893.51/1123; J. P. Morgan & Co. to Morgan, Greenfell & Co., November 4, 1912, SD 893.51/1131.

21. Calhoun to Knox, October 22, 1912, SD 893.51/1156; Calhoun to Knox, October 29, 1912, SD 893.51/1159.

22. McKnight to J. P. Morgan & Co., November 20, 1912, SD 893.51/1170.

23. Group to Zhou Xueshi, October 3, 1912, SD 893.51/1163; Calhoun to Knox, November 5, 1912, SD 893.51/1170; Williams to Knox, November 29, 1912, SD 893.51/1171.

24. McKnight to J. P. Morgan & Co., November 5, 1912, SD 893.51/1175.

25. McKnight to J. P. Morgan & Co., December 9, 1912, SD 893.51/1188; Morgan, Greenfell & Co. to J. P. Morgan & Co., December 12, 1912, SD 893.51/1191; J. P. Morgan & Co. to Morgan, Greenfell & Co., ibid.

26. Report on conference of group members, December 13, 1912, SD 893.51/1195; J. P. Morgan & Co. to Morgan, Greenfell & Co., December 31, 1912, SD 893.51/1208; Knox to Straight, December 11, 1912, Straight Papers; J. P. Morgan & Co. to Morgan, Greenfell & Co., December 26, 1912, SD 893.51/1203.

27. Morgan, Greenfell & Co. to J. P. Morgan & Co., December 11, 1912, SD 893.51/1221.

28. Knox to American group, January 2, 1913, SD 893.51/1203; Straight to Knox, January 16, 1913, SD 893.51/1240.

29. Calhoun to Knox, January 23, 1913, SD 893.51/1253; J. P. Morgan & Co. to McKnight, January 25, 1913, SD 893.51/1261; McKnight to J. P. Morgan & Co., April 19, 1913, SD 893.51/1417.

30. Calhoun to Knox, January 22, 1913, SD 893.51/1254.

31. Calhoun to Knox, January 29, 1913, SD 893.51/1264.

32. Morgan, Greenfell & Co. to J. P. Morgan & Co., January 28, 1913, SD 893.51/1265.

33. Calhoun to Knox, February 4, 1913, SD 893.51/1274.

34. Calhoun to Knox, February 9, 1913, SD 893.51/1282; McKnight to J. P. Morgan & Co., February 15, 1913, SD 893.51/1302.

35. Leishman to Knox, February 12, 1913, SD 893.51/1294; Knox to E. T. Williams, February 27, 1913, Knox Papers, Correspondence relating to China; Calhoun to Knox, February 25, 1913, SD 893.51/1358.

36. Foreign Office to Hong Kong–Shanghai Bank, April 10, 1913, and enclosure no. 1 in C. Addis to Foreign Office, April 16, 1916, FO 405/211; Ernest Young, pp. 124–25.

37. Huntington-Wilson to Taft, October 5, 1912, SD 893.51/1083; J. P. Morgan & Co. to Morgan, Greenfell & Co., February 14, 1913, SD 893.51/1307; R. S. Miller, memorandum, February 21, 1913, SD 893.51/1341; Straight to McKnight, November 22, 1912, Straight Papers; Knox to H. P. Davison, February 20, 1913, SD 893.51/1342; Knox to American group, February 26, 1913, SD 893.51/1317; Straight to Knox, February 27, 1913, SD 893.51/1325; Knox to E. T. Williams, FRUS, 1913, pp. 166–67; Addis to Foreign Office, January 13, 1913, FO 405/47.

38. Bryce to Grey, April 1, 1913, FO 405/398; Bryce to Grey, March 24,

1913, FO 405/359. According to Bryce, the Japanese minister to the United States felt that the United States might "use the isolation they have now obtained for the purpose of endeavoring to obtain special advantages for themselves and generally posing as the true and only friend of China." Bryce was not alarmed by this possibility, however. "It is quite likely that they may assume the attitude of disinterested friendship and endeavor to obtain credit for it, but I hardly think that they will use that credit for the purpose of pressing for concessions or other advantages for their own citizens, for it is rather their desire to appear as being entirely detached from what in this country are called the 'interests,' which were supposed to have enjoyed too much influence with the late administration."

39. Wilson proved true to his word as he vigorously promoted American economic enterprise in China throughout his presidency. Paul Reinsch, the new minister to China, was particularly active in this regard. Reinsch favored "any development of enterprise which increases American commercial interests in China, . . . [t]he organization of an American investment bank, . . . participation of American capital in railway building, and the development of mines and oil fields through American companies and under American business methods." Commenting on the concession obtained by the Standard Oil Company in Shaanxi province, Jordan noted that the venture "is of the mercenary type of exploitation from which American policy has studiously held aloof in recent years. Dr. Reinsch has undoubtedly played a considerable part in inaugurating this movement." Ironically, the Standard Oil agreement provided that "no concessions whatever for petroleum-bearing properties in China [shall] be given to other foreigners." Apparently, the principle of monopoly, of which the Taft administration was so fond, also appealed to the Wilson administration. As the *North China Daily News* reported, "It is rather surprising to see a Democratic President in the same field with the Standard Oil Co. but when American businessmen decide to participate generously in anything, they do not do it by halves." See Jordan to Grey, April 14, 1914, FO 220/115; Jordan to Grey, February 15, 1914, FO 216/69; *North China Daily News*, April 2, 1913; Reinsch to Bryan, July 3, 1914, SD 893.51/2152.

40. Straight to Bryan, March 5, 1913, FRUS, 1913, pp. 167–68; Straight to Bryan, March 7, 1913, SD 893.51/1337; Bryan to Straight, March 8, 1913, ibid.; Straight to Bryan, March 8, 1913, SD 893.51/1338; *New York Times*, March 11, 1913, p. 4; Straight to McKnight, March 14, 1913, Straight Papers; William Jennings Bryan, *Memoirs*, pp. 362–63; Wilson statement on U.S. participation in consortium, March 18, 1913, FRUS, 1913, pp. 170–71; American group to Bryan, March 19, 1913, ibid., pp. 171–72; Bryan to ministers of Great Britain, Germany, France, Japan, and Russia, April 1, 1913, ibid., pp. 177–78; *New York Times*, March 20, 1913, p. 2; Straight to Bryan, June 27, 1913, SD 893.51/1445.

41. Huntington-Wilson, *Memoirs of an Ex-Diplomat*, chapter 34; Huntington-Wilson to President Wilson, March 19, 1913, Wilson Papers; Kahn, p. 444; *New York Times*, March 19, 1913, p. 1; Croly, p. 453; Straight to Bland, March 25, 1913, Straight Papers; Knox to John A. Sleicher, March 21, 1913, Knox Papers; *New York Times*, March 23, 1913, p. 2; "The Effect of the Chinese Loan Veto," *Literary Digest* 46 (April 6, 1913): 758; "Rescuing China from the Cross of Gold," ibid., p. 692; *Wall Street Journal*, March 21, 1913, p. 1; Bashford to Bryan, October 13, 1913, SD 711.93/36; Miscellaneous messages to the president included in SD 893.51/1356; Consul General Thomas Sammons (Yokohama) to Franklin K. Lane, March 23, 1913, Wilson Papers; Adee to Wilson,

March 24, 1913, ibid.; *New York Times*, March 20, 1913, p. 1; Adee to Wilson, March 20, 1913, SD 893.51/1355; Consul General Wilder (Shanghai) to Bryan, March 24, 1913, SD 893.51/1392; FRUS, 1913, p. 175.

    42. Kahn, p. 438.

CHAPTER 6

    1. Thomas Jefferson was the first American statesman to lay down basic guidelines of American recognition policy. In 1792, Jefferson declared that the United States would "acknowledge any government to be rightful which is formed by the will of the nation, substantially declared." Jefferson's dictum was taken to indicate a de facto approach to recognition, which left open the possibility of a moral component in the formulation of American policy. John Quincy Adams, during his tenure as secretary of state, abandoned the moral option in diplomatic recognition. As Adams said, American recognition policy would not be dictated by morality but by an "acknowledgment of existing facts." Following Adams's amoral formula, the United States, through the early part of the nineteenth century, adhered to a strictly de facto approach to the problem of recognition: If a new government was firmly established, it deserved diplomatic recognition. Jefferson's dictum regarding the "will of the nation, substantially declared" was a decidedly secondary consideration. The Civil War forced the American Department of State to reassess Adams's de facto approach and to adopt a more self-interested approach to the problem of recognition. Secretary of State William H. Seward argued that constitutional legitimacy was the key factor in the matter of recognition, that it was the foremost test of a regime's domestic permanence and stability and that, in its absence, foreign nations should not extend diplomatic recognition. Seward's reformulation of American recognition policy gave the United States the flexibility to use recognition as a diplomatic device to be employed as an adjunct to the nation's foreign policy. Paul Leicester Ford, ed., "The Writings of Thomas Jefferson," in Graebner, *Ideas and Diplomacy*, p. 54; "Memoirs of John Quincy Adams," ibid., pp. 130–31; George Baker, ed., "The Works of William H. Seward," ibid., pp. 298–301; Ti Chiang Chen, *The International Law of Recognition*, p. 271.

    2. Roger Greene to Knox, November 22, 1911, SD 893.00/894.

    3. Knox to John Fowler, January 26, 1912, SD 893.00/969.

    4. Wu Tingfang to secretary of state, January 8, 1912, SD 893.00/1065.

    5. Alvey A. Adee to secretary of state, May 16, 1913, SD 893.00/1669; Knox to John Fowler, January 26, 1912, SD 893.00/969; Knox to German embassy, February 6, 1912, SD 893.00/l029.

    6. Meribeth Cameron, "American Recognition Policy Toward the Republic of China," p. 214.

    7. Japanese embassy to secretary of state, February 27, 1912, SD 893.00/1105; Secretary of state to Japanese Embassy, March 1, 1912, SD 893.00/1114; Cameron, p. 215.

    8. "Recognition of the Chinese Republic," *Independent* 72 (January 25, 1912):209.

    9. A. E. Lafferty to Knox, February 21, 1912, SD 893.00/1097.

    10. Huntington-Wilson to Taft, February 26, 1912, SD 893.00/1108.

    11. *Washington Post*, April 1, 1913, p. 6.

    12. J. W. Hammer to Taft, July 19, 1912, SD 893.00/1378.

    13. L. Oppenheim, *International Law: A Treatise*, p. 124; H. Lauterpacht,

Recognition in International Law, pp. 92, 109; Charles Hyde, *International Law Chiefly as Interpreted and Applied by the United States*, p. 664.

14. Huntington-Wilson to *Outlook Magazine*, October 10, 1912, SD 893.00/1468.

15. FRUS, 1912, pp. 61–62; American consul (Qingdao) to Knox, August 1, 1912, SD 893.00/1392.

16. Memorandum on recognition of "Republican Government of China," February 4, 1913, SD 893.00/1529.

17. *New York Times*, January 4, 1913, p. 8.

18. George Anderson to Knox, January 11, 1912, SD 893.00/1066.

19. Calhoun to Knox, August 3, 1912, SD 893.00/1447; Bashford and Lewis to Knox, September 16, 1912, SD 893.00/1464.

20. Greene to Knox, August 10, 1912, SD 893.00/1422.

21. Calhoun to Knox, August 3, 1912, SD 893.00/1444.

22. "The Chinese Republic: Financial Influences," *Outlook* 102 (November 30, 1912):13; Sulzer to Knox, January 13, 1913, SD 893.00/1787.

23. John Foster to Arthur Brown, February 10, 1913, SD 893.00/1788.

24. Calhoun to Knox, March 29, 1912, SD 893.00/1282.

25. FRUS, 1913, pp. 73–74; Jordan to Grey, April 12, 1912, FO 405/516.

26. The ever-present Willard Straight outlined the pragmatic rationale for a policy of international cooperation: "If in this country we should attempt to finance the reorganization of the Chinese administration and to furnish funds for China's industrial development we would find ourselves in the jealous regard of the other Powers, the object of their political, if not their armed opposition. We could not therefore undertake this task unless we were prepared to uphold China with our active military support." Willard Straight to Arthur Brown, February 18, 1913, SD 893.00/1447.

27. Cameron, p. 224.

28. Japanese embassy to Knox, February 27, 1912, SD 893.00/1105; Minister Bryan (Tokyo) to Knox, April 19, 1912, SD 893.00/1318.

29. Calhoun to Knox, September 3, 1912, SD 893.00/1438; Huntington-Wilson to Calhoun, September 4, 1912, ibid.; Calhoun to Knox, February 21, 1913, SD 893.00/1453; Arthur Brown to secretary of state, February 18, 1913, SD 893.00/1441.

30. American memorandum to the powers, July 20, 1912, SD 893.00/1303.

31. French embassy to secretary of state, August 31, 1912, SD 893.00/1379.

32. E. T. Williams to secretary of state, April 1, 1913, SD 893.00/1628; Williams to secretary of state, March 18, 1913, SD 893.00/1607; Lu Zhengxiang to secretary of state, March 25, 1913, SD 893.00/1571; State Department to all powers having treaty relations with China, April 2, 1913, SD 893.00/1558A; Bryan to E. T. Williams, April 24, 1913, SD 893.00/1633A.

33. Bryan to E. T. Williams, April 24, 1913, SD 893.00/1633A.

34. Yuan, who had recently bypassed constitutional procedures in concluding the Reorganization Loan without parliamentary approval, and who was engaged in a bloody campaign of repression against his political foes, thanked Wilson "most heartily" for his message of recognition, stating that the sole aim of his government "will be, to preserve this [republican] form of government and to perfect its workings, to the end that they [the Chinese people] may enjoy its unalloyed blessings—prosperity and happiness within, through the union of law and liberty, and peace and friendship without, through the faithful execution of all established obligations." *Peking Daily News*, May 5, 1913.

35. Jordan to Grey, May 3, 1913, FO 405/546.

CHAPTER 7

1. Liew, p. 141.
2. *Peking Daily News*, September 7, 1912, p. 5, quoted in Edward Friedman, *Backward Toward Revolution: The Chinese Revolutionary Party*, p. 31.
3. Ernest Young, p. 99.
4. Ibid., p. 104.
5. Ibid., p. 105.
6. Ibid., pp. 115–16; Tenney (Nanjing) to Calhoun, January 1, 1913, SD 893.00/1538; Frank W. Hadley (Shanghai) to Beijing legation, March 4, 1913, SD 893.00/1611; "Civil War between North and South; possibilities of," March 14, 1913, FO 228/1861.
7. Williams to Bryan, April 18, 1913, SD 893.00/1657.
8. *China Press*, May 18, 1913.
9. Elizabeth Perkins to Enoch Bell, April 5, 1912, ABCFM; Edward Smith to Barton, December 10, 1912, ibid.; Goucher to Bashford, June 3, 1912, Goucher Papers; Lyman Peet to Barton, October 21, 1912, ABCFM.
10. Walker to Barton, January 4, 1913, ABCFM; Sheffield to Barton, February 1, 1913, ibid.
11. Sheffield to Barton, ibid.
12. Henry Martin (Beijing), "Notes on Governmental Conditions in China," February 13, 1913, ABCFM; Walker to Bell, June 26, 1912, ibid.; Walker to Barton, January 4, 1913, ibid.
13. Goodnow to Nicholas Murray Butler, June 26, 1913, Archives of the Carnegie Endowment for International Peace [hereafter CEIP]; Goodnow to Butler, August 16, 1913, ibid.; Paul Reinsch, *An American Diplomat in China*, p. 31. The Carnegie Endowment for International Peace was founded in 1910 to improve worldwide diplomatic relations. Several influential businessmen and retired government officials, including former secretaries of state John W. Foster and Elihu Root, as well as George W. Perkins and Robert Bacon, former partners of J. P. Morgan, were trustees of the Endowment. Burch, 2:204–5.
14. Goodnow to Butler, June 26, 1913, CEIP; *Peking Gazette*, December 11, 1913, Goodnow Papers; Goodnow to Butler, February 16, 1914, ibid.
15. W. W. Rockhill to Ts'ai T'ing-kan, June 23, 1914, Rockhill Papers; Goodnow to Nicholas Murray Butler, August 16, 1913, Goodnow Papers; Ernest Young, pp. 172–73.
16. Speech by Dr. Charles Eliot, Conference on Recent Developments in China, Clark University, November, 1912, SD 893.00/1643.
17. Butler to Goodnow, January 24, 27, February 2, 1914, CEIP.
18. Fernand Farjenal, *Through the Chinese Revolution*, pp. 293–95. Jordan summed up the dispute between Yuan and his republican opponents as follows: "Men like Sun Yat-sen and Huang Hsing have really nothing in common with Yuan Shih-k'ai and the older class of officials. The former extol constitutional methods and wish to make their application a means of curtailing the powers of the President. The latter sees little virtue in a Parliament which has become a veritable pandemonium, and continues to govern the country to a large extent on old lines." Jordan to Grey, May 19, 1913, FO 405/572.
19. Ernest Young, p. 123; Stabb to Addis, April 25, 1913, FO 228/456; Foreign Office to Hong Kong–Shanghai Bank, April 10, 1913, FO 405/211; *North China Daily News*, April 28, 1913.

20. Henry Martin to headquarters, May 10, 1913, ABCFM.

21. Lucy Mead to Miss Calder, April 23, 1913, ibid.

22. London *Times*, May 3, 1913, p. 7; Williams to Bryan, March 11, 1913, SD 893.00/1635; Williams to Bryan, April 1, 1913, SD 893.00/1628.

23. Williams to Bryan, May 16, 1913, SD 893.00/1700; Cheshire to Bryan, May 17, 1913, SD 893.00/1715.

24. "The Chinese President's Challenge," *Journal of the American Asiatic Association* 14 (August 1913): 205–6; Williams to Bryan, July 26, 1913, SD 893.00/1790; Williams to Bryan, July 18, 1913, SD 893.00/1811; Wilder to Williams, July 20, 1913, SD 893.00/1852.

25. Quoted in Williams to Bryan, July 18, 1913, SD 893.00/1811.

26. London *Times*, July 19, 1913, p. 9.

27. *New York Times*, August 6, 1913, p. 6.

28. Bryan to Williams, July 20, 1913, SD 893.00/1770A; John B. Moore to American consular officers in China, July 23, 1913, SD 893.00/1778; Foreign Minister Lu to Williams, July 23, 1913, SD 893.00/1784; Jordan to Chinese Foreign Ministry, July 25, 1913, SD 893.00/1823.

29. Williams to Bryan, July 25, 1913, SD 893.00/1845; Williams to Bryan, July 26, 1913, SD 893.00/1790; Williams to Bryan, July 29, 1913, SD 893.00/1832.

30. Cheshire (Guangzhou) to Williams, July 22, 1913, SD 893.00/1859; Bryan to Chinese minister, October 6, 1914, SD 893.00/2188.

31. Williams to Bryan, August 5, 1913, SD 893.00/1886; Williams to Bryan, July 14, 1913, SD 893.00/1850; Bryan to Wilson, November 8, 1913, Wilson Papers, vol. 6.

32. Williams to Bryan, July 14, 1913, SD 893.00/1755; Williams to Bryan, July 21, 1913, SD 893.00/1771; Secretary of the Embassy G. Bailey Blanchard to Bryan, August 6, 1913, SD 893.00/1866; Williams to Bryan, August 15, 1913, SD 893.00/1887.

33. Ch'en, p. 134.

34. Edward Smith to Barton, July 23, 1913, ABCFM.

35. C. A. Nelson, "The Second Revolution in China," ibid.; F. Lionel Pratt, "General and Ecumenical Developments in China, 1914–15," *China Mission Year Book*, pp. 74–75, 88–91; "Main Events of the Year 1913 as they related to the Missions," ABCFM; Walker to Bell, October 8, 1913, ABCFM.

36. Bryce to Wilson, June 12, 1913, Wilson Papers, 2: 36; Williams to Bryan, August 22, 1913, SD 893.00/1890.

37. *China Year Book*, 1914, p. 549; Reinsch, p. 2; Goodnow, "The Present Constitutional Crisis," *Peking Daily News*, November 25, 1913, Goodnow Papers; "Dissolution of the Kuomintang," *Journal of the American Asiatic Association* 14 (January 1914):375.

38. Walker to Gardner, December 24, 1913, ABCFM; Wilder to Barton, November 7, 1913, ibid.

39. Report for the Year 1913, Archives, M. E. Mission; Goodrich to Barton, September 3, 1913, ABCFM.

40. Ernest Young, p. 150.

41. Ibid., pp. 150–51.

42. Ch'en, p. 138.

43. Friedman, p. 167.

44. Jordan to Grey, February 9, 1914, FO 228/1883.

45. Reinsch to Bryan, July 25, 1915, SD 893.01/18.

46. *China Year Book*, 1916, pp. 434–35.

47. *North China Herald*, November 29, 1913, p. 621.

48. Ernest Young, p. 168; Jordan to Langley, February 8, March 8, 1914, Jordan Papers, FO 350/12.

49. Wilder to Bryan, May 7, 1913, SD 893.00/1702.

50. *Washington Post*, November 6, 1912, p. 6.

51. *New York Times*, October 11, 1913, p. 17.

52. Walker to Bell, October 8, 1913, ABCFM; General Work Report, Lintsing Station, North China, May 1, 1913–May 1, 1914, ibid.; Annual Report for the Year 1913, Archives, M. E. Mission; Report of Evangelistic Work of Fenzhou Station, 1913, ABCFM.

53. James and Jennie Curnow to Goucher, April 30, 1913, Goucher Papers.

54. Bertha Reed to headquarters, November 27, 1915, ABCFM; Educational Report, Fenzhou Station, 1915, ibid.

55. Editorial, *The Chinese Christian Advocate*, October 1915, p. 2; Gilbert Reid, "Autocracy for China or Not?" *National Review* 18 (August 14, 1915): 121–22.

56. "Conditions in China in 1914 as Viewed from Beijing," *Journal of the American Asiatic Association* 14 (June 1914): 143–48; William Rockhill, "Brief Review of the Present Situation in China" (speech before Central Asian Society of London), November 5, 1914, Rockhill Papers.

57. Goodnow, "Reform in China," *American Political Science Review* 9 (May 1915):209–26.

58. Goodnow, "The Parliament of the Republic of China," *American Political Science Review* 8 (November 1914):560.

59. Goodnow to Butler, February 26, 1914, CEIP.

60. Goodnow to Butler, January 2, February 26, 1914, CEIP.

61. Reinsch to Bryan, December 1, 1913, SD 893.00/2049; Bryan to Joseph Tumulty, December 2, 1914, SD 893.51/146a.

62. "Inaugural Address of the President to the Council of Government," December 15, 1913, FO 350/12.

63. W. H. Wilkinson (Hankou) to Jordan, April 11, 1914, FO 228/1907; Ernest Young, pp. 178–84.

64. Lansing to Reinsch, November 4, 1914, FRUS, Supplement, p. 190.

65. Reinsch to Bryan, December 22, 1914, SD 793.00/216.

66. Reinsch to Bryan, February 10, 1915, SD 793.00/257; Reinsch to Bryan, February 1, 1915, SD 793.00/219.

67. Reinsch to Bryan, March 7, 1915, SD 793.00/224; Commercial attaché (Beijing) to Department of Commerce, March 30, 1915, SD 793.00/272; Reinsch to Bryan, January 24, 1915, SD 793.00/210; Memorandum, E. T. Williams to Bryan, April 13, 1915, SD 793.00/292; Reinsch to Bryan, April 5, 1915, SD 793.00/284; Consul Pontius (Amoy) to Reinsch, March 8, 1915, SD 793.00/299; Reinsch to Bryan, March 31, 1915, SD 793.00/276; Bashford to Wilson, March 12, 1915, Wilson Papers.

68. Bashford to Bryan, March 18, 1915, SD 793.00/316; see also statement of American missionaries in China included in consul general (Shanghai) to Reinsch, February 25, 1915, SD 793.00/277.

69. Bryan to Japanese minister, March 13, 1915, SD 793.00/240a; Memorandum of E. T. Williams to Bryan, February 15, 1915, SD 793.00/224; Consul General Heintzleman (Mukden) to Reinsch, March 3, 1915, SD 793.00/282; Bryan to Wilson, March 25, 1915, SD 793.00/280.

70. Williams to Bryan, February 26, 1915, Bryan Papers; Lansing to Bryan, March 1, 1915, SD 793.00/182.

71. Bryan to Japanese minister, March 13, 1915, SD 793.00/182.

72. Reinsch to Bryan, April 14, 1915, SD 793.00/294; Bryan to Reinsch, April 15, 1915, ibid.

73. "Must China Fight" [editorial], *The China Press*, March 24, 1915, SD 793.00/313.

74. Jordan to Langley, February 2, 1916, Jordan Papers, FO 350/15; Jordan to Grey, May 5, 8, 1915, FO 228/2308; Reinsch to Bryan, March 13, 1915, SD 793.00/250; Reinsch to Bryan, March 8, 1915, SD 793.00/245.

75. Smith to Barton, March 8, 1914, ABCFM; General work report, Lintsing Station, North China, May 1, 1913–May 1, 1914, ibid.; E. H. Parker, "The Chinese Revolution," *Asiatic Quarterly Review* 34 (July 1912):1–20, esp. 17–19.

76. Ernest Young, pp. 212–13.

77. Gardner Harding, *Present-Day China*, p. 183; B. L. Putnam-Weale, *The Fight for the Republic in China*, pp. 146–47, 149.

78. FRUS, 1915, pp. 66–67; Ernest Young, p. 215.

79. Goodnow, "Republic or Monarchy," Goodnow Papers.

80. Goodnow, "The Parliament of the Republic of China," Memorandum to Yuan, August 15, 1915, Goodnow Papers; FRUS, 1915, pp. 58–59.

81. Jordan to Grey, November 1, 1915, FO 228/2939.

82. Smith (Chengdu) to Jordan, January 4, April 14, June 22, and July 20, 1915, FO 228/1942; Mead (Chongqing) to Jordan, July 27, 1915, ibid.; Smith (Chengdu) to Jordan, February 2, 1916, FO 228/2753; Tokyo legation to secretary of state, September 24, 1915, SD 893.01/37.

83. Jordan to Grey, August 15, 1915, FO 405, No. 277 (135730).

84. Ibid.

85. Reinsch to Lansing, October 2, 1915, SD 893.01/30; Heintzleman (Mukden) to MacMurray, August 31, 1915, SD 893.01/33; MacMurray to Lansing, September 7, 1915, SD 893.01/35.

86. MacMurray to Lansing, September 4, 1915, SD 893.01/24; Chinese Nationalist League of America to Wilson, September 4, 1915, SD 893.01/26.

87. Putnam-Weale, pp. 220–35.

88. MacMurray to Lansing, August 25, 1915, SD 893.01/22.

89. "Government in China," *Journal of the American Asiatic Association* 15 (December 1915):330; Putnam-Weale, pp. 222–23.

90. MacMurray to Lansing, September 2, 1915, SD 893.01/23.

91. Jordan to Grey, September 10, 1915, FO 405, No. 228 (144613).

92. MacMurray to Lansing, September 10, 1915, SD 893.01/25.

93. *New York Times*, October 9, 1915, p. 15; Putnam-Weale, p. 225.

94. Baron Ishii to C. Green in Green to Grey, October 13, 1915, FO 405, No. 232 (150178); Green to Grey, September 20, 1915, FO 405, No. 241 (156032); Guthrie to Lansing, October 26, 1915, SD 893.01/38.

95. Jordan to Grey, October 15, 1915, FO 405, No. 230 (148381); Grey to Jordan, October 18, 1915, FO 405, No. 236 (153204); Jordan to Grey, October 19, 1915, FO 405, No. 237 (153583); Jordan to Grey, October 21, 1915, FO 405, No. 238 (155265); Guthrie to Lansing, October 26, 1915, SD 893.01/38.

96. Lansing to Reinsch, October 28, 1915, SD 893.01/40; Lansing to Guthrie, October 26, 1915, SD 893.01/38; Reinsch to Lansing, October 28, 1915, SD 893.01/41.

97. Friedman, p. 181.

98. Lansing to Wilson, October 27, 1915, SD 893.01/73; Wilson to Lansing, October 31, 1915, SD 893.01/78.

99. Jordan to Grey, October 1, 1915, FO 405, No. 258 (159898).

100. Reinsch to Lansing, November 12, 1915, SD 893.01/59; Grey to Green, October 29, 1915, FO 405, No. 270 (160042).

101. Grey to Jordan, November 5, 1915, FO 405, No. 279 (1655820); Reinsch to Lansing, December 18, 1915, SD 893.01/60; Lansing to Reinsch, December 10, 1915, SD 893.01/61.

102. Reinsch to Lansing, November 19, 1915, SD 893.01/63; State Department memorandum, "The Monarchical Movement in China and American Policy," SD 893.01/66.

103. Grey to Jordan, December 18, 1915, FO 405, No. 314 (194568); Jordan to Grey, December 21, 1915, FO 405, No. 316 (195483).

104. Jordan to Grey, January 7, 1916, FO 405, No. 12 (4329); Reinsch to Lansing, January 3, 1916, SD 893.01/64.

105. Goffe to Jordan, March 10, 1916, FO 228/2736; Alston to Foreign Office, March 3, 1917, FO 228/2658; Jordan to Langley, October 20, 1915, Jordan Papers, FO 350/13; Jordan to Grey, October 27, 1915, FO 228/2397; Friedman, pp. 181–85; Ernest Young, pp. 219–40.

106. *Peking Daily News*, January 20, 1916, quoted in Friedman, p. 185.

107. Reinsch to Lansing, January 29, 1916, SD 893.01/75; Reinsch to Lansing, February 5, 1916, SD 893.01/79; Reinsch to Lansing, March 4, 1916, SD 893.01/86; Reinsch to Lansing, February 24, 1916, SD 893.01/90.

108. G. E. Morrison to Louis E. Broome, March 31, 1916, quoted in Ernest Young, p. 210.

109. Reinsch, p. 197.

CHAPTER 8

1. Wu Tingfang, Qing minister to the United States and later the rebels' minister for foreign affairs, attested in his memoirs to the reluctance of the Americans to invest in China: "Up to a few years ago business men in America, especially capitalists, had scarcely any idea of transacting business in China. I well remember the difficulty I had in raising a railway loan in America. It was in 1897. I had received positive instructions from my government to obtain a big loan for the purpose of constructing the proposed railway from Hankow to Canton. I endeavored to interest well-known bankers and capitalists in New York City but none of them would consider the proposals. They invariably said that their money could be just as easily, and just as profitably, invested in their own country, and with better security, than was obtainable in China." Wu Tingfang, *America Through the Spectacles of an Oriental Diplomat*, pp. 71–72.

2. From the perspective of American financiers, free competition in the China loan business, when coupled with the already substantial risks caused by internal political conditions there, jeopardized the profitability of the entire enterprise. In particular, the Americans were justifiably concerned about the chilling effect of competition on interest rates. Interest rates already had fallen from the 8–10 percent range charged the Qing in the mid-1890s to the 5–7 percent range offered to the Qing a decade later. Competition would accelerate this downward trend, thereby making it impossible for the bankers to earn the risk premium that they felt conditions warranted. Hence, the desire of the Americans for a monopoly. The Chinese demand for foreign funds also was sufficiently inelastic to permit

the existence of such a monopoly. Not only did China lack the internal financial structure necessary to generate huge sums for development, but even if that were not the case, interest rates charged by native Chinese financiers traditionally were far above those to which Western financiers, even under monopoly conditions, were accustomed. As a result, the temptation to borrow from foreigners was even stronger. See Chung-li Chang, *The Income of the Chinese Gentry*, pp. 192–93; Albert Feuerwerker, *China's Early Industrialization*, pp. 18, 24; Feuerwerker, *The Chinese Economy, ca. 1870–1911*, pp. 7, 14, 44; Robert F. Dernberger, "The Role of the Foreigner in China's Economic Development, 1840–1949," in Dwight Perkins, ed., *China's Modern Economy in Historical Perspective*, pp. 45–46.

3. Wilson's decision to go it alone in China was not as naïve as it has been made to appear. Following Wilson's decision to withdraw from the consortium and to recognize the Republic, Yuan pledged prompt and favorable action to American investors on a number of pending projects, including petroleum development by Standard Oil, the Huai River Conservancy project, a Bethlehem Steel contract, currency reform, river and harbor improvements, and the granting of a monopoly to the British-American Tobacco Company. While Yuan was unable to deliver on his promises, the mere existence of such opportunities helps to establish a realistic basis for Wilson's decision to break with Taft's cooperative approach to Chinese affairs (see Pugach, p. 89). Recent reexaminations of Wilson's economic policies corroborate this interpretation. As Burton Kaufman has observed, Wilson was extremely aggressive in supporting policies and legislation designed to enhance America's ability to compete for foreign markets. Among Wilson's initiatives were amending the Federal Reserve Act to permit foreign branch banking, exempting the U.S. export business from the antitrust laws, subsidizing the merchant marine, and strengthening the export-support function of the Department of Commerce. These measures certainly were consistent with—indeed prerequisites of—an independent, competitive approach to China such as that adopted by Wilson. See Kaufman, passim.

4. Warren I. Cohen, *The Chinese Connection*, p. 48.

5. Curry, pp. 188–90; Carl P. Parrini *Heir to Empire: United States Economic Diplomacy, 1916–1923*, pp. 173–80; Beers, pp. 75–87.

6. Cohen, *The Chinese Connection*, p. 49.

7. Ibid., pp. 49–50; Curry, pp. 152–54.

8. Curry, pp. 188–92; Beers, pp. 86–91; Cohen, *The Chinese Connection*, pp. 48–51.

9. Michael J. Hogan, *Informal Entente: The Private Structure of Cooperation in Anglo-American Economic Diplomacy, 1918–1928*, pp. 84–86.

10. Beers, p. 116.

11. Hogan, p. 86; Lansing to Wilson, June 20, 1918, FRUS, pp. 169–71.

12. Curry, p. 189.

13. Ibid., p. 194; Beers, pp. 143–44; Field, p. 176, notes that "the Consortium plan, as originally issued by the American Government in 1918, envisaged something more nearly approaching a monopoly than the organization which was finally formed in 1920."

14. Cohen, *The Chinese Connection*, pp. 53–55.

15. Ibid., p. 51.

16. Curry, p. 203.

17. Parrini, pp. 178–80.

18. Ibid., p. 176.

19. Link, *Wilson: The New Freedom*, pp. 347–48; Kenneth J. Grieb, *The*

United States and Huerta, pp. 36–37; Mark T. Gilderhus, *Diplomacy and Revolution: U.S.–Mexican Relations Under Wilson and Carranza*, pp. 1–2; Henry F. Pringle, *The Life and Times of William Howard Taft*, pp. 700–711; Robert Freeman Smith, *The United States and Revolutionary Nationalism in Mexico, 1916–1932*, pp. x–xi; P. Edward Haley, *Revolution and Intervention: The Diplomacy of Taft and Wilson with Mexico 1910–1917*, p. 11.

20. Haley, pp. 33–34, 50, 69.

21. Larry D. Hill, *Emissaries to a Revolution: Woodrow Wilson's Executive Agents in Mexico*, pp. 6–9.

22. Gilderhus, p. 2; Grieb, p. 36.

23. N. Gordon Levin, *Woodrow Wilson and World Politics: America's Response to War and Revolution*, p. 124; Smith, p. 33.

24. Gilderhus, p. 5; Grieb, p. 44.

25. Smith, p. 35, quoting John Bassett Moore, "Our Purposes in Mexico," November 24, 1913; Wilson to Sir William Tyrell, November 22, 1913, in Ray Stannard Baker, *Woodrow Wilson, Life and Letters*, 4:292.

26. Gilderhus, p. 15; Bryan to Vice Consul Silliman, July 23, 1914, FRUS, 1914, pp. 568–69.

27. Levin, pp. 178–87; Gilderhus, pp. 10–15.

28. Gilderhus, pp. 17–19.

29. Ibid., pp. 104–5; Smith, pp. 37–42.

30. Smith, p. 85.

31. Levin, p. 42.

32. Ibid.

33. Joan Hoff Wilson, *Ideology and Economics: U.S. Relations with the Soviet Union, 1918–1933*, p. 15

34. Levin, passim.

35. Burch, 2:173–74.

36. The American psychiatrist Harry Stack Sullivan called this phenomenon "parataxic distortion"; it warps "our political vision and induce[s] us to mistake one revolutionary movement for another, to see threats where there are none, or conversely, to perceive friendships and affinities where none exist, or reliable instruments of policy where there are only weak clients or cynical adulants." Edmund Stillman and William Pfaff, *Power and Impotence: The Failure of American Foreign Policy*, p. 74.

37. Iriye, p. 138.

38. Cohen, *America's Response to China*, p. 112.

39. Ibid., p. 116; Dorothy Borg, *American Policy and the Chinese Revolution, 1925–1928*, p. 2.

40. Iriye, p. 157.

41. Cohen, *America's Response to China*, pp. 121–22.

42. Ibid., p. 130; Iriye, pp. 178–80; Dorothy Borg, *The United States and the Far Eastern Crisis of 1933–1938*.

43. *Washington Star*, February 13, 1932, quoted in Iriye, p. 180.

44. Cohen, *America's Response to China*, p. 162.

45. Stanley K. Hornbeck, memorandum, May 26, 1941, in "China, Assistance to 1939–41," Box 52, Hornbeck Papers.

46. Hunt, *The Making of a Special Relationship*, p. 306.

Bibliography

MANUSCRIPTS

American Board of Commissioners for Foreign Missions. Papers. Houghton Library, Harvard University, Cambridge.
Bashford, James. Diaries. 54 vols. Missionary Research Library, New York City.
Bryan, William Jennings. Papers. Library of Congress, Washington.
Carnegie Endowment for International Peace. Archives. Columbia University, New York City.
Eliot, Charles. Papers. Widener Library, Harvard University, Cambridge.
Goodnow, Frank. Papers. Johns Hopkins University, Baltimore, Maryland.
Goucher, John. Papers. Missionary Research Library, New York City.
Hornbeck, Stanley K. Papers. Hoover Institution, Stanford, California.
Huntington-Wilson, F. M. Papers. Ursinus College, Collegeville, Pennsylvania.
Knox, Philander C. Papers. Library of Congress, Washington.
Methodist Episcopal Mission. Archives. Division of World Missions, New York City.
Phillips, William. Recollections. Columbia University Oral History Project, New York City.
Presbyterian Foreign Missions. Archives. Presbyterian Historical Society, Philadelphia, Pennsylvania.
Reid, Whitelaw. Papers, Library of Congress.
Rockhill, William. Papers. Houghton Library, Harvard University, Cambridge.
Straight, Willard. Papers. Cornell University, Ithaca, New York.
Taft, William Howard. Papers. Library of Congress, Washington.
Wilson, Woodrow. Papers. Library of Congress, Washington.

Public Documents

Congressional Record, 1911–16.
Foreign Relations of the United States, 1900–1917.
Great Britain, *Parliamentary Debates*.
Great Britain, Foreign Office. Confidential Print, FO 228.
———. Confidential Print, John Jordan Papers, FO 350.
———. Confidential Print, China, FO 371, 405.
MacMurray, John Van Antwerp, ed. *Treaties and Agreements with and Concerning China*, 1894–1919.
United States. Commerce Department. *Historical Statistics of the United States, Colonial Times to 1970.* Washington, D.C.: Government Printing Office, 1975.
United States. State Department. Records relating to the internal affairs of China, 1900–1929.
———. Records relating to the relations between China and other states, 1910–29.
———. Records relating to the political relations between the United States and China, 1910–29.

Newspapers

Atlanta Constitution
Boston Advertiser
Boston Globe
Boston Herald
China Press
Christian Science Monitor
Journal of Commerce and Commercial Bulletin
New York Herald
New York Journal of Commerce and Commercial Review
New York Times
New York Tribune
North China Daily News
North China Herald
Peking Daily News
Peking and Tientsin Times
St. Louis Post-Dispatch
San Francisco Examiner
The Times (London)
Wall Street Journal
Washington Post

Periodicals

American Political Science Review
Assembly Herald (Presbyterian)
Atlantic Monthly
Asiatic Quarterly Review
Baptist Missionary Review
China Christian Advocate (Methodist Episcopal)
Chinese Intelligencer (Reformed Church in America)

Contemporary Review
Current Opinion
Far Eastern Review
Harper's
Independent
International Review of Missions
Journal of the American Asiatic Association
Literary Digest
Missionary Herald (Congregationalist)
Missionary Intelligencer
Missionary Review of the World
National Review
New Republic
Outlook
World's Work

MISSIONARY BOARD REPORTS

American Baptist Foreign Mission Society. *Annual Reports.*
American Board of Commissioners for Foreign Missions. *Annual Reports.*
China Continuation Committee. *Proceedings.*
Foreign Missions' Conference of North America. *Annual Reports.*
Methodist Episcopal Church. Board of Foreign Missions. *Reports.*
Presbyterian Church in the United States. China Council. *Reports.*
Protestant Episcopal Church. Board of Missions. *Annual Reports.*

YEARBOOKS

China Mission Year Book. 1910–20.
Journal of the American Asiatic Association. 1898–1920.
Methodist Episcopal Year Book.

SECONDARY SOURCES

Adams, Brooks. *America's Economic Supremacy.* New York: Macmillan, 1900.
Adshead, S. A. M. *The Modernization of the Chinese Salt Administration, 1900–1920.* Cambridge, Mass.: Harvard University Press, 1970.
Bailey, Thomas A. *A Diplomatic History of the American People.* 9th ed. Englewood Cliffs, N.J.: Prentice-Hall, 1974.
Baker, Ray Stannard. *Woodrow Wilson: Life and Letters.* Vol. 4, 1913–1914. New York: Doubleday, Doran, 1931.
Barnett, Richard. *Intervention and Revolution: The United States in the Third World.* New York: World, 1968.
Bashford, James W. *China: An Interpretation.* New York: Abingdon Press, 1916.
Bays, Daniel. *China Enters the Twentieth Century: Chang Chih-tung and the Issues of a New Age, 1895–1909.* Ann Arbor: University of Michigan Press, 1978.
Beale, Howard. *Theodore Roosevelt and the Rise of America to World Power.* New York: Collier Books, 1956.
Beard, Charles A. *The Idea of the National Interest: An Analytical Study in American Foreign Policy.* New York: Macmillan, 1934.

Beaver, R. Pierce. *All Loves Excelling: American Protestant Women in World Mission.* Grand Rapids, Michigan.: Eerdmans, 1968.

Beers, Burton. *Vain Endeavor: Robert Lansing's Attempts to End the American-Japanese Rivalry.* Durham, N.C.: Duke University Press, 1962.

Beisner, Robert. *Twelve Against Empire: The Anti-Imperialists, 1898–1900.* New York: McGraw-Hill, 1971.

Berger, Meyer. *The Story of the New York Times, 1851–1951.* New York: Simon & Schuster, 1951.

Beveridge, Albert J. *The Russian Advance.* New York: Harper, 1903.

Blakeslee, George H., ed. *Recent Developments in China.* New York: G. E. Stechert Co., 1913.

Bland, J. O. P. *Recent Events and Present Policies in China.* Philadelphia: Lippincott, 1912.

Borg, Dorothy. *American Policy and the Chinese Revolution, 1925–1928.* New York: Octagon, 1968.

———. *The United States and the Far Eastern Crisis of 1933–1938.* Cambridge, Mass.: Harvard University Press, 1964.

Borst-Smith, Ernst. *Caught in the Chinese Revolution: A Record of Risks and Rescues.* London: Unwin, 1912.

Brandt, Conrad. *Stalin's Failure in China.* Cambridge, Mass.: Harvard University Press, 1958.

Bryan, William Jennings, and Bryan, Mary Baird. *The Memoirs of William Jennings Bryan.* Chicago: Winston, 1925.

Burch, Philip H., Jr. *Elites in American History.* 3 vols. New York: Holmes & Meier, 1981.

Cameron, Meribeth E. "American Recognition Policy Toward the Republic of China," *Pacific Historical Review* 2 (June 1933):214–30.

———. *The Reform Movement in China, 1898–1912.* Stanford, California: Stanford University Press, 1931.

Chang, Chung-li. *The Income of the Chinese Gentry.* Seattle: University of Washington Press, 1962.

Chang, Kia-ngua. *China's Struggle for Railway Development.* New York: John Day, 1943.

Chang, Tennyson Po-hsun. "China's Revolution, 1911–1912, and Its Foreign Relations." Ph.D. dissertation, Georgetown University, 1948.

Ch'en, Jerome. *Yuan Shih-k'ai.* Stanford, California: Stanford University Press, 1961.

Cheng, Emily. "United States Policy During the Chinese Revolution." Ph.D. dissertation, University of South Carolina, 1964.

Chi, Madeleine. *China Diplomacy, 1914–1918.* Cambridge, Mass.: Harvard University Press, 1970.

Chou Ts'e-tsung. *The May Fourth Movement: Intellectual Revolution in Modern China.* Stanford, California: Stanford University Press, 1967.

Clyde, Paul H., ed. *United States Policy Toward China: Diplomatic and Public Documents, 1839–1939.* Durham, N.C.: Duke University Press, 1940.

Cohen, Warren I. *America's Response to China: An Interpretive History of Sino-American Relations.* New York: John Wiley, 1971.

———. *The Chinese Connection.* New York: Columbia University Press, 1978.

Coons, Arthur G. *The Foreign Public Debt of China.* Philadelphia: University of Pennsylvania Press, 1930.

Crane, Daniel M. "The Reaction of the American Press to the Chinese Revolution of 1911." M.A. thesis, University of Virginia, 1970.

————. "The United States and the Chinese Republic: Profit, Power and the Politics of Benevolence." Ph.D dissertation, University of Virginia, 1974.

Croly, Herbert. *Willard Straight*. New York: Macmillan, 1924.

Curry, Roy Watson. *Woodrow Wilson and Far Eastern Policy, 1913-1921*. New York: Bookman Associates, 1957.

David, Elmer. *History of the New York Times, 1851–1921*. New York: New York Times, 1921.

deBary, William T., ed., *Sources of Chinese Tradition*. New York: Columbia University Press, 1960.

Dennett, Tyler. *Americans in Eastern Asia*. New York: Macmillan, 1922.

Dingle, Edward J. *China's Revolution, 1911–1912: A Historical and Political Record of the Civil War*. New York: McBridge, Nast and Co., 1912.

Dulles, Foster Rhea. *China and America: The Story of Their Relations Since 1784*. Princeton, N.J.: Princeton University Press, 1946.

Eckstein, Alexander. *China's Economic Development: The Interplay of Scarcity and Ideology*. Ann Arbor: University of Michigan Press, 1975.

Elvin, Mark. "The Mixed Court of the International Settlement at Shanghai," In Center For East Asian Studies, *Papers on China*, Vol. 17. Cambridge, Mass.: Harvard University, December 1963.

Emery, Edwin. *The Press and America: An Interpretative History of Journalism*. Englewood Cliffs, N.J.; Prentice Hall, 1962.

Esherick, Joseph N. *Reform and Revolution in China: The 1911 Revolution in Hunan and Hubei*. Berkeley: University of California Press, 1976.

Fairbank, John K. *The United States and China*. 3d ed. Cambridge, Mass.: Harvard University Press, 1971.

————. Reischauer, E.O., and Craig, A.M. *East Asia: The Modern Transformation*. Boston: Houghton Mifflin, 1965.

Farjenal, Fernand. *Through the Chinese Revolution*. New York: Frederick A. Stokes, 1916.

Feuerwerker, Albert. *China's Early Industrialization*. Cambridge, Mass.: Harvard University Press, 1958.

————. *The Chinese Economy, ca. 1870–1911*. Michigan Papers in Chinese Studies, No. 5. Ann Arbor: University of Michigan Press, 1969.

————, Murphy, Rhoads, and Wright, Mary C., eds. *Approaches to Modern Chinese History*. Berkeley: University of California Press, 1967.

Field, Frederick V. *American Participation in the China Consortium*. Chicago: University of Chicago Press, 1931.

Fifield, Russell H. *Woodrow Wilson and the Far East*. New York: Cromwell, 1952.

Finney, Charles Grandison. *Lectures on Revivals of Religion*. Edited by William McLoughlin. Cambridge, Mass.: Belknap Press, Harvard University Press, 1960.

Fitzgerald, C. P. *The Birth of Communist China*. Baltimore: Penguin Books, 1964.

Foner, Philip S. *The Spanish-Cuban-American War and the Birth of American Imperialism, 1895–1902*. 2 vols. New York: Monthly Review Press, 1972.

Foster, Charles I. *An Errand of Mercy: The Evangelical United Front, 1790–1837*. Chapel Hill: University of North Carolina Press, 1960.

Friedman, Edward. *Backward Toward Revolution: The Chinese Revolutionary Party*. Berkeley: University of California Press, 1974.

————, and Selden, Mark, eds. *America's Asia: Dissenting Essays on Asian-American Relations*. New York: Pantheon, 1971.

Fung, Edmund S. K. *The Military Dimension of the Chinese Revolution: The New Army and its Role in the Revolution of 1911.* Vancouver: University of British Columbia Press, 1980.

Gage, Daniel J. "Paul S. Reinsch and Sino-American Relations." Ph.D. dissertation, Stanford University, 1939.

Gardner, John B. "The Image of the Chinese in the United States." Ph.D. dissertation, University of Pennsylvania, 1961.

Gasster, Michael. *Chinese Intellectuals and the Revolution of 1911: The Birth of Modern Chinese Radicalism.* Seattle: University of Washington Press, 1969.

Gilderhus, Mark T. *Diplomacy and Revolution: U.S.-Mexican Relations Under Wilson and Carranza.* Tucson: University of Arizona Press, 1977.

Goldstein, Jonathan. *Philadelphia and the China Trade, 1682–1846: Commercial, Cultural and Attitudinal Effects.* University Park: Pennsylvania State University Press, 1978.

Graebner, Norman, ed. *Ideas and Diplomacy.* New York: Oxford University Press, 1964.

Graham, Malbone W. *American Diplomacy in the International Community.* Baltimore: Johns Hopkins University Press, 1948.

Grayson, Benson Lee, ed. *The American Image of China.* New York: Ungar, 1979.

Grieb, Kenneth J. *The United States and Huerta.* Lincoln: University of Nebraska Press, 1969.

Grisinger, Kenneth. "The Policy of the United States Toward the Early Republican Movement in China, 1911–1916." Ph.D. dissertation, Claremont College, 1950.

Griswold, A. Whitney. *The Far Eastern Policy of the United States.* New York: Harcourt, Brace, 1938.

Haley, P. Edward. *Revolution and Intervention: The Diplomacy of Taft and Wilson with Mexico, 1910–1917.* Cambridge, Mass.: MIT Press, 1970.

Harding, Gardner. *Present-Day China.* New York: Century, 1916.

Hartz, Louis. *The Liberal Tradition in America.* New York: Harcourt, Brace & World, 1955.

Hill, Larry D. *Emissaries to a Revolution: Woodrow Wilson's Executive Agents in Mexico.* Baton Rouge: Louisiana State University Press, 1973.

Hogan, Michael. *Informal Entente: The Private Structure of Cooperation in Anglo-American Economic Diplomacy, 1918–1925.* Columbia: University of Missouri Press, 1977.

Holcombe, Arthur. *The Chinese Revolution: A Phase in the Regeneration of a World Power.* Cambridge, Mass.: Harvard University Press, 1930.

Hornbeck, Stanley K. *Contemporary Politics in the Far East.* New York: Appleton, 1916.

Houston, David F. *Eight Years with Wilson's Cabinet, 1913–1920.* Garden City, N.Y.: Doubleday, Page, 1926.

Hu Sheng. *Imperialism and Chinese Politics.* Peking: Foreign Language Press, 1955.

Hu Shih. *The Chinese Renaissance.* Chicago: University of Chicago Press, 1934.

Hummel, Arthur W., ed. *Eminent Chinese of the Ch'ing Period.* 2 vols. Washington, D.C.: U.S. Government Printing Office, 1943.

Hunt, Michael H. *Frontier Defense and the Open Door: Manchuria in Chinese-American Relations, 1895–1911.* New Haven, Conn.: Yale University Press, 1973.

————. *The Making of a Special Relationship: The United States and China to 1914*. New York: Columbia University Press, 1983.

Huntington-Wilson, F. M. *Memoirs of an Ex-Diplomat*. Boston: Bruce Humphries, 1945.

————. *The Perils of Hifalutin*. New York: Duffield, 1918.

Hyde, Charles. *International Law Chiefly as Interpreted and Applied by the United States*. Boston: Little, Brown, 1945.

Iriye, Akira. *Across the Pacific: An Inner History of American–East Asian Relations*. New York: Harcourt, Brace and World, 1967.

Isaacs, Harold. *Scratches on Our Minds: American Images of China and India*. New York: John Day, 1958.

————. *The Tragedy of the Chinese Revolution*. New York: Atheneum, 1966.

Israel, Jerry. *Progressivism and the Open Door: America and China, 1905–1921*. Pittsburgh: University of Pittsburgh Press, 1971.

Jansen, Marius B. *The Japanese and Sun Yat-sen*. Cambridge, Mass.: Harvard University Press, 1954.

Jenks, Leland H. *Our Cuban Colony: A Study in Sugar*. New York: Vanguard, 1928, reprinted 1972.

Johnston, Reginald F. *Confucianism and Modern China*. New York: Appleton Century, 1935.

Kahn, Helen. "The Great Game of Empire: Willard Straight and American Far Eastern Policy." Ph.D. dissertation, Cornell University, 1968.

Kaufman, Burton. *Efficiency and Expansion: Foreign Trade Organization in the Wilson Administration 1913–1921*. Westport, Conn.: Greenwood Press, 1974.

Kennan, George F. *American Diplomacy 1900–1950*. Chicago: University of Chicago Press, 1951.

————. "A Fresh Look at Our China Policy," *New York Times Magazine*, November 22, 1964, pp. 27, 140–47.

Kent, Percy Horace. *The Passing of the Manchus*. London: Edward Arnold, 1912.

Kimball, Warren F. "Seduction Without Satisfaction: Textbooks and the Teaching of the History of American Foreign Policy and Diplomacy," *Newsletter of the Society for Historians of American Foreign Relations* 11 (June 1982): 14–18.

Kolko, Gabriel. *The Triumph of Conservatism: A Reinterpretation of American History, 1900–1916*. New York: Macmillan, 1963.

Kotenev, Anatol M. *New Lamps for Old: An Interpretation of Events in Modern China and Whither They Lead*. Shanghai: North China Daily News and Herald, 1931.

————. *Shanghai: Its Mixed Court and Council*. Shanghai: North China Daily News and Herald, 1925.

LaFeber, Walter. *The New Empire: An Interpretation of American Expansion, 1860–1898*. Ithaca, N.Y.: Cornell University Press, 1963.

Langley, Lester D. *The Cuban Policy of the United States: A Brief History*. New York: Wiley, 1968.

Latourette, Kenneth Scott. *A History of Christian Missions in China*. New York: Macmillan, 1929.

Lauterpacht, H. *Recognition in International Law*. Cambridge, Eng.: Cambridge University Press, 1947.

Levin, N. Gordon. *Woodrow Wilson and World Politics: America's Response to War and Revolution*. New York: Oxford University Press, 1968.

Levinson, Joseph R. *Confucian China and Its Modern Fate: A Trilogy.* Berkeley: University of California Press, 1968.
————. *Liang Ch'i-chao and the Mind of Modern China.* Berkeley: University of California Press, 1967.
Li, Chien-nung. *The Political History of Modern China, 1840–1928.* Stanford, Calif.: Stanford University Press, 1956.
Li, Tien-yi. *Woodrow Wilson's China Policy, 1913–1917.* [Kansas City]: University of Kansas Press, 1952.
Liew, K. S. *Struggle for Democracy: Sung Chiao-jen and the 1911 Chinese Revolution.* Berkeley: University of California Press, 1971.
Link, Arthur S. *Wilson: The New Freedom.* Princeton, N.J.: Princeton University Press, 1956.
————. *Woodrow Wilson and the Progressive Era, 1910–1917.* New York: Harper, 1954.
Litell, Franklin H. *From State Church to Pluralism.* New York: Macmillan, 1971.
Lynd, Staughton. *Intellectual Origins of American Radicalism.* New York: Random House, 1968.
McCormick, Frederick. *The Flowery Republic.* New York: Appleton, 1914.
McCormick, Thomas. *China Market: America's Quest for Informal Empire, 1893–1901.* Chicago: Quadrangle, 1967.
McFeely, William S. *Grant: A Biography.* New York: Norton, 1981.
MacNair, Harley Farnsworth. *China in Revolution.* Chicago: University of Chicago Press, 1931.
Madden, John T. *America's Experience as a Creditor Nation.* New York: Prentice-Hall, 1937.
Marty, Martin. *The Modern Schism.* New York: Harper & Row, 1969.
Matthewson, Timothy M. "George Washington's Policy toward the Haitian Revolution." *Diplomatic History* (Summer 1979): 321–36.
May, Ernest R., and Thomson, James C., Jr. *American-East Asian Relations: A Survey.* Cambridge, Mass.: Harvard University Press, 1972.
May, Henry F. *The End of American Innocence.* New York: Knopf, 1959.
Meisner, Maurice. *Li Ta-chao and the Origins of Chinese Marxism.* Cambridge, Mass.: Harvard University Press, 1967.
Millard, Thomas F. *Our Eastern Question.* New York: Century, 1916.
Miller, Jesse. "China in American Policy and Opinion, 1906–1909." Ph.D. dissertation, Clark University, 1940.
Moon, Parker Thomas. *Imperialism and World Politics.* New York: Macmillan, 1926.
Morse, Hosea Ballou. *The International Relations of the Chinese Empire.* 3 vols. New York: Longmans, Green, 1910–18.
————, and MacNair, H. F. *Far Eastern International Relations.* Boston: Houghton Mifflin, 1931.
Moulder, Frances V. *Japan, China, and the Modern World Economy.* Cambridge, Eng.: Cambridge University Press, 1977.
Mullowney, John J., ed. *A Revelation of the Chinese Revolution.* New York: Fleming H. Revell, 1941.
Oppenheim, L. *International Law: A Treatise.* 7th ed. New York: Longmans, 1948.
Osgood, Robert. *Ideals and Self-Interest in America's Foreign Relations.* Chicago: University of Chicago Press, 1953.
Overlach, T. W. *Foreign Financial Control in China.* New York: Macmillan, 1919.

Parrini, Carl. *Heir to Empire: United States Economic Diplomacy, 1916–1923.* Pittsburgh: University of Pittsburgh Press, 1969.

Perkins, Dwight, ed. *China's Modern Economy in Historical Perspective.* Stanford, Calif.: Stanford University Press, 1975.

Pringle, Henry. *The Life and Times of William Howard Taft.* New York: Farrar & Rinehart, 1939.

Pugach, Noel H. *Paul S. Reinsch: Open Door Diplomat in Action.* Millwood, N.Y.: KTO Press, 1979.

Putnam-Weale, B. L. *The Fight for the Republic in China.* New York: Dodd, Mead, 1917.

Reid, John Gilbert. *The Manchu Abdication and the Powers.* Berkeley: University of California Press, 1935.

Reinsch, Paul S. *An American Diplomat in China.* London: William Heinemann, 1922.

Remer, C. F. *Foreign Investments in China.* New York: Macmillan, 1933.

Rhoads, Edward J. M. *China's Republican Revolution: The Case of Kwangtung, 1895–1913.* Cambridge, Mass.: Harvard University Press, 1975.

Richardson, James D., ed. *A Compilation of Messages and Papers of the Presidents.* New York: Bureau of National Literature, 1917.

Roy, M.N. *Revolution and Counter-Revolution in China.* Calcutta: Renaissance Publishers, 1940.

Schiffrin, Harold Z. *Sun Yat-sen and the Origins of the Chinese Revolution.* Berkeley: University of California Press, 1968.

Schirmer, Daniel. *Republic or Empire: American Resistance to the Philippine War.* Cambridge, Mass.: Schenkman, 1972.

Scholes, Walter, and Scholes, Marie. *The Foreign Policies of the Taft Administration.* Columbia: University of Missouri Press, 1970.

Schram, Stuart. *Mao Tse-tung.* New York: Simon & Shuster, 1967.

Schwartz, Benjamin. *Chinese Communism and the Rise of Mao.* Cambridge, Mass.: Harvard University Press, 1951.

———. *In Search of Wealth and Power: Yen Fu and the West.* Cambridge, Mass.: Harvard University Press, 1964.

Sharmon, Lyon. *Sun Yat-sen: His Life and Its Meaning.* New York: John Day, 1934.

Sinclair, Andrew. *Corsair: The Life of J. Pierpont Morgan.* Boston: Little, Brown, 1981.

Smith, Robert Freeman. *The United States and Revolutionary Nationalism in Mexico, 1916–1932.* Chicago: University of Chicago Press, 1972.

Snow, Edgar. *Red Star Over China.* New York: Grove Press, 1961.

Staley, Eugene. *War and the Private Investor.* Garden City, N.J.: Doubleday, Doran, 1935.

Steele, A. T. *The American People and China.* New York: McGraw-Hill, 1966.

Stillman, Edmund, and Pfaff, William. *Power and Impotence: The Failure of American Foreign Policy.* New York: Random House, 1966.

Stover, Leon. *The Cultural Ecology of Chinese Civilization.* New York: Pica Press, 1974.

Sun Yat-sen. *Memoirs of a Chinese Revolutionary.* Taipei: China Cultural Service, 1953.

———. *San Min Chu I: The Three Principles of the People.* Shanghai: Commercial Press, 1929.

Sutton, Donald S. *Provincial Militarism and the Chinese Republic: The Yunnan Army, 1905–1925.* Ann Arbor: University of Michigan Press, 1980.

Tang Leang-li. *China in Revolt.* London: Noel Douglas, 1927.

———. *The Foundations of Modern China.* London: Noel Douglas, 1928.

Tebbel, John. *The Compact History of the American Newspaper.* New York: Hawthorne Books, 1963.

Teitelbaum, Louis M. *Woodrow Wilson and the Mexican Revolution (1913–1916).* New York: Exposition Press, 1967.

Teng, Ssu-yu, and Fairbank, John K., eds. *China's Response to the West.* Cambridge, Mass.: Harvard University Press, 1954.

Thompson, John Stuart. *China Revolutionized.* Indianapolis: Bobbs-Merrill, 1913.

Ti Chiang Chen. *The International Law of Recognition.* New York: Praeger, 1951.

Varg, Paul. *The Making of A Myth: The United States and China, 1897–1912.* East Lansing: Michigan State University Press, 1968.

———. *Missionaries, Chinese and Diplomats: The American Protestant Missionary Movement in China, 1890–1952.* Princeton, N.J.: Princeton University Press, 1958.

Vevier, Charles. *The United States and China, 1906–1913: A Study in Finance and Diplomacy.* New Brunswick, N.J.: Rutgers University Press, 1955.

Williams, William A. *The Tragedy of America Diplomacy.* Cleveland: World, 1959.

Willoughby, Westel W. *Foreign Rights and Interests in China.* Baltimore: Johns Hopkins University Press, 1927.

Wilson, Joan Hoff. *Ideology and Economics: U.S. Relations with the Soviet Union, 1918–1933.* Columbia: University of Missouri Press, 1974.

Wright, Mary, ed. *China in Revolution: The First Phase, 1900–1913.* New Haven, Conn.: Yale University Press, 1968.

Wright, Stanley F. *China's Struggle for Tariff Autonomy: 1843–1938.* Shanghai: Kelly & Walsh, 1938.

———. *The Collection and Disposal of the Maritime and Native Customs Revenue Since the Revolution of 1911, With an Account of the Loan Services Administered by the Inspector General of Customs.* 2d ed., rev. and enlarged. Shanghai: Statistical Department, Inspectorate General of Customs, 1927.

Wu, Tingfang. *America Through the Spectacles of an Oriental Diplomat.* Taipei: Ch'eng Wen, 1968 Reprint.

Young, Ernest P. *The Presidency of Yuan Shih-k'ai: Liberalism and Dictatorship in Early Republican China.* Ann Arbor: University of Michigan Press, 1977.

Young, Marilyn. *The Rhetoric of Empire: American China Policy, 1895–1901.* Cambridge, Mass.: Harvard University Press, 1968.

Index

DATE DUE

			PRINTED IN U.S.A.